MAKING SENSE O

Practices for Change in Difficult Times

"Despite our nation's rapidly changing demographics, the subjugation and marginalization of racial and ethnic communities continues. We can seek to address the ongoing barriers that are preventing ethnoracial harmony, or we can ignore the obvious—the visibility and prominence of race and ethnicity throughout our society and the world. It is essential that our nation's educational institutions centrally value explicit and carefully crafted practices to foment classrooms that address diversity along many dimensions. While some progress clearly has been made since the overt and codified racism of times past, subtle forms of unconscious and implicit racism now hide in the public discourse. As a result, this book is important in the canon because the chapters are a clarion call for educators to stand firm on race and critique and address structural and institutional racism in its various forms. The contributions in this book overcome the theory and practice divide by specifying and advocating for pedagogy and practice that creates the space for all humans to be treated with dignity and provided educational opportunity."

—JULIAN VASQUEZ HEILIG, PH.D.
DEAN OF THE UNIVERSITY OF KENTUCKY COLLEGE OF EDUCATION

"In this wonderfully edited volume, Dr. Jessica Heybach and Dr. Sheron Fraser-Burgess pick up and advance one of the most challenging issues in education: talking and teaching about race and racism. Heybach, Fraser-Burgess, and the authors assembled in this text challenge readers to consider the complexities of supporting students in "speaking race" while also bridging the theory and practice divide. Throughout this brilliant and challenging book, powerful practical experiences regarding teaching race are explored, exposing research and scholarship that encourage all educators to thoughtfully engage dialogue and instruction around race and racism in the one place that encourages rigorous examination of ideas: classrooms."

—JOSEPH FLYNN, PH.D.
ASSOCIATE PROFESSOR, CURRICULUM AND INSTRUCTION OF THE COLLEGE OF
EDUCATION AND ASSOCIATE DIRECTOR OF ACADEMIC AFFAIRS, CENTER FOR
BLACK STUDIES DIVISION OF ACADEMIC AFFAIRS FOR
NORTHERN ILLINOIS UNIVERSITY

"*Making Sense of Race in Education* is a true testament to what happens when Critical Race Theory meets real educational practices. Every chapter tells a story of a dedicated critical educator who strives to bring open, reflective, and genuine conversations of race, racism, and racists to their classrooms and beyond. Their narratives are testimonies of their struggles to create open spaces where race is the lens used to look at issues of privilege and oppression. "

—YOLANDA MEDINA, PH.D.
BOROUGH OF MANHATTAN COMMUNITY COLLEGE/CUNY,
CRITICAL STUDIES OF LATINX IN THE AMERICAS, BOOK SERIES EDITOR

THE ACADEMY BOOK SERIES IN EDUCATION

Steven P. Jones and Eric C. Sheffield, *Editors*

The *Academy Book Series in Education* focuses serious attention on the often-missed nexus of educational theory and educational practice. The volumes in this series, both monographs and edited collections, consider theoretical, philosophical, historical, sociological, and other conceptual orientations in light of what those orientations can tell readers about successful classroom practice and sound educational policy. In this regard, the *Academy Series* aims to offer a wide array of themes including school reform, content specific practice, contemporary problems in higher education, the impact of technology on teaching and learning, matters of diversity, and other essential contemporary issues in educational thought and practice.

BOOKS IN THE SERIES

Why Kids Love (and Hate) School: Reflections on Difference
Why Kids Love (and Hate) School: Reflections on Practice
Making Sense of Race in Education: Practices for Change in Difficult Times
A Case for Kindness: A New Look at the Teaching Ethic

Steven P. Jones is a professor in the College of Education at Missouri State University and Executive Director of the Academy for Educational Studies. He is author of *Blame Teachers: The Emotional Reasons for Educational Reform*—a book that investigates how and why so many people try to justify educational change by deriding the efforts and effectiveness of our public school teachers. A former high school English teacher in Jefferson County, Colorado, Jones received his B.A. in English from the University of Denver, his M.A. in Educational Administration from the University of Colorado (Boulder), and his Ph.D. in Curriculum and Instruction from the University of Chicago.

Eric C. Sheffield is Professor and Department Chair of Educational Studies at Western Illinois University in Macomb. He is also founding editor of the Academy for Educational Studies' peer reviewed journal, *Critical Questions in Education*. A former English teacher in Putman County Florida, Sheffield received his B.A. in Philosophy from Illinois College, and his M.Ed (English Education) & Ph.D (Philosophy of Education) from the University of Florida.

The editors of the *Academy Book Series in Education* are interested in reviewing manuscripts and proposals for possible publication in the series. Scholars who wish to be considered should email their proposals, along with two sample chapters and current CVs, to the editors. For instructions and advice on preparing a prospectus, please refer to the Myers Education Press website at http://myersed press.com/sites/stylus/MEP/Docs/Prospectus%20Guidelines%20MEP.pdf. You can send your material to:

Steven P. Jones
Eric C. Sheffield
academyedbooks@gmail.com

MAKING SENSE OF RACE IN EDUCATION

Practices for Change in Difficult Times

MAKING SENSE OF RACE IN EDUCATION

Practices for Change in Difficult Times

Edited by Jessica A. Heybach
and Sheron Fraser-Burgess

GORHAM, MAINE

Published by Myers Education Press, LLC
P.O. Box 424 Gorham, ME 04038

Myers Education Press is an academic publisher specializing in books, e-books, and digital content in the field of education. All of our books are subjected to a rigorous peer-review process and produced in compliance with the standards of the Council on Library and Information Resources.

Library of Congress Cataloging-in-Publication Data available from Library of Congress.

13-digit ISBN 978-1-9755-0189-1 (paperback)
13-digit ISBN 978-1-9755-0188-4 (hard cover)
13-digit ISBN 978-1-9755-0190-7 (library networkable e-edition)
13-digit ISBN 978-1-9755-0191-4 (consumer e-edition)

Printed in the United States of America.

All first editions printed on acid-free paper that meets the American National Standards Institute Z39-48 standard.

Books published by Myers Education Press may be purchased at special quantity discount rates for groups, workshops, training organizations, and classroom usage. Please call our customer service department at 1-800-232-0223 for details.

Cover design by Sophie Appel

Visit us on the web at **www.myersedpress.com** to browse our complete list of titles.

TABLE OF CONTENTS

RACE: STILL THE WORLD'S MOST DANGEROUS IDEA

J. Q. ADAMS

R ACE AS A MEME and its transmission in a fifth-wave multimedia culture can have dire national and global consequences, exacerbated as a result of the incredible speed of human population growth in the last 200 years. The earth's population has grown from one billion in 1820 to almost eight billion today. In the last 500 years race has become the most dangerous idea in the world; it has become the ultimate "other" maker, dividing people not based on their character but on their phenotypical characteristics. This "othering" has become the shorthand of racial supremacy in American society and the de facto affirmative action plan of its White people. While we are 155 years past slavery, multiple manifestations of neo-slavery strategies such as Jim Crow, class stratification, and White flight continue to reaffirm the privileges of Whites and the disadvantages of people of color.

Our nation's obsession with color hierarchy continues to redefine itself as the visual palate shifts to tan, as a result of the decrease in immigration from predominantly White European countries and the increasing number of persons with tan and brown faces coming in from Central and South America and Asia. Combine that with a steadily growing mixed-race birth population, and it becomes clear that the face of America is changing right in front of our eyes. While most Americans say they don't believe in "racism" (Horowitz, Brown, and Cox, 2019), the reaction to the Obama presidency on the part of a significant vocal minority clearly revealed that the

deep-seated racial animosity of the past was alive and well. This was clearly
documented in the fear-driven, record-breaking increase in gun sales and
membership in racially extremist organizations (see Southern Poverty Law
Center, 2018). And when it comes down to racial identity politics, the "one
drop rule" of hypo-descent still applies to presidents and anyone else. A half
Black and half White Barack Obama could not claim to be White; his racial
identity was chosen for him by a society still wedded to the mindset of slavery and White supremacy. Obama was Black by default!

In the era of Trump, the president's rhetoric has clearly continued to
awaken racially divisive ideas that have always been part of the colonial and
American narrative. These ideas justified slavery and made it a constitution-
ally sanctioned component of our nation's economic system, granting it a
permanent place within the DNA of this country.

In our synchronized contemporary society, we seldom take the time to
examine the psycho/social blueprint of race, though its impact still under-
girds what we accept as our nation's normative behavior. This social construct has major consequences, especially for people of color, in how they
are evaluated in our schools, communities, and workplaces. The unequal
treatment of African American males, particularly by law enforcement, has
been a recurring phenomenon throughout the history of this country. It
reflects the collective beliefs of a nation born in an ambiguous self-iden-
tity: on the one hand, God-fearing and righteous; on the other, perpetuating
human trafficking on a global scale and committing centuries of genocidal
atrocities on the indigenous peoples who occupied the lands that were stolen
to form the colonies and later the United States.

While the ideas of democracy, liberty, and freedom form their historical
narrative, hegemony conceals the reality of the intersectionality of gender
in the hierarchy of patriarchy, class in the hierarchy of the aristocracy, and
race in the hierarchy of skin color and privilege. This has led to an ongoing
belief in American exceptionalism, which is accepted and revered by most
Americans. Among the middle and lower classes this idea acts as a defense
mechanism for maintaining the status quo, fostering certain levels of dem-
agoguery, and even nurturing a suspicion of science that leads to political, economic, and social uncertainties that compromise decisions that can
save lives and protect against ever greater damage to the planet. In upper
classes it serves to justify all manner of economic corruption. Despite this,
Americans generally continue to believe that the United States is the greatest

nation in the world and a model for anything that matters to civilized, democratic, and free-market, capitalist people. This hypnotic mythology leads to a Pavlovian dependence on consumerism and pharmacology to steer our focus away from the real goal of capitalism—that is, global economic domination—and to prevent any serious analysis and critique of capitalism either as an appropriate economic or social model or as the cornerstone of racism.

The idea of race in the twenty-first century separates us at a time when unity is more important than ever; it disconnects us when connection is critical and creates fear between us that dampens the possibilities of building trust. It must be the role of human beings to transcend, transform, and transmute this idea of race into a celebration of what it is to be human in all its unique variety, while seeking to satisfy our universal needs equitably. It is incumbent upon our educators at all levels to challenge the mythology of race in all its many forms and to champion our common humanity by preparing this generation to be the antidote to the viral infection called race.

References

Horowitz, J. M., Brown, A., & Cox, K. (2019). *Race in America 2019*. Pew Research Center. Retrieved from https://www.pewsocialtrends.org/2019/04/09/race-in-america-2019/

Southern Poverty Law Center. (2018). *Hate map*. Retrieved from https://www.splcenter.org/hate-map

ACKNOWLEDGMENTS

THE EDITORS THANK STEVEN P. Jones and Eric C. Sheffield for the opportunity to edit this timely collection for the Academy of Educational Studies. We also thank the contributing authors for their insightful chapters and commitment to this project. May these chapters encourage the courageous and risky work related to race that is needed in all classrooms.

LEARNING TO SPEAK RACE:

Negotiating Race, Racism, and Racists in the Classroom

JESSICA A. HEYBACH

IT WAS A BRISK fall evening outside as I stood at the front of my undergraduate classroom. I was responsible for the education of roughly 30 students—some young, some old, some aspiring teachers, some just checking the box for the required general education diversity courses—all of them seemingly disinterested in talking about race in public. Based on appearance, we were a fairly homogeneous group—overwhelmingly White, a few Latinx students, and no Black students—assembled together in a third-floor classroom. Try as I might, there was little eye contact and few were willing to jump into the deep end to deal with my verbal prompts. The sense of constraint, possibly fear, was palpable. I turned their attention to our institution and asked some rhetorical questions regarding race relations on campus. Race had historically been a complicated topic on this campus and in this college town. Situated between a large urban city and a horizon of corn fields, it is a town that defies the categories of rural, suburban, and urban. Instead, the demographics and the story of this town include aspects of all these categories. Locals often call for the end of programs that bring community members from the city to this town for university life or permanent housing. The campus itself is, generally speaking, alive with diverse populations, but somehow this particular Wednesday evening class did not represent the usual diversity found in our courses.

My students' body language signaled to me that they were uncomfortable and disinterested in talking about race. Finally, one young man raised his hand and asked, "Why isn't there a Center for White Studies on campus?" I was taken aback by the question. I paused, and asked: "What do you mean?" He responded: "Well...there is a Center for Black Studies and a Center for Latino Studies, and a Center for Women Studies.... Why is there no Center for White Studies?" This was not a question I anticipated, but then again, all the good questions seem to be the ones we fail to anticipate as instructors. I could have quickly responded with a quip about historic White supremacy and male supremacy in the academy, or provided the typical "Some would argue that the institution was built by and for the White population and thus, higher education has already committed too much time and energy to the study of Whites." But my years of teaching told me that few students would have been willing to speak after such a response from the woman at the front of the room. I knew this because many heads nodded in agreement with the student who raised the question, and it appeared that others were intrigued by these buildings on campus. My aim in this moment was not to didactically teach them the answer to the question posed—I'd learned enough to know that such a move by instructors can quickly shut down student inquiry. My aim was to get them to "speak race" into the public space of the classroom and speak through the emotional difficulties that surround the topic. I gave students time to talk to each other about what they thought was the purpose of specialized "Centers" on campus. As they fumbled through a small group conversation, I was already thinking that we should go visit these spaces to hear from those who run them why they are essential to campus life.

The following week, we met at one of the centers on campus and were ushered into a large common space to hear from the director. The director gave a brief overview of the center and the work it does on campus, and then opened up the discussion to student questions. In the course of the evening, the conversation unraveled. At one point the director commented that they[1] "hated White women...and Asian women...." The director commented that

1 I am using the plural pronoun throughout to conceal the gender of the director. My use of the plural pronoun does not signal that the entire center agreed with the ideas expressed.

their reputation on campus was one of brutal honestly, and they were more than willing to speak uncomfortable truths to those with White privilege. As the rhetoric continued, my chest hollowed out and sunk into my feet—what had I done? All these years later, I am still discomfited by these memories. I was in many ways as stunned as my students were to hear a university administrator say these words in public on the campus of a public university. The feeling of wanting to evaporate, slide onto the floor, and crawl out the back door will remain ever-fresh in my mind. I scanned the room to check my students' faces, but none of them looked over toward me. Instead, they were glued to the director's rhetoric.

One of the White female students raised her hand and retold her story of racial tension and harassment from a roommate in the dorms on campus. She recounted what it was like to live with someone of a different race who hated her. She asked the director point blank, "Why does my roommate hate me just because I'm White?" She added, "and, I think everyone can be racist, not just White people." The director replied that there was no such thing as racism against Whites—"it didn't exist." The student was visibly shaken by this comment. I don't remember if she replied to the answer that was given by the director or not. Instead, I was astonished that this otherwise silent student had been so provoked that she was willing to engage the director, who had just declared their hatred for White women. Why had she not offered this story in the safety of our classroom, but instead waded into a contentious discussion of race with the director? At one point the director scanned the room and commented that the class was "all White" and that they "wouldn't understand," further remarking that *anyone* could attend events at the Center but that "they wouldn't want to." One male student shot his hand up—"I'm not White! I'm Mexican." He continued, asking the director, "But what about all these posters on the wall, what about what Martin Luther King said about not judging people based on their skin color, don't you agree with that?" She replied, "Those are nice ideas, but it's more complicated than that."

The conversation ended right as an event was about to begin at the center. The director said we were welcome to stay, but that "we would probably feel uncomfortable when her students walked in." My students quickly filed out of the building and gathered outside. Many of them were visibly upset. One student, filled with anger, said: "I'm writing a letter to the president of the university—we should all write letters." Another commented: "Well that just set race relations back a few hundred years." I myself had little to offer at that late hour. I quickly asked students to write a reflection to share next week in class. We parted ways, and I quickly grabbed my phone to call a colleague who knew the director. She said, "Let me come to your class next week and talk to your students, and I'll bring another instructor with me who knows the director well." I hung up and considered the potentially explosive nature of what had just happened. What if the students did write to the president? What will happen to my evaluations this semester? How can I make sure these students understand the depth of what the director just spoke about without inciting more hatred?

The next class period arrived, and the class quickly erupted in chatter: hands were raised, students were having side conversations, talking to each other, and were more than willing to talk to me at the front of the room. They actively wanted to understand why the director "said all those things." Upon reflection, I realize that this moment offered a common shared experience about race that they could talk through from the same starting point. They didn't have to explain the prior scenarios that were prompting their questions; instead, the common lived experience allowed them to finally talk about race in real time. The guest speakers arrived and first listened to my students' reactions but offered little in the way of a response. Once students were done talking, the speakers shared some of the personal background of the director and attempted to provide a context as to why there is hatred of Whites within non-White communities. They described how hatred was built up through experience—both personal experience and the larger sociopolitical historical experience of race in America. In short, they coaxed students to recognize that hatred was not an abstract idea about the other; rather, it was rooted in how others had been treated. However, the bulk of the evening's conversation was spent talking about power, and how racism as an explicit form of power had, and continues to be, wielded by "White" institutions. The speakers gently nudged my students to move away from an individualistic understanding of race, racism, and even racists, and instead to adopt a structural understanding of how power operates in the United States. A structural understanding of how power had operated on U.S. college campuses helped reveal to my students why those specialized "centers" came to be and remain relevant today.

I recount this story not because it provides an answer to the question of race in education, but because it remains the most honest discussion of race I have had with students in a classroom throughout my 20 years as a university instructor. It was void of platitudes. It avoided the trappings of consensus and the easy answers of unity and equality. This event exposed, in plain sight, how those who occupy different positionalities experience race, racism, and racists. The rhetoric of the director reminded me that much of what has been said about race may simply be too nice and polite to actually be heard. In classrooms we often tap dance around the issue and struggle to "speak race" into public learning spaces. And yet, classrooms remain our last, great hope as a nation for the critical analysis of race—and educators remain the stewards of this inquiry.

The public square seems unlikely to produce this type of inquiry, given the status of 24-hour news, talk radio, social media, and meme culture. The public square is overrun with sound bites and snark—discourse has become sport—and thus is an improbable space for reasoned, frank, fearless speech and dialogue. Such speech has been described by Cornel West (2004) as *parrhesia*—"the lifeblood of any democracy" (p. 209). These practices demand what Amy Gutmann (1999) describes as a "non-repressive" education: a pedagogical space where information and knowledge are not concealed, and inquiry into what Deborah Britzman (1998) deemed "difficult knowledge" is a mandate. Without such practices and spaces, it is unlikely that we will produce citizens who are able to grapple with the complexity of race, racism, and racists in America. This edited collection offers a window into such practices.

Chapter 1, *Higher Education Faculty Countering Systemic Racism: Reflexive Positionality about Black Girls' Experiences of School Discipline*, by Sheron Fraser-Burgess, Kiesha Warren-Gordon, Maria Hernández Finch, and Maria B. Sciuchetti, follows an analysis of a higher education faculty book club. The book in question is *Pushout: The Criminalization of Black Girls in Schools* (Morris, 2016). These faculty sought to transform their classroom pedagogies by stepping away from the classroom to foster their practices of positionality and reflexivity in relation to conceptions of social justice.

Chapter 2, *Relieving Tension and Empowering Students: Addressing Societal Racism in U.S. Classrooms Through Critical Discourse Analysis*, by Christina J. Cavallaro, Cole Kervin, Sabrina F. Sembiante, and Traci P. Baxley, describes how critical discourse analysis can be brought into the K–12 classroom to analyze texts and assist educators in difficult discussions regarding race. Using this methodology, the authors offer a sample analysis of the article "Zimmerman Is Acquitted in Killing of Trayvon Martin"

(Alvarez & Buckley, 2013).

Chapter 3, *The World Without Art Is Eh: Aesthetic Engagement and Race in the Classroom*, by Ritu Radhakrishnan, argues that public school teachers should more readily include aesthetic experiences in the classroom to explore issues of race. Radhakrishnan draws on aesthetic theory, critical pedagogy, and visual thinking strategies to offer pedagogical options for educators to engage students in discussions of race.

Chapter 4, *Ignorance Is Not Bliss: Why Early Childhood Educators Need to Teach Young Children about Race and Racism*, by Terry Husband, argues that early childhood educators should resist the practice of omitting race and racism from the classroom. Husband discusses implicit racial bias, lack of diversity in texts and curriculum, racial socialization, and racial identity development as justifications for the inclusion of this topic in the early childhood classroom.

Chapter 5, *The Pedagogical Dilemmas of Addressing Blackface and White Privilege in the Classroom*, by Mary Beth Hines, describes an alternative high school classroom incident involving Blackface within a small group assignment. Hines chronicles student, administrator, and teacher reactions and offers an analysis of student positionality through the lens of White privilege as a means to confront racism in the classroom.

Chapter 6, *It's Messy: You Can't Just Talk about Race*, by Michael Hernandez, Paul Markson III, and Kathryn Young, offers a discussion among three colleagues regarding how they address race in their high school and college classrooms. Authors pay particular attention to concepts such as intersectionality, implicit bias, honesty, citizenship, moral responsibility, and empathy to normalize discussions of race and to combat the usual silence surrounding race in the classroom.

Chapter 7, *Processes and Protocols for Creating and Sustaining Cross-Racial Dialog Among K–12 Educators*, by Susan Adams and Jamie Buffington-Adams, describes necessary practices for fostering cross-racial dialogue among educators. The authors advocate the use of agreements, shared leadership, and specific discussion protocols that can nurture the concept of "critical friendship" and allow colleagues to discuss the contested terrain of race.

Chapter 8, *Changing Narratives: Understanding the Struggle of Muslim Americans Today*, by Wafa Mohamad, describes the lived experience of being Muslim in America in a post-9/11 context. Mohamad chronicles the rise of hate crimes and Islamophobia in the political arena within the United States, and then turns her attention to the lack of representation of Muslim populations in the official curriculum of K–12 settings. Mohamad ultimately argues that education can be a site of transformation for Muslim identity in America.

Chapter 9, *Restorative Justice: The Alternative to Excessive Suspensions and Expulsions and the Zero Tolerance Policy*, by Kimberly R. James, Runell J. King, and Jovan T. Thomas, offers an overview of current research related to the practice of restorative justice and the impact this practice has had on educational settings. The authors describe a variety of restorative practices that can be utilized to foster a more humane educational environment.

The authors whose work appears in this collection break from the usual divide that isolates either theorizing race in education or engaging race in the classroom through myriad practices. Of course, theoretical discussions are essential to clarifying why discussions of race, racism, and racists are warranted in educational settings, but if the scholarship on race remains forever caught in an either/or trap (either practice or theory), both will have limited efficacy in addressing the difficulties and complexities of race in educational settings. This collection seeks to overcome the theory/practice divide that has shaped much of the educational scholarship regarding race.

References

Alvarez, L., & Buckley, C. (2013, July 13). Zimmerman is acquitted in Trayvon Martin killing. *The New York Times*. Retrieved from http://www.nytimes.com/2013/07/14/us/george-zimmerman-verdict-trayvon-martin.html? mcubz=2

Britzman, D.P. (1998). *Lost subjects, contested objects: Toward a psychoanalytic inquiry of learning*. Albany, NY: State University of New York Press.

Gutmann, A. (1999). *Democratic education*. Princeton, NJ: Princeton University Press.

Morris, M.W. (2016). *Pushout: The criminalization of Black girls in schools*. New York, NY: New Press.

West, C. (2004). *Democracy matters: Winning the fight against imperialism*. New York, NY: Penguin.

CHAPTER ONE

HIGHER EDUCATION FACULTY COUNTERING SYSTEMIC RACISM:

Reflexive Positionality about Black Girls' Experiences of School Discipline

SHERON FRASER-BURGESS, KIESHA WARREN-GORDON,
MARIA HERNÁNDEZ FINCH, & MARIA B. SCIUCHETTI
BALL STATE UNIVERSITY

HIGHER EDUCATION FACULTY PREPARE teachers, counselors, and other practitioners for professional work in K–12 schools. Within this function, the structural factors that perpetuate educational inequality are prominent research areas in the academy (Doyle, 2007; Giroux & Giroux, 2004). For example, teacher education commonly addresses opportunity gaps along the lines of race and socioeconomic status, for which it must prepare its candidates to advance positive social change (Howard, 2010). With the goal of cultivating "democratic, critical, socially responsible employees," there is an important role for higher education faculty to play in advancing K-12 education that is socially just (Boyles, 2007, p. 576).

The focus of this chapter is making meaning of the faculty's role in promoting equity in the context of institutional responses to Black girls in K–12 education. Despite having such potential for positive influence, the demographics of the primarily Anglo American and middle-class status of higher education faculty and persons preparing to become academics varies dramatically from the K–12 population that they serve as an end goal. According to the National Center for Educational Statistics:

> In fall 2015, of all full-time faculty at degree-granting postsecondary institutions, 42 percent were White males, 35 percent were White females, 6 percent were Asian/Pacific Islander males, 4 percent were Asian/Pacific Islander females, 3 percent each were Black females and Black males, and 2 percent each were Hispanic males and Hispanic females. (McFarland et al., 2017, p. 2)

This disparity exposes areas where social class, race, and gender identities can hinder higher education faculty's nuanced understanding of the K–12 environment. This chapter addresses the racialized implementation of discipline policies as an exemplar.

Background

In 2017, a group of faculty and doctoral students at a Midwestern university participated in a book study on Morris's (2016) *Pushout: The Criminalization of Black Girls in Schools*. Morris centered the plight of young Black girls who confront excessively punitive policies and practices that schools implement in racialized ways. Initiated by an educational psychology department faculty member from the university's Teachers College, the eventual all-female group was disciplinarily diverse, coming from academic backgrounds that include special education, educational psychology, educational studies, and criminology. There was also ethnic and racial diversity among the group, which consisted of persons who identified as Black/African-American, Latinx and Anglo American. In the initial phase, one of the participants was also visually impaired and another was blind.

In each member's professional role, she regularly encountered practitioners and staff who work with Black girls who experienced heavy-handed discipline (Crenshaw, Ocen, & Nada, 2016). These practices included frequent in-school and out-of-school suspensions, expulsions, and being "pushed out" into the juvenile justice system early in their schooling. For example, the educational psychologists encountered girls who were systematically tested and placed into special education categories; for the counseling psychologists, their practicing school counselors shared concerns regarding the dire prospects that the girls had for post-secondary education because of their early encounters with the juvenile justice system. Education professors glimpsed the precursors of this pathway in Black and female first- and second-graders whom teachers routinely identified as problem students and sent out into the hallway or to the principal's office. The criminologist in the group, who was an expert in female victimology, underscored the established link between life outcomes of abuse and the early patterns that the higher education faculty observed and that were also described in Morris's work.

In the course of a spring semester, summer, and a fall semester of a calendar year, the group of faculty met monthly. Different members voluntarily facilitated one-hour meetings that corresponded roughly to each chapter of the text. In the reflection modality, discussion prompts typically encouraged participants to relate their lived experiences to the girls and the stories that Morris narrated. The disparity between the faculty participants' background and that of the girls was evident in terms of socioeconomic status, race, and exposure to risk factors (Crenshaw et al., 2016). Throughout the duration of the book study, there was an ongoing effort to engage with the text from various vantage points and conceptual frameworks. These perspectives included interpreting the text discursively in terms of critical race theory (Ladson-Billings, 2005; Howard & Navarro, 2016), identifying with the girls' gender oppression and intersectionality (Crenshaw, 1989) and applying the therapeutic social justice lens in order to consider possible kinds of intervention (Goodman et al., 2004).

Rationale

The collaborative narrative research that evolved into this chapter emerged out of the evident dissonance (Festinger, 1985) arising from the disparity of lived experiences between the faculty and the Black girls in Morris's work. There was a significant gulf in cultural horizons that challenged the way that the faculty participants were making meaning of the text (Alcoff, 2006). Problematically, it was more likely than not that the members of the university study group could not relate substantially to the "pushed-out" Black girls whom Morris profiled. Although there were individual convergences of identification—for example, with racism, female voicelessness, and body stigmatization—no member of the group had ever experienced the degree of surveillance, tracking, and criminalization described in the work.

An additional consideration motivating this chapter was the professional and moral imperative of social justice. Everyone in the group
expressed deep compassion for the girls' condition, but in order to be agents
of social change, activists need to add agency to sympathy (Freire, 1972).
This critical reflection is essential to social justice praxis in one's field (Freire,
McLaren & Giroux, 1988). The implicit research question became the following: In the face of the systemic criminalization of young Black girls that
Morris (2016) chronicles and the critical distance engendered by divergent
lived experiences, how do higher education faculty make meaning of their
professional role in actuating the social justice ideal?

Theoretical Framework

According to Mezirow (1990), to make meaning "means to make sense
of an experience...make an interpretation of it. When we subsequently use
this interpretation to guide decision-making or action, then making meaning
becomes learning" (p. 2). To conceptualize the myriad perspectives that the
participants brought to the reflection and its meaning for their professional
lives, the general construct of *positionality* was invoked. It is an interpretive
framework with hermeneutic and discursive conceptualizations. Interpre-
tatively, positionality acknowledges the contextual and partial nature of
knowledge garnered through lived experiences and identification with the
dominant or othered social group (Alcoff, 1988, 2006; Maher & Tetreault,
1993). According to Linda Martín Alcoff (1995), who introduced the concept in relation to the theorizing of feminine gender identity,

> The concept of positionality includes two points: first, as already
> stated, that the concept of woman is a relational term identifiable
> only within a (constantly moving) context; but, second, that the
> position that women find themselves in can be actively utilized
> (rather than transcended) as a location for the construction of
> meaning, a place from where meaning is constructed, rather than
> simply the place where a meaning can be discovered (the meaning
> of femaleness). (p. 454)

In this reading, gender is the embodiment of an advantageous sociocultural
location that can generate beliefs, shape values, and inform judgments by

its very status in relation to the broader society. It is an awareness that identifying with the social marker (e.g., race, social class, gender, LGBTQ+) provides a site for meaning-making and instantiation of a form of subjectivity as a worthwhile and important ontological stance for being in the world.

Sensoy and DiAngelo (2017) explain positionality as recognizing "that where you stand in relation to others shapes what you see and understand" (p. 15). This relative social standing can correlate with identification with a dominant or subordinate group respectively, and with the power to control the prevailing narrative and dictate the institutional culture. Conversely, one can be found to be lacking this status or be dominated by persons who possess such influence (p. 73). In this sense, one's positionality can convey forms of privilege or the lack thereof.

This first-person inquiry draws on these conceptions of positionality to explore faculty interpretation of Black girl's experiences and its implications for preparation of educational practitioners. To activate the positional analysis, the study appealed to *reflexivity* as a distinct construct apart from reflection. Mezirow (1990) defines reflective action, or reflexivity, as being different from merely being thoughtful or reflective. Rather:

> Reflective action, understood as action predicated on a critical assessment of assumptions, may also be an integral part of decision making. Thoughtful action is reflexive but is not the same thing as acting reflectively to critically examine the justification for one's beliefs. Reflection in thoughtful action involves a pause to reassess by asking: What am I doing wrong? The pause may be only a split second in the decision-making process. Reflection may thus be integral to deciding how best to perform immediately; reflection becomes an integral element of thoughtful action. (Mezirow, 1990, p. 6)

Reflexivity involves capturing the grounds of one's beliefs in self-assessment. One limitation of reflexivity in the literature is that it does not acknowledge the social context and one's embeddedness in it as a consideration in the self-examination heuristic. Even critical reflection can fail to consider the influence that personal and cultural value systems have on reasoning about beliefs and actions (Nairn, et al., 2012)

When reflexivity is combined with imputing positionality it understands reflective action as originating from one's being embedded in social context. Using positionality as a reflective tool for self-assessment can be a *critically* constructive interpretation of one's situated racial, social, and gender identification. This criticality of critical positionality relates to self-reflecting on identity aspects as realized in somatic engagement with the world and its sources of power, dominance, and oppression. As a socially constructed stance, *critical positionality* both utilizes identity as a source of meaning and acknowledges the discursive dominance of prevailing cultural norms, their shaping of institutional policy and practices, and their judgments and beliefs. It is an evaluative self-examination in regard to holding beliefs characteristic of systems of dominance, oppression, or sub-ordinance intersubjectively in light of existent moral, ethical, and democratic norms of social justice.

Research Reflection: Prompting Critical Positionality

Two Black faculty members who were scheduled to facilitate the final chapter discussion opted to provoke reflexive positionality using Morris's (2016) final chapter. An email was sent to all of the faculty participants on the listserv (approximately 22 people) inviting them to read the Maher and Tetreault (1993) piece on positionality as the reflective prompt. Eight group members attended the final book meeting, including three Black faculty, two persons who identified as LatinX and three as Anglo American. Seven were university faculty members.

During the meeting, they were invited to complete a simple descriptive identity inventory about the primary sources of their group identification as a lens through which they understood the condition and plight of the "pushed out" Black girls. After the meeting, everyone was invited to submit a structured reflection in response to a series of questions (see below) as one way of getting outside one's embeddedness in interlocking systems of domination of race, socioeconomic status, and so forth (hooks, 1994).

This reflexive positional piece was intended to articulate the conscious dissonance that gaps in lived experience can represent as a source of tension along the lines of one's sources of identification and belonging (Fraser-Burgess, 2018). The call for submissions encouraged persons completing the reflection to share the ways in which they wrestle alternately with detachment and proximity in their teaching and mentoring of educational practitioners vis-à-vis the criminalization of young Black girls. In this vein, they were asked to address the questions below, which constituted the structuring

of critical positionality. Each question probed the positional stance by urging its interpretation in light of particular identity and structural considerations. Some of these factors pertain to the intersectional social status of the
girls, and others query the theory-to-practice implications.

- How does positionality, insofar as it does, inform and address your assumptions about the worthiness of young Black girls for interventions,
  or your qualifications to do so?

- How does or can your positionality differentially inform the meaning of
  the love and concern that you bring to these relationships [with practitioners who work with Black girls]?

- Is positionality a part of the reasoning that guides your thinking about
  the prospects for having an impact on the success or failure of Black
  girls being tracked in this way?

- How does your positionality (in the relevant forms) relate to or inhibit
  "centering Black girls" in your pedagogy and practice?

In each case, participants were urged to complicate their self-appraisal vis-
à-vis positionality.

The collaborative product would collectively represent a multi-perspec-
tival experience of engaging with Black girl's stories, plight and struggles,
where the claim to identifying with them is merely preliminary. The reflection could take any form (narrative, expository, prose, dialogue, etc.). The
length was to be 500–1,000 words, providing basic demographic information, including background on the specific discipline in which one teaches
and the kind of practitioners one is preparing.

Telling their story in this way employs a methodology of narrative
engagement that is counter to prevalent discourses. Goodall (2010) argues
that the power of narrative is "to alter perceptions of reality, to change
minds, and to influence choices of action" (p. 28). As a form of research, it
is an attempt to challenge established discourses of deficiency that have been
reified into oppressive systemic practices. Such a counter narrative research
methodology, in contrast to logo-centric research frames, engages in story-
telling that promotes "specialized ideas about community and social issues"
that depart from the established frameworks (Ginwright, 2002, p. 550).

Research Reflections

In addition to the two Black facilitators, two other faculty members sub-mitted reflections over a six-month period. Each of the participants are the co-authors of this chapter. Their reflections are provided verbatim below.

Sheron

I am a woman of the twentieth century African Diaspora. Of Caribbean extraction, commonwealth colonized mentality characterized my formative years of schooling on the Jamaican island. In my young consciousness then, the ideology of Eurocentric superiority co-existed with nationalist pride that was mediated by Christian Pentecostal fervor. After my family emigrated when I was 11 years old, I eventually earned a Ph.D. in philosophy that opened the doors of the professoriate and landed me in the American Mid-west at 40 years old. Preparing teacher candidates and academics who will teach them has been the primary focus of my faculty labor for over a decade.

There has been little in the intervening years prior to academic work and the journeyed pathways of belonging and exclusion, then and after, that positioned me to identify with the girls in Morris's work. Nowhere was this gap more present than with Heaven, the 17-year-old girl featured in chapter five of Morris's *Pushout* (2016). In her interview, she explained that she had been academically unfocused in school and more concerned with being in a romantic relationship, which she achieved at age 14 when she moved in with her boyfriend for short bursts of time. At the time of her conversation with Morris, she was in a juvenile hall facility and had not attended her high school for five months.

In making sense of the text, an immediate awareness was the extent to which the anecdote was another challenge to the myths of meritocracy that my socialization had reified and exposed a tension around race and the role of effort that had been a latent issue for me. I encountered this internalized false narrative previously and authentically presented my critiques in lectures and classroom discussions with teacher candidates who were predominantly Anglo American. "Meritocracy is an ideology that is predicated on the dominant group's use of power to stigmatize the other and advance White supremacy," I would claim. Meeting Heaven in the text as the embodiment of the harm of systemic practices of disproportionate discipline exposed an additional layer of conflict that the positionality questions excavated.

The first two questions relate to the underlying reasons for these harsh policies:

- How does positionality, insofar as it does, inform and address your assumptions about the worthiness of young Black girls for interventions or your qualifications to do so?

- How does or can your positionality differentially inform the meaning of the love and concern that you bring to these relationships (with practitioners who work with Black girls)?

Morris (2016) links the excessively punitive discipline to an underlying idea that these girls deserve harsh punishments because of their choices. It is believed for instance that they are too loud, lack motivation or ambition or, even worse, any working moral compass to guide their choices. Morris raised this point in the chapter: "Rarely is there reflection upon the extent to which our reactions to girls' behaviors are rooted in whether they are being 'good girls' or whether they have actually presented a harm or threat to safety, personal or public" (p. 178).

I had been the perennial "good girl" as an immigrant who was oriented towards achievement. It was one of the main labels on which my way of navigating school and life was predicated and a facet of my school experience in elementary school and eventually middle and high school, which in retrospect brought me so much satisfaction. I completed assignments and received affirmation through excellent grades and teacher rewards. I reveled in the simple satisfaction of their approval. I learned to read the social mores and conform to the "good girl" expectations. In middle school the undertow of economic factors on my family and their choices increasingly infringed upon my simple demarcation of the world into good people and bad ones instead of categories of limited means versus more than sufficient resources, but it was a categorization that made my youthful world uncomplicated.

Morris's injunction presented the case for the further excavation of a basic principle of my consciousness and moral constitution. Although I had moved a long way from it being a defining label, it was a challenge to concede its vacuous designation all the way down to decisions such as whether to remain in school. Heaven's experience illustrated that choices are real only in the context of awareness of multiple options. Eliciting this critical reflection was supported by the reminder that there were many underlying factors that made Heaven's path more burdensome. Her troubled family provided little support, and her schools lacked the resources and engaged teachers that could generate excitement about learning. There was no place in Heaven's world where she felt that she belonged and that could support her educational goals. As a democratic society that tolerates such stark educational fortunes, in a way, we all are culpable.

Despite trying to be the good girl, I could relate to Heaven's alienation. For despite my laser-like focus on academic achievement, my professional status is bounded and delimited by worry about other's perceptions of my being the "Angry, Black woman." A minority in the professoriate, my presence in the room is not always welcome in that it ostensibly challenges dominant frames. My experiences as an academic mirror Heaven's in a few important ways where racism is experienced as gendered. Even now self-love can be hard. Morris states:

> We must also consider how expressions of Black femininity (e.g. how girls talk, dress, or wear their hair) are pathologized by school rules. In our haste to teach children social rules, we sometimes fail to examine whether these rules are rooted in oppression—racial, patriarchal, or any other form.... School-based policies and practices that expose Black girls to the disproportionate application of discipline, that emphasizes society's dominant and negative constructs of Black femininity, or that seek to punish them for clothing and/or hairstyle choices must be eliminated and instead replaced by a pedagogy that embraces the healing and liberating power of talking. (Morris, 2016, p. 178)

It stands to reason that if being a good girl did not protect me from the stigmas associated with the Black female body, it is a nebulous standard to apply to Heaven. Although she made poor decisions, there was also a social responsibility that schools and families neglected (Sensoy & DiAngelo, 2017). So this mythology can be a red herring where a confluence of social problems augment the risk to which these girls are exposed.

The pre-service teachers in our program are firm converts to the "good girl" gospel generally and typically also express an appreciation for diversity. Pezzetti (2017) argues that preservice teachers view themselves as nonracist people but struggle to make sense of implications of diversity for their classrooms. How does one convey that holding on to this belief poses a barrier for being able to advocate for girls like Heaven? In addition, teacher candidates typically do not have a firm basis for comparison because of racialized gender privilege.

The remaining two questions of the structured reflection, as listed below, query the theory-to-practice implications of getting beyond the good girl myth; the first does so in terms of the likelihood of sufficiently problematizing this mythology to engender a change in the teaching mindset of Anglo-American teacher candidates. The second question, "centering Black girls" equates to decentering the normative hold of the dominant good girl narrative.

- Is positionality a part of reasoning that guides your thinking about the prospects for having an impact on the success or failure of Black girls being tracked in this way?

- How does your positionality (in the relevant forms) relate to or inhibit "centering Black girls" in your pedagogy and practice?

A robust body of work points to resistance as one outcome of the disparity of lived experiences that White preservice teachers can exhibit in social foundations classes and that show up on teacher evaluations of their professors (e.g., Galman, 2009; Evans-Winters & Hoff, 2011). However, Lowenstein (2009) maintains that it is possible to disrupt these patterns by immersing teacher candidates in field experiences that confront them with the imperative of culturally relevant pedagogy. It is her belief that teacher candidates can think "in complex ways" about "social issues" and bring assets to this experience, on which teacher education can capitalize (p. 186).

Consistent with this basic premise, my teacher education instruction takes place for the most part in settings where teacher candidates are immersed in culturally diverse communities as a part of their coursework. Beginning with the aim of schools in a democratic society to which we all subscribe, I problematize the current unequal state of education as falling short of these ideals. Ayers (2010) proposes that cultural assumptions and deficit views can shape the way that teachers "see" students. I invoke this metaphorical statement to impart to teacher candidates the implications of their positionality and its related power and privilege. My hope is that it reveals pathways to their advocacy. While limited options are available to transform classroom curriculum and pedagogy, each emergent teacher has complete control over the way she "sees" and will see her students as future and fellow citizens. In this way, I can re-center advocacy for girls like Heaven and create a classroom environment to interrogate the belief that there was an absence of deep internal choice to move in constructive directions alone that condemned a girl like Heaven to an early presence in the juvenile justice system.

Maria H.F.

I identify as a culturally and linguistically diverse (CLD) woman whose parents were refugees. My childhood was marked by significant economic struggle and with overt racism and constant surveillance directed at us, particularly when we spoke our heritage language in public spaces. On a personal level, I suppose I related to some of the girls in the text through that lens, in that you could never just "be," but instead were simultaneously asked to discard your identity and to see it as inferior, but also persistently reminded of its pervasiveness and finality. There were many discordant feelings that overlaid one another, such as simultaneous shame and defiance. I *liked* being CLD but was constantly faced with being encouraged to forget it and to never forget it (in a negative manner) in the school setting, as were my siblings. To forget my language would be to forget my mother and her love. We would not be able to communicate. I thought in that language and could not do schoolwork without it. There were some teachers who really made an effort to get to know me and my family beyond surface food differences and stereotypes, and that made all the difference in my career choices and academic trajectory. That relational ability, which is very valued in my culture of origin, is something that I try to bring to the table when working in schools and as an academic in the field of psychology. Though I cannot, nor would I want to pretend to, fully understand what the young women in the text experienced, perhaps my feelings while growing up of "otherness" and of feeling in a "Catch-22" would allow me to be able to listen first and to know that there is likely much more under the surface.

- How does your positionality (in the relevant forms) relate to or inhibit "centering Black girls" in your pedagogy and practice?

In my pedagogy and practice I attempt, not always successfully, to first listen deeply to my students and the children we work with in the schools.
Providing validation, belief in the individual student's worth and ability,
and seeing them from a multidimensional intersectional strengths and cultural assets perspective can help center the focus on the student rather than
on yourself or the broader norming system. Perhaps the hardest challenge
in centering Black girls comes at the system level, where we have to really demonstrate the need to start making significant changes in how discipline and dress codes and other mechanisms of norming and oppression are
implemented, and why making changes has value when there is systemically
a lot of inertia and satisfaction with the status quo.

- How does positionality, insofar as it does, inform and address your assumptions about the worthiness of young Black girls for interventions
  or your qualifications to do so?

I think that the situation in schools surrounding disproportionate discipline
and its deleterious effects as well as a lot of the culturally construed categories such as "persistent disobedience" found in schools create a dire situation and necessitate that *everyone* do what they can to make major changes.
We need changes in our own thinking, to check our assumptions regularly,
and to dismantle regressive punitive systems that do not improve academic
outcomes for everyone. We need to start asking: "Who benefits?" and "Why
am I doing what I am doing and why am I responding in this way?" etc.

My personal positionality and qualifications are not a 100% perfect
fit, but in my professional role I can help schools to disaggregate data such
as discipline data, and can make consultative suggestions that could differentially help Black girls both as a group and individually. There first needs
to be an intervention for the system; then we can look at individual cases.
If some of the problematic practices and bias that disproportionately affect
Black girls are addressed first, intervention could be better tailored to the
small group and individual levels.

- How does or can your positionality differentially inform the meaning of
  the love and concern that you bring to these relationships?

Having been a girl who very much benefited from being seen wholly by a
few teachers, especially the one that referred me to a gifted program despite

the prevailing logic that individuals who are CLD can't make it in a gifted program due to the English-language demands, I think my positionality encourages me to look beyond the initial referral concern and to remember the joy and utter creativity of childhood. I hope that I can help children have a space in which to dream *and* achieve. I hope that they can sense that I do care about them and that I see them. I don't want to erase their culture or who they are, but instead want to foster a sense of value and of being valued.

- Is positionality a part of reasoning that guides your thinking about the prospects for having an impact on the success or failure of Black girls being tracked in this way?

Yes. As I stated before, things are really tough out there and we all have a responsibility to do what we can, when we can. My professional role, which is part of my positionality and actually *stemmed* from my positionality, allows me to use data and research findings to influence both schools and future school leaders. The intersectional needs of Black girls must be seen holistically rather than by separating race, gender, and economic resources status. Therefore, for example, disaggregation of discipline data at a given school can take place for intersectional groups (e.g., Black girls by grade level and by type or location of "infraction") so as not to erase or mask any unique issues. I see many of these issues as systemic first and foremost. We need to interrogate our practices regularly and very critically root out policies and practices that undermine the well-being of the children we are serving, sometimes in very wounding and personal ways. I did not like people making assumptions about my family members, or me, and this has informed my approach.

Kiesha

As an African American female who is Professor of Criminology and Criminal Justice at a four-year institution of higher education and a mother of three children, I cannot separate who I am from what I do in my professional work space. The reality is that every aspect of my work is to protect girls and boys that look like my children—children of color. I am the only female faculty member of color in my department, and the majority of my students have career aspirations of working within some aspect of the criminal justice system. Given that the majority of these students identify as Anglo

Americans and are from rural areas and that for many of them the career trajectory will lead them to working with people different from themselves, it is imperative that I work to teach them the importance of understanding how their positionality and White privilege shape how they act on stereo-types and view "others."

As I think of my work and the girls represented in Morris's *Pushout* (2016), I cannot help but think about how my teaching with predominantly Anglo males will shape the views and interactions with adolescent girls of color who are in vulnerable situations and in need of support—for instance, when those male teachers interact with a young girl of color like Jmiya Rick-man, who is autistic and when in kindergarten had her hands and feet cuffed by police after throwing a tantrum. For a little girl who is acting out due to emotional issues, being cuffed can cause lasting trauma.

It is important that I teach my students to go beyond stereotypes and to look at others from a position of understanding cultural competence and humanity. By looking just at the act of young women of color, like Jennifer, selling her body for money and not examining why she is taking part in the act and the cultural implications of such acts in her community does not leave room for authentic support and help for the victim and will contribute to the continued stereotypes of adolescent girls of color. It is important for future criminal justice professionals to recognize the fragility of working with people who do not look like themselves.

Mistrust is inherent in police-minoritized community relationships. Anglo individuals working with young girls of color must also understand that this level of mistrust impacts the way in which these girls will choose to take advantage of support being offered. Focusing on developing culturally competent skills that will allow them to be able to communicate with young girls of color is vital. My goal is that by challenging my criminal justice stu-dents to develop cultural competency skills, they will begin to think beyond stereotypical norms and see young women of color as individuals who need support that goes beyond locking them away from society.

Maria S.

When I sat down to write this reflection, I was challenged. I wrestled with *wanting to say the right thing* and *needing to be authentic* while also *stay-ing true to myself and my beliefs*. I understood that my positionality plays a pivotal role in the framing of my interpretations and reflections on the experiences of the young Black girls in Morris's *Pushout* (2016). I struggled to find the balance between acknowledging my positionality without over-shadowing the purpose of this reflection on the plight of young Black girls that Morris captured in *Pushout*.

I am a first-generation Portuguese-American, first-generation college student, and a military veteran. I am a mother, a teacher, and a scholar. I grew up in a single-parent household in a very small town in New England. All these parts of myself strongly influence the lens through which I view, interpret, and interact with the world around me. For me, it has always been important to recognize and disclose my positionality to the preservice teach-ers in my classes. I find that it is essential for me to explain who I am, where I come from, and what circumstances and experiences have ultimately led me to being in the classroom working with them in order to contextualize future discussions.

My professional work focuses on preservice teacher preparation to meet the needs of students with disabilities from culturally, linguistically, and socioeconomically diverse backgrounds, with a primary focus on stu-dents who engage in challenging behaviors. My research focuses on explor-ing school-based factors and practices that perpetuate the exclusion from school of diverse students with disabilities and identifying interventions and alternative practices.

Given the focus of my research, I was familiar with much of the hard data (e.g., statistics) that Morris shared in *Pushout*. What has historically been missing in the literature, however, is what Morris captured: the voice of Black girls directly impacted by punitive and exclusionary policies and practices in schools. For this reason, I was much less familiar with the expe-riences and larger issues facing young Black girls—how many of the school-based policies that I had been researching and teaching about impacted young Black girls specifically.

Often the literature subsumes young Black girls in discussions of either African American students or girls without addressing the intersectional-ity of race and gender and the implications of that intersectionality on the unique experiences faced by young Black girls. I must admit, uncomfortable as it is, that I was perpetuating the isolated exploration of these larger issues without consideration of the intersectionality of race, gender, and socioeco-nomic status in particular. When I was discussing the marginalization of youth of color when it comes to school-based behavior policies, codes of conduct, etc., all too often I discussed the impact of such policies on young Black males. I had not considered the unique experiences and challenges faced by young Black girls—I certainly never talked about the issues of dress codes, despite having these discussions on a personal level with other mothers of daughters.

For me, the "worthiness" of young Black girls for intervention and access to free, fair, equitable education that is neither punitive nor dismissive of their cultural experiences and norms is paramount. I struggle with framing it as a matter of "worthiness" because for me it feels like it should be so much more. It should not be a question of "worthiness"—Yes, of course young Black girls are worthy. But it is easy for me to say they are worthy and another thing entirely to acknowledge that young Black girls are growing up in a society and navigating systems that at any given moment are feeding them the message that they are *not* worthy. For me, it is pressing that we find a way to immerse young Black girls with the messages that they are worthy, but also that they are entitled to, deserve, and should be receiving these things. I understand that much of what I am saying comes from my particular lens informed by my experiences and privilege. I have to acknowledge and often *check myself* that although I relate to isolated experiences shared by some of the girls in the book, the contexts within which we experienced them were vastly different. I was, and still am, afforded privileges because of the way I look; the ways in which people around me responded to, or did not respond, to my deviant, unruly behaviors were vastly different than those experienced by the young Black girls in *Pushout*. This is undoubtedly linked to issues of privilege imbedded in my Whiteness.

For me, a considerable takeaway in moving forward is considering my language when talking with young Black girls and young Black women. Although I want to relate to the young Black girls I encounter in my work, at least to some degree, and not come across as an outsider, I have to remember that I can have dialogue through which a relationship may ensue.

Much of my day-to-day activity involves working directly with undergraduate pre-service teachers and graduate students who are practicing teachers, behavior clinicians, and school administrators. From these interactions, I see how the education workforce continues to be comprised predominately of White, middle-class females, with the exception of administrators, who tend to be White, middle- or upper-class males. And although I have had a small number of male pre-service or in-service students, I have had far fewer African

American students. Those of us in education know that our education force does not mirror the student population that it serves. I often wonder what message this sends to students in classrooms across the country.

Synthesis & Summary

This structured reflection as counternarrative research was an inquiry by and about higher education faculty and their pedagogy of emerging education professionals and practitioners who interact with Black girls on a consistent basis. It drew on both positionality and reflexivity to explore the possibilities of meaning making for actuating the social justice ideal. In the face of the systemic criminalization of young Black girls and the dissonance generated by critical distance of divergent lived experiences, it was hoped that each person's narrative response to the generated questions of critical positionality would offer emergent pedagogical possibilities that moved beyond sympathy as motivation to agency. Being reflexively positional would be productive in this regard by engaging the underlying assumptions of each faculty member's subject positionality within the social and political context and in light of the predominantly White students with whom they are working.

Positionality can be efficacious in this regard because it has a two-fold meaning that represents the discursive nature of group identity in being embedded in social relations. As a construct pertaining to gender identity and race/ethnicity, positionality offers that each location can be a source of knowledge, because each is a subject site for beliefs, values, and judgments. Either the dominant or othered standing of each group identity provides a rich sociocultural location from which persons can engage in meaning-making and construct narratives of agency.

The alternate face of positionality also recognizes the partial nature or situatedness of beliefs and that institutions can function in ways that equate regimes of knowledge, science, and principles with the dominant group's beliefs. As such, the kind of social status one holds and its related degree of influence and power are linked for instance to one's gender identity, racial or ethnic group membership, and its relative social standing.

The dual nature of the positionality construct places a reflective demand on the subject that inhabits it to actively and consistently engage with the twin aspects in reflexive positionality. Salient intersubjective considerations in such an analysis include who experiences inequality, forms of oppression that society visits upon the least powerful, and the political manifestation of injustice.

The positionality critique is complicated by the fact that each of the faculty members belongs to a racially or ethnically othered group and has experienced some form of racism or marginalization. None of the Anglo-American participated in the study. As women in academia, they are still fewer in number relative to men. However, their status as minoritized faculty members and the associated subordinated status mediated their gender and racial identification. They are tasked with preparing predominately White students in an institutional space that has been shown to replicate the existing racialized and gendered social order and its social hierarchies in which White male racial dominance has the greatest capital. Therefore, all wrestle in their faculty role with reconciling their professional tasks with attendant narratives of marginalization from the mainstream culture. Their reflexively positional narratives articulated a convergence of social status and professional role and indicate beliefs, preliminary convictions, or stances around which they are individually converging. Below we foreground the key points that each faculty expressed.

Confronted with the divergence of life outcomes between the girls featured and her own history as a studious teenager, for Sheron there was an initial recourse to an individualistic interpretation of the meaning of the text. Acknowledging that the implicit question there is one of the degree of responsibility the girls hold, Sheron problematized the notion of meritocracy and its animating role in the false narratives of colonialist imperialism, which influenced her formative years. In this self-assessment she imputed the trope of the angry, Black woman as a professional parallel in higher education, in which responsibility plays a small part in a matrix of systemically oppressive factors.

Maria H.F. calls into question the syntax of discipline in the K–12 schools as being political and views her role as helping the higher education students see the status quo with the critical lens of the role of power. Among her pedagogical tools are the ability of statistical information to make evident the various demographic and institutional axes of Black girls' vulnerability. Such pedagogical strategies are exercised, she makes clear, in a learning environment in which she shares some aspects of positionality with her pre-professional students. Like them she is racially different from the Black girls who are the subject of her advocacy, while as a LatinX woman there rare clear poins of divergence from her higher education students. It is an identification in which she strives to articulate a discourse of social justice where these gaps of lived experience endure, are respected, but do not serve as a barrier to social action.

For Kiesha, as an African-American woman and mother, her positionality is such that the social status of her minor children as minoritized persons have a reflexive influence. It plays a role in the normative framing of the disparity between her students' lives and the Black girls that they are being prepared to encounter as police officers and other law-enforcement professionals. Arguing that the disparity does not equate to deficiency, in spite of the poor decisions that contribute to poor outcomes for some of the Black girls, she strives to provide cultural competency training in her classroom. Critical positionality is evidenced in this curricular intervention, which she believes holds the greatest promise for closing the experiential divide and motivating social justice.

Maria S. evidences reflexive positionality as she lists the various markers with which she identifies and their relationship to identifying with Black girls confronting this crisis. Just as she prefers not to be defined predominantly with any one identifier but sees herself as inhabiting interlocking identities, in the same way she strives to foster acknowledgement of such a right for Black girls. This moral aspiration encourages pre-professional students to focus on the commonalities and shared humanity among themselves, their professor, and the Black girls (Lowenstein, 2009).

In reflective self-assessment in relation to the systemic sources of racism, in her pedagogy Maria S. differentiates the individual recognition of shared humanity from wrestling with the implications for Black girls who must navigate systems of stigma and fear of them. Being able to acknowledge and foster efforts to disrupt this status quo is an essential part of the work of becoming an advocate and White ally (Titone, 2009). Maria S. views countering the male gendered bias about Black youth criminalization as Morris' (2016) does as being primary in advancing social justice. Her reflection evinces the intersectional (Crenshaw, 1989) nature of the Black girls' criminalization in which they are objects of overlapping forms of oppression. Only by recognizing, for example, that stringent K – 12 rules and punishments linked to cultural and ethnic hair, dress and tone are carriers and precursors of systemic tracking of Black girls can pre-professionals become aware of ways stand up for them in school settings.

Conclusion

Morris's (2016) *Pushout* amplified the dire conditions that confront young Black girls, where previously it was thought that only Black boys were vulnerable to the pipelines of mass incarceration. The girls featured in the work experience systemic racism in gendered ways that Morris carefully excavates. Assimilated into the very fabric of mainstream American education, their oppression can be hiding in the plain sight of schools. The higher education faculty in this chapter tell stories of figuratively stepping away from their teaching practice by holding their sociocultural location up to a critical light. They ponder ways that they possess and lack the power to relate to the factors that make one vulnerable to racism and female oppression. Nevertheless, they remain committed to advancing a discourse of social justice for these girls, in spite of the disparities between their lived experiences.

References

Alcoff, L. M. (1988). Cultural feminism versus post-structuralism: The identity crisis in feminist theory, *Signs 13*(4), 425-436.

Alcoff, L.M. (1995). Cultural feminism versus post-structuralism: The identity crisis in feminist theory. In N. Tuana & R. Tong (Eds.), *Feminism and philosophy: Essential readings in theory, reinterpretation, and application* (pp. 434–451). Boulder, CO: Westview Press.

Alcoff, L.M. (2006). *Visible identities: Race, gender, and the self.* Oxford: Oxford University Press.

Ayers, B. (2010). *To Teach: The journey in comics.* New York, NY: Teachers College Press.

Boyles, D. (2007). Marketing sameness: Consumerism, commercialism, and the status quo. In J. Smart (Ed.), *Higher education: Handbook of theory and research*, 22 (pp. 537-582). Dordrecht: Springer.

Crenshaw, K. (1989). Demarginalizing the intersection of race and sex: A Black feminist critique of antidiscrimination doctrine, feminist theory and antiracist politics. *University of Chicago Legal Forum*, 139–168. Retrieved from https://philpapers.org/rec/CREDTI

Crenshaw, K., Ocen, P., & Nada, J. (2016). *Black girls matter: Pushed out,*

overpoliced, and under-protected. Retrieved from http://www.aapf.org/recent/
2014/12/coming-soon-blackgirlsmatter-pushed-out-overpoliced-and-under
protected

Doyle, W.C. (2007). The political economy of redistribution through higher education subsidies. In J. Smart (Ed.), *Higher education: Handbook of
theory and research*, 22, (pp. 335–411). Dordrecht, Netherlands: Springer.

Evans-Winters, V.E., & Hoff, P.T. (2011). The aesthetics of White racism in
preservice teacher education: A critical race theory perspective. *Race, Ethnicity and Education, 14*(4), 461–479. doi:10.1080/13613324.2010.548376

Freire, P. (1972). *Pedagogy of the oppressed*. New York, NY: Herder and
Herder.

Freire, P., Giroux, H., & McLaren, P. (1988). *Teachers as intellectuals: towards a critical pedagogy of learning*. Westport, CT: Bergin and Garvey, Inc

Festinger, L. (1985). *A theory of cognitive dissonance*. Stanford, CA: Stanford University Press.

Fraser-Burgess, S. (2018). Identity politics and belonging. In P. Smeyers
(Ed.), *International Handbook of Philosophy of Education* (pp. 851-865).
Cham, Switzerland: Springer International Publishing.

Galman, S. (2009). Doth the lady protest too much? Pre-service teachers
and the experience of dissonance as a catalyst for development. *Teaching
and Teacher Education, 25*(3), 468–481. doi:10.1016/j.tate.2008.08.002.

Ginwright, S. (2002), Classed out: The challenges of social class in black
community change. *Social Problems, 49*(4), 544-562.

Giroux, H. & Giroux, S. (2004). *Take back higher education: Race, youth,
and the crisis of democracy in the post-civil rights era*. New York, NY: Palgrave Macmillan.

Goodall, Jr., H.L. (2010). *Counter-narrative: How progressive academics
can challenge extremists and promote social justice*. Walnut Creek, CA: Left
Coast Press.

Goodman, L.A., Liang, B., Helms, J.E., Latta, R.E., Sparks, E., & Weintraub, S.R. (2004). Training counseling psychologists as social justice agents: Feminist and multicultural principles in action. *The Counseling Psychologist, 32*(6), 793–836. doi:10.1177/0011000004268802

hooks, b. (1994). *Teaching to transgress: Education as the practice of freedom.* New York, NY: Routledge.

Howard, T.C. (2010). *Why race and culture matter in schools: Closing the achievement gap in America's classrooms.* New York, NY: Teachers College Press.

Howard, T.C., & Navarro, O. (2016). Critical race theory 20 years later. *Urban Education, 51*(3), 253–273. doi:10.1177/0042085915622541

Ladson-Billings, G. (2005). The evolving role of critical race theory in educational scholarship. *Race, Ethnicity, & Education, 8*(1), 115-119.

Lowenstein, K. (2009). The work of multicultural teacher education: Reconceptualizing white teacher candidates as learners. *Review of Educational Research, 79*(1), 163-196.

Maher, F. & Tetreault, M.K. (1993). Frames of positionality: Constructing meaningful dialogues about gender and race. *Anthropological Quarterly, 66*(3), 118-126.

McFarland, J., et. al. (2017). Characteristics of post-secondary faculty. *The Condition of Education.* Retrieved from https://nces.ed.gov/programs/coe/indicator_csc.asp

Mezirow, J. (1990). How critical reflection triggers transformative learning. In J.M. & Associates (Ed.), *Fostering critical reflection in adulthood: A guide to transformative and emancipatory learning* (pp. 1–20). San Francisco, CA: Jossey-Bass.

Morris, M.W. (2016). *Pushout: The criminalization of Black girls in schools.* New York, NY: New Press.

Nairn, S., Chambers, D., Thompson, S., McGarry, J., & Chambers, K. (2012). Reflexivity and habitus: Opportunities and constraints on transformative learning. *Nursing Philosophy, 13*(3), 189–201. doi:10.1111/j.1466-769x.2011.00530.x

Pezzetti, K. (2017) "I'm not racist; my high school was diverse!" white pre-service teachers deploy diversity in the classroom. Whiteness and Education, 2(2), 131-147.

Sensoy, O. & DiAngelo, R.J. (2017). *Is everyone really equal? An introduction to key concepts in social justice education.* New York, NY: Teachers College Press.

Titone, C. (2009). Educating the White teacher as ally. In J. Kincheloe, et al., (Ed.) *White reign: Deploying whiteness in America*, (pp. 159-176). New York, NY: St Martin Press.

CHAPTER TWO

RELIEVING TENSION AND EMPOWERING STUDENTS:

Addressing Societal Racism in U.S. Classrooms Through Critical Discourse Analysis

CHRISTINA J. CAVALLARO, COLE KERVIN,
SABRINA F. SEMBIANTE, TRACI P. BAXLEY

Introduction

"I THINK IT WAS a rookie error in teaching about race" (Wootson, Jr., 2016, para. 13), said Paul Ketchum, Assistant Professor of Criminal Justice at the University of Oklahoma. This was Ketchum's response to a lecture given by a Norman North High School teacher, James Coursey, who told his philosophy class that "to be White is to be racist, period" (para. 5). Reporting on the incident, Norman Public Schools Superintendent Joe Siano stated that "racism is an important topic that we discuss in our schools.... We regret that the discussion was poorly handled" (para. 13). Across the country, other teachers have found themselves in similar situations when attempting to foster classroom discussions surrounding race and racial issues. For instance, in Dedham, Massachusetts, school officials are currently investigating an incident involving a high school Spanish teacher who was dismissed after she facilitated a class discussion on immigration that offended a student who had recently immigrated from Guatemala (Bowen, 2017). Another situation, this one in Spring Hill, Florida, involved releasing a middle school teacher as a result of an assignment in which students were asked to evaluate their level of comfort in hypothetical situations, such as when "a group of Black men are walking towards [them] on the street," or "[their] new roommate is Palestinian or Muslim" (Schladebeck, 2017, para. 4). The experiences of these three teachers epitomize the conundrum many teachers face across the nation while attempting to address issues of racism in their classrooms. Many teachers are encouraged by administrators to examine relevant issues concerning race but are often not given adequate preparation to do so, leaving them unequipped to discuss these sensitive topics in appropriate ways. In this chapter we describe an approach that presents teachers with educational and academic entry points to facilitate these important, sometimes taboo, discussions of race with students in their classrooms as a means to a social justice-oriented education.

Social Justice

Social justice is both a goal and a process (Bell, 2016) in which teachers must provide safe spaces where issues of racism, sexism, classism, and other forms of institutional and individual discrimination are discussed in order to help students process and respond to local, national, and global events (Shields & Mohan, 2008). Social justice can be defined as the full and equitable participation of all people within a society that is "mutually shaped to meet their needs" (Bell, 2016, p. 3). To achieve this, social justice requires confronting the ideological frameworks and institutional patterns that perpetuate hierarchical structures—often concerning race—in which power, social, and economic advantages are afforded to certain social groups at the expense of others. Social justice-based education enables students to develop awareness, knowledge, and skills not only to examine issues of social justice and injustice, but also to develop agency and commitment to work collaboratively toward the goal of disrupting and changing oppressive structures (Bell, 2016). In working toward social justice, teachers must move beyond simply transmitting information to students and begin to create safe, welcoming, and inclusive spaces where students are able to engage in discussion and share potentially varying perspectives. In this way they can be encouraged to explore the nature of power, privilege, disparity, and oppression in order to "make sense of things" (Shields & Mohan, 2008). Teachers cannot fulfill their responsibility to promote equity, social mobility, and a democratic society without discussing these often-controversial issues (Coles-Ritchie & Smith, 2017; Noddings & Brooks, 2017).

Barriers for Teachers to Acknowledge and Overcome
Despite calls encouraging teachers to discuss racial issues within social justice-oriented education, several challenges have emerged that stifle these types of classroom discussions. While teachers may want to discuss these issues, especially given the research that confirms the benefits of such discussions for students (i.e., Banks, 2015; Gay, 2010; Ladson-Billings, 2009; Milner IV, 2017), teachers are often unprepared to address such politically and racially charged topics (Boyd & Glazier, 2017) or they view topics of race as too controversial, sensitive, or emotional (Coles-Ritchie & Smith, 2017) to be included in instruction. Few pre-service preparation programs and in-service professional development opportunities support teachers in understanding how to discuss issues of social inequity in their classrooms, sheltering them from experiences or exposure to appropriate practical approaches (Gorski, 2008). This leaves teachers ill-equipped to broach the topic of race in constructive ways (Sleeter, 2008). As a result, too many teachers have yet to recognize the value of engaging students in discussions concerning race. Additionally, the predominantly White, middle-class teacher population stands as highly disproportionate to the racial and socioeconomic makeup of students from historically marginalized groups (Sleeter, 2016). Rather than dismiss these differences, teachers must recognize their privilege and take action in ways that address White privilege and make it unacceptable (Epstein, 2017). In order to be able to address topics of race, teachers must critically examine their own experiences and perspectives to understand the racial distance that exists between them and their own students (Singleton, 2015). Further, teachers must be conscious of the institutionalized racism at play within society, schools, and classrooms in order to expose and weaken the hidden systems that work to oppress and privilege (Epstein, 2017).

Students are constantly exposed to issues connected to race through their daily experiences in their schools, communities, and social groups, and in their media exposure. While these issues may remain untouched or ignored in their schools, this does not prevent students from experiencing the realities of racism in the forms of microaggressions, bullying, verbal abuse, and other racially fueled events in their daily lives outside of coursework (Harwood, Mendenhall, Lee, Riopelle, & Browne Huntt, 2018). Therefore, as teachers bridge students' home and school realms, they require the tools and strategies that allow them to address a variety of racial issues through discussion and in their planned curriculum (Coles-Ritchie & Smith, 2017). The effort to find ways to overcome the obstacles to talking and teaching about topics of race as a means of achieving social justice is ongoing within the research. However, further efforts are needed.

In this chapter we introduce an approach that helps teachers to facilitate discussions about sensitive social justice-themed topics of race in an equitable and educational manner. We present steps that teachers can use with students to critically examine texts that reveal the potential underlying messages of social inequity and prejudice surrounding race. These steps are aligned with Common Core English Language Arts Standards (2017) that encourage students to read science and social studies texts to retrieve various informational matter and background knowledge. Using this practical, holistic approach, teachers can guide students through an analysis of textbooks, newspaper articles, and other forms of media in order to facilitate classroom discussions around racial issues of prejudice, injustice, and related public and political controversy.

Our approach is based on prior work in educational and applied linguistics that has exposed how the organization of language creates messages of racism within comedic texts (Weaver, 2011), children's literature (Sembiante, Baxley, & Cavallaro, 2017), and newspaper articles (Teo, 2000). As we discuss our framework, we will provide examples of the steps that can be used to analyze texts in a manner that can facilitate discussions surrounding topics of social justice. This approach, rooted in Critical Discourse Analysis (CDA), allows one to analyze a text by focusing on discourse and the relations between discourse and other social elements (Fairclough, 2013). Employing a CDA-informed framework exposes students to the socially constructed discourses of social justice issues, which can only be derived from their meaning and significance in specific historical, political, and social contexts (Appiah, 1989; Coles-Ritchie & Smith, 2017) that have long-term and enduring effects on people and communities (Brown, Gutierrez, Okmin, & McCullough, 2017). With regard to topics of race, CDA also exposes students to elements of "new racism" (Bonilla-Silva, 1999; Coles-Ritchie & Smith, 2017)—that is, the idea that gives those who are considered White more social opportunities and advantages than people of color, and the option for people with unearned White privilege to ignore race-based discrepancies and take for granted the privileges that they enjoy. These elements of "new racism" are often disguised, indirect expressions of racial prejudice in the media that take the form of discursive strategies that blame disparities on historically marginalized groups' social, economic, and cultural disadvantages (Sniderman, Piazza, Tetlock, & Kendrick, 1991; Teo, 2000). Further, teachers who do not discuss race and racial issues in their classes participate in silencing the dialogue of individuals and communities (Delpit, 2006). The failure to acknowledge events that affect all members of society, especially those who have been historically marginalized, can be detrimental. It is particularly damaging to students of color who face racism in their communities and attend school only to have their lived experiences of injustice ignored. By accumulating evidence of these inequities through analyzing texts, as the steps for analysis will showcase, teachers can facilitate critical discussions that legitimize the anger and frustration of culturally and linguistically diverse students while creating safe spaces for broaching these topics.

The George Zimmerman Trial and the Trayvon Martin Case

For this chapter, we chose to analyze an article that was published in a recognized media publication covering a polarizing event surrounding race. The article, titled "Zimmerman Is Acquitted in Killing of Trayvon Martin," by Lizette Alvarez and Cara Buckley, was published in *The New York Times* on July 14, 2013, following the acquittal of George Zimmerman on charges of murdering Trayvon Martin. Not only was this event the first of many high-profile trials involving the deaths of and brutality toward unarmed Black Americans; it was also the event in which the #BlackLivesMatter movement was conceived (Capehart, 2015; Garza, 2016).

George Zimmerman, the 29-year-old neighborhood watch volunteer who fatally shot unarmed Black teenager Trayvon Martin in Sanford, Florida, ignited a national debate on racial profiling and civil rights (Alvarez & Buckley, 2013; Capehart, 2015; Garza, 2016). According to reports, Zimmerman was driving through his townhouse complex on the evening of February 26, 2012, when he saw 17-year-old Trayvon Martin walking through the rain wearing a hooded sweatshirt (or "hoodie"). Zimmerman notified police but then disregarded their advice by exiting his vehicle to confront

Martin. As reported, Martin responded by punching Zimmerman and slamming him to the ground. Zimmerman, fearing that his life was in danger, then shot Martin in an act of self-defense. Zimmerman was protected by Florida's "stand your ground" law, which is a self-defense law that allows someone who fears great bodily harm or death to use lethal force to protect him or herself, even if retreating from danger is an option (Justifiable Use of Force, 2017). This law forced prosecutors to prove beyond a reasonable doubt that Zimmerman's safety was not in jeopardy, diverting attention away from the fact that Zimmerman's approaching Martin began the chain of events that led to Martin's death. Jurors decided that although there was no doubt that Zimmerman had fatally shot Martin, he had done so out of self-defense after being attacked by the teen, resulting in Zimmerman's acquittal on second-degree murder and manslaughter charges (Alvarez & Buckley, 2013). The outcome of this case caused many to question a judicial system in which a man could legally shoot an unarmed Black teenager without experiencing any repercussions. Many, especially people involved at the community level, were frustrated that the U.S. justice system would protect such racial prejudice. These frustrations led to the #BlackLivesMatter movement as a response to the anti-Black racism permeating U.S. society (Garza, 2016). Given the implications of such a racial climate in society, this is an important issue that should be deliberated in the classroom. Students need to be provided spaces in which to discuss these issues and understand what they mean, both at the personal and wider societal levels.

The Theory Behind Our Approach

We use a CDA framework called the Functional-Critical Analytical Model (FCAM) (Sembiante, Baxley, & Cavallaro, 2017) to guide our approach to the challenge of how teachers can work with their students to reveal and question underlying messages of racial inequity in texts (Figure 1). This framework shows how combining Critical Literacy (CL) and Systemic Functional Linguistics (SFL) informs a language analysis around social justice themes. Below we provide more discussion about CL and SFL and the ways in which their combination informs and builds, one upon the other, to foster our CDA framework.

Critical Literacy

CL is an instructional approach to literacy that seeks to identify the power relationships construed in text, exposes which perspectives are legitimized, and reveals which groups are privileged over others (Beck, 2005). For students, becoming critically literate means developing the skills to engage with texts in a discerning manner that transcends merely accepting the message of a text at face value. Instead, through CL, students develop the agency to critique and question a text from a teacher who shows them how to interpret the meaning of a message within the larger societal context, and with reference to systemic social justice issues. Students are encouraged to challenge the disparities they encounter in texts across a range of social constructs such as socioeconomic status, race, class, gender, and sexual orientation (Shor, 1992; 1999). If one of the purposes of schooling is to produce citizens who contribute to the democracy of U.S. society (Dewey, 1916; Sleeter, 2005), then CL plays a crucial part in preparing students to recognize the role and potential of written language as a tool "to analyze the division of power and resources in their society and transform discriminatory structures" (Blackledge, 2000, p. 18). Teachers can cultivate the awareness afforded by CL through activities that allow students to actively construct knowledge (Freire, 1970). For example, by facilitating discussions around social issues that affect students, teachers can provide students with the opportunity to question the status quo, build their understanding of social inequity, and create spaces in which to take action.

Systemic Functional Linguistics
If CL calls for critically interrogating, interpreting, and contextualizing who is dis/empowered in texts (Provenzo, 2005), then SFL provides a method for analyzing texts for evidence of these power relationships. SFL is a theory and method stemming from CDA. A central tenet of SFL is the idea that language choices are made purposefully, based upon the goal of communication (Schleppegrell, 2011). Thus, when texts are written in ways that intentionally or implicitly perpetuate prejudiced ideologies and systemic inequities, SFL offers the means to identify how the language is working to communicate those meanings (Eggins, 2004). For example, SFL encourages teachers and students to consider the language used to construct experiences in the world (e.g., who is being talked about, what actions/events are taking place, when and how actions/events are taking place), to interact with others (e.g., how ideas are negated or affirmed, how and what attitudes are conveyed), and to organize the ideas in a text (e.g., what order is information presented in,

how is the information connected) (Halliday & Matthiessen, 2014). In turn, these questions help students to attend to particular language features and their functions within texts. By teaching students to recognize and identify the language features that construct prejudice, students are positioned to point out evidence of bias and may feel more empowered to dismiss or challenge these bigoted discourses.

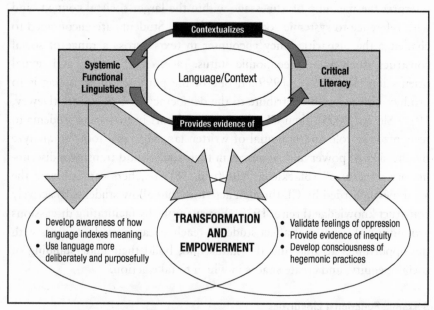

FIGURE 1. The Functional-Critical Analytical Model (FCAM). This figure shows how to engage recursively with the Systemic Functional Linguistics and Critical Literacy analytical frameworks to effect transformation and empowerment.

The Power of Discourse

Comprising one of the many factors contributing to social inequity, the role of discourse has the power to (re)produce or challenge dominant, oppressive structures as it reflects and constructs social entities and relations (Fairclough, 1992; van Dijk, 1993). Any instance of discourse is both a social interaction and a piece of text (Fairclough, 1992). Therefore, discourse refers to any written or spoken product that can be analyzed through a CDA approach. In knowing that discourse is never neutral, holistically analyzing discourse can promote a critical understanding of power structures and the assumptions and biases that support them (van Dijk, 1993). The application of CDA in the classroom extends from critical pedagogy and the work of Paulo Freire, as it can engage students in critiquing and challenging dominant discourses and practices with the goal of creating a better learning environment and a better world (Freire, 1970). Freire advocates for education that provides students with the space to recognize connections between their personal experiences and the social context in which they are embedded. Discourse "is the encounter between [people], mediated by the world in order to name the world" (p. 69). Discourse analysis provides a way for students to draw on their own experiences and recognize personal biases as they uncover power structures and their relations. This analysis provides the foundation for discussion around varying attitudes, ideologies, norms, and values, and their relation to existing structures. Through such critical discussion, students and teachers are able to discover ways to take action against oppressive elements of reality as they engage in their own discourse, from which knowledge and social transformation can emerge.

Describing the Steps for Analyzing Texts

In addressing how, or in what way, educators should connect racial issues in the schools with the larger public and political debate about issues of race in America, we provide teachers with an opportunity to critically examine texts in the classroom in a manner that reveals the underlying messages of social inequity and prejudice. To achieve this, we have developed a set of steps for analyzing texts (Table 1), derived from the CL and SFL concepts, that helps teachers guide students through a critical examination of newspaper articles and other forms of media. The table consists of three properties of language, each of which has its own guiding questions (and related probing questions) that represent the steps teachers can follow to critically analyze texts. These guiding and probing questions help teachers to think about different parts of the text and, specifically, the type of language that should be looked at more closely to find evidence of the larger social justice themes. As teachers are able to become more critical of texts, they also become more prepared to engage their students in being critical consumers of text. In the next section we will review the contents of the table to clarify and present examples of the language features for every property of language. In the subsequent section, we will present a model analysis wherein these steps are implemented.

Property of Language	Guiding Questions	Probing Questions	Language Features to Analyze	Example
People and Experiences	What content and action are communicated in the text? (This tells us what the text is about.)	Who is being talked about?	Participant	George Zimmerman # of times mentioned: 1 **Mr. Zimmerman** # of times mentioned: 29 *"The neighborhood watch volunteer"* Associated with "defense lawyers," "his parents," "His wife, Shellie, and several of his friends" **Trayvon Martin** # of times mentioned: 13 **Mr. Martin** # of times mentioned: 22 *"The hoodie-clad teenager"* Associated with Sybrina Fulton and Tracy Martin (parents, attorney)
		What actions/ events are happening?	Process	Find all instances of **verbs** and <u>who</u> they are associated with: —Relational (describes states of being, having, or naming): "<u>We</u> **are** outraged" —Mental (describes thoughts, feelings, perceptions): "<u>He</u> **assumed** the hoodie-clad teenager was a criminal" —Material/Behavioral (describes physical changes or actions): "<u>the</u> **teenager knocked** <u>him</u> to the ground, **punched** <u>him</u> and **slammed** <u>his</u> head repeatedly against the sidewalk"
		When and how are these actions/ events taking place?	Circumstance (preposition-al & adver-bial phrases)	Find the additional information regarding time, place, manner: —"after three weeks" —"outside the courtroom" —"with fear and trauma"
			Classifier or Epithet (adjectives)	Identify descriptors for Zimmerman and for Trayvon (and everyone on each of their sides): —"the **small** city" —"a **routine** homicide"
Relationships	What are the relationships being built by the text between participants and with the reader? (this tells us about the power, hierarchy, position, perspectives)	How is negation and affirmation used in the text?	Postive Negative	Analyze the marked use of negative— and with whom, and in what light, for what function (keep in mind that positive and negative stem from expectation): —"His history was **not** as a racist" —"He likely would **never** have been charged"
		What are the attitudes and stances conveyed in the text?	Probability Usuality Inclination Obligation	Find every modal auxiliary and indicate which of these four categories it stands in. Also indicate if it is high, medium, low: —"Mr. Zimmerman **could** have been justified" *probability, medium* —"We **will** pursue civil rights charges" *probability, high* —"We **must** conduct ourselves" *obligation, high*

Property of Language	Guiding Questions	Probing Questions	Language Features to Analyze	Example
Cohesion and Coherence	How is the information organized? (This tells us the sequence in which we should under-stand the events, and insight into the reasoning for the order of ideas.)	What is the order of the information presented?	Genre Stages	Introduction (Statement of Event) Background Information Details of Event Actions Following Event Discussion/Closing
		How is the information connected throughout the text?	Theme/Rheme	Subject vs. Object of a sentence
			New/Given	New information and how it is picked up, integrated, and expanded in each new sentence.
			Referents (also nomin-alizations)	Referents like "he, she, it, they," etc.

TABLE 1. Steps for Analyzing Texts

The steps of the table are organized around three properties of language: the language used to talk about what is happening, such as the events, states of being, experiences (People and Experiences); the language used to inter-act with and showcase relationships between people and characters (Rela-tionships); and the way the text is organized according to a specific purpose or genre (Cohesion and Coherence) (Halliday & Matthiessen, 2014). These properties of language are addressed through the three guiding questions presented in the table: *What content and action is communicated in the text? What are the relationships being built by the text between participants and with the reader?* and *How is the information organized?* The guiding questions help to point out the language features that will drive the analysis of the text and provide linguistic evidence of the social justice themes. Each property of language has different guiding questions, but the same analysis approach is used for each.

To understand the main content of the text, we must answer the prob-ing questions of *Who is being talked about? What actions/events are taking place?* and *When and how are these actions/events taking place?* Each prob-ing question can be answered by finding certain linguistic features, as listed in each row, under the "Language Features to Analyze" and "Example" col-umns. Within the property of language governing people and experiences, the linguistic features of nouns, verbs, and adjectives are central to under-standing ways that people and events are discussed in texts. As one way to analyze the manner in which people and experiences are portrayed in the text, teachers can ask students to identify all the nouns and adjectives used for the main participants. For example, in the news article, George Zimmerman is referred to as "the neighborhood watch volunteer," "Mr. Zimmerman," and "a wannabe cop," among other labels, while Trayvon Martin is referred to as "an unarmed black teenager," "a hoodie-clad teenager," "Mr. Martin," etc. These are all terms that teachers could have asked students to look for, compare, and discuss. Analyzing the differences in these types of labels and terms, whether it be the societal meaning, connotation, or simply the amount of times the label is used, is one way in which teachers can push students to think critically about the potential biases within the text.

Another way to analyze how people and experiences are construed is to identify the verbs and prepositional phrases. Verbs work to showcase the actions and events taking place, while prepositional phrases give more information regarding the manner, time, or place of the action. In the excerpt, "Mr. Zimmerman spent 16 months filled with fear and trauma," the verb "filled" and the prepositional phrase "with fear and trauma" work together to render action and provide insight into Zimmerman's feelings, further showcasing the text's implicit message.

The second property of language—relationships—represents the connection or hierarchy between the participants in a text, such as Zimmerman and Martin, and how relationships are built by the text between participants and with the reader (in this case, with the teacher and his or her students). An analysis of relationships will reveal the power, hierarchy, positioning, and perspectives portrayed in the article. To understand more about these relationships, we answer the probing questions tied to relationships: *How are negation (e.g., the use of not, no, never) and affirmation (e.g., information stated affirmatively or positively) used in the text?* and *What are the attitudes and stances conveyed in the text?* To answer these probing questions, teachers can have students identify and compare the use of positives and negatives. We can see the power of an analysis that focuses on positives and negatives by looking at an example from the article that states: "Mark O'Mara, one of Mr. Zimmerman's lawyers, said, 'George Zimmerman was never guilty of anything except firing the gun in self-defense'" (Alvarez & Buckley, 2013, para. 13). Here, the phrase "was never guilty" is negated by "never," yet the phrase "was always innocent" could have been used to achieve the same meaning, just in a more positive manner. Additionally, modal verbs—such as might, may, must, could, should, can, and will—tell us more about the relationships by shifting the level of probability, usuality, inclination, and obligation in a text. For example, "should" or "will" are much stronger in communicating probability than "may" or "might." These words help to nuance, temper, lessen, or heighten the probability, usuality, inclination, and obligation of a situation. For instance, when the NAACP spokespersons stepped forward to provide commentary on the situation, as described in the article, the meaning of their statement that "we will pursue civil rights charges" would be much different than if they had said "we might pursue civil rights charges." The use of "will" has a higher degree of probability and intensity than "might," and aligns with the outrage that the case sparked for many across the nation. Adverbs, or words that modify adjectives, verbs, or other adverbs (e.g., likely, probably, typically), can also be used to nuance the meaning of what is being said by increasing or decreasing probability, usuality, inclination, and obligation.

The third property of language—cohesion and coherence of a text—deals specifically with how text is organized and structured to achieve a certain purpose. All texts have a purpose and therefore have a purposeful organization (called genre stages) contingent on the genre of the text. For example, narrative stories typically have genre stages of exposition, rising action, climax, falling action, and resolution. A verbal interaction of language even has genre stages. Consider meeting a new person: the conversation begins with an introduction, followed by multiple exchanges, then a closing phrase. Texts, and the way in which texts are organized, reflect the norms and expectations of the social context in which the text occurs, whether it is verbal or written, or fiction or nonfiction. Furthermore, studying the organization of text provides insight into potential social issues that the text presents. To analyze the cohesion and coherence of a text is to study the order in which information is presented, which provides insight into the manner in which the author wants readers to understand the issue.

Using the Steps to Analyze Texts

In this section we illustrate how to implement the steps that teachers can take to conduct a textual analysis, with examples from our own analysis of the aforementioned *New York Times* article entitled "Zimmerman Is Acquitted in Killing of Trayvon Martin," by Lizette Alvarez and Cara

Buckley (2013). Following this section, a table is provided to showcase the themes and supporting examples in a consolidated manner.

Prior to conducting a textual analysis, teachers should consider the intended goals and objectives of the lessons. Just as with any lesson preparation, the activities and materials should be aligned with the goals and objectives. Because our goal with this example analysis is to foster a text-based classroom discussion on racial issues, we chose to analyze a newspaper article reporting on the Trayvon Martin case. We chose this event because it was emblematic of some of the racial issues in U.S. society and was extensively covered in the media. Thus, the article served as a good source to analyze and to foster classroom discussion that connects to larger political societal issues. However, a teacher can select any genre or form of text to analyze, depending on the desired purpose and outcome of the lesson.

After selecting the article, the teacher will identify the major themes presented in the text. Identifying the major themes prior to engaging in the text analysis helps to ensure that students will focus on areas that lead to achieving the lesson's goals and objectives. The major themes are meant to extend beyond the main ideas and details of the text. For example, we identified two major themes in Alvarez and Buckley's (2013) article: (1) Zimmerman is portrayed as the victim, and (2) race changes the rules and norms of the case. Teachers would identify the main themes that they find in an article and turn these into critical questions to be presented for students' consideration. This means that our themes would then be put forward to students as: (1) How is Zimmerman presented as the victim? and (2) How does race change the rules and the norms of this case? These themes would be aligned with a teacher's purpose of addressing one facet of the U.S. racial climate in the classroom. Presenting these themes as questions will also help students to engage in the analysis and subsequent discussion from an unbiased, text-based perspective rather than in a personally defensive or reactionary manner. Following this step, we began to use Table 1, Steps for Analyzing Texts, to connect the themes with the three properties of language and their respective language features that serve as textual evidence.

Theme 1: How is Zimmerman presented as the victim?
Framing the themes as questions continuously scaffolds students to think in terms of providing answers, or evidence to support the theme. To discover textual evidence of the theme, we began by answering the questions

presented in the table for each property of language, beginning with the guiding questions. This can be done for as many of the properties of language as the teacher feels are appropriate, depending on the purpose of the lesson. After reading the article, we found that George Zimmerman was often characterized as the victim, as opposed to Trayvon Martin. There was not neutrality between the two, as George Zimmerman and Trayvon Martin were not positioned as equals. To strengthen our finding, we analyzed all three properties of language to provide textual evidence for this theme. We found evidence primarily around relationships (the second property of language) and cohesion and coherence (the third property of language). To answer the guiding question about relationships (*What are the relationships being built by the text between participants and with the reader?*), we had to look for evidence of power, hierarchy, positions, and perspectives. Using Table 1, we looked for uses of negation and affirmation that are used in the text. We also looked for the use of modal verbs to indicate probability, usuality, inclination, and obligation. By locating this type of language in the article, we found that modal verbs positioned Zimmerman as a victim by deflecting or casting doubt on assigning blame to him. For example, the modal verb "could" in the following sentence from the article works in this way:

- "In finding him not guilty of murder or manslaughter, the jury agreed that Mr. Zimmerman *could* have been justified in shooting Mr. Martin because he feared great bodily harm or death" (Alvarez & Buckley, 2013, para. 3).

In this example, the probability of Zimmerman being guilty of his action of shooting is being questioned and lessened through the use of "could." The use of adverbs that further support the theme of how Zimmerman is presented as the victim was found in the following excerpt describing the feelings of Zimmerman's lawyers:

- "And while defense lawyers were elated with the verdict, they also expressed anger that Mr. Zimmerman spent 16 months filled with fear and trauma when *all he was doing* was defending himself" (para. 3).

In this excerpt, the use of "all" as an adverb to describe the action of Zimmerman "defending himself" functions to lessen the severity of what he was doing, indirectly justifying his actions of shooting and killing Trayvon Martin and portraying Zimmerman as the victim.

We can find more evidence of Zimmerman being portrayed as a victim through the text by focusing on cohesion and coherence (the third language property) and the guiding question, *How is information organized?* It is characteristic of newspaper articles to be organized in stages beginning with background information of the main event, followed by details of the event, and ending with a discussion and conclusion. When considering the related probing question, *What is the order of the information presented?*, we see that the background information sets up the article to favor Zimmerman by portraying him as the victim. The audience is primed to see him in this light, as opposed to Martin. This is accomplished by initially including background information solely pertaining to Zimmerman. Just as we have done here, a teacher would go through the article (or other form of text) to identify themes and then conduct a preliminary analysis following the steps as described in order to ensure that there is textual evidence in support of these themes. Teachers can make note of the language that they found using the steps, which would prepare them to lead and facilitate the class activity. However, teachers would leave the actual analysis and search for textual evidence to the students as part of the activity. As the students engage in their own analysis, the teacher can scaffold the activity for students by using, showing, or posing the guiding and probing questions to students, as well as teaching them to look for the related language features that help to answer the questions.

Theme 2: How does race change the rules and norms of the case?

Again, while the theme that we found was that race changes the rules and norms of the case, we frame the theme as a question in order to turn it into an educational, discussion-fueling activity for the classroom and to encourage students to seek supportive textual evidence in an objective, academic manner. Before presenting the theme in question form to students, teachers will have preliminarily analyzed the properties of language conducive to their lesson in order to identify examples to support the theme. After analyzing all three properties of language, we found supportive textual evidence primarily with regard to people and experiences (the first language property) and relationships (the second language property). Under the guiding question, *What content and action is communicated in the text?*, we found language features to answer the probing question of *Who is being talked about?*, which called for looking at labels. Often, labels were assigned to Martin and Zimmerman that were indicative of or related to race. The following excerpts included multiple labels for Martin and Zimmerman.

- "George Zimmerman, *the neighborhood watch volunteer* who fatally shot Trayvon Martin, *an unarmed black teenager*, igniting a national debate on racial profiling and civil rights, was found not guilty late Saturday night of second-degree murder" (Alvarez & Buckley, 2013, para. 1).

- "After three weeks of testimony, the six-woman jury rejected the prosecution's contention that Mr. Zimmerman had deliberately pursued Mr. Martin because he assumed the *hoodie-clad* teenager was a criminal and instigated the fight that led to his death" (para. 2).

- "Mr. O'Mara disputed the notion that Mr. Zimmerman engaged in racial profiling. 'His history was not as a *racist*,' he said" (para. 21).

- "The public outcry began after the police initially decided not to arrest Mr. Zimmerman, who is *half-Peruvian*..." (para. 24).

These excerpts include multiple labels referring to race and ethnicity. The labels exude power, as they function as the participant. This emphasizes the focus on who and what is being discussed or partaking in an action. In the first quote, Zimmerman is given the label "neighborhood watch volunteer," while Martin is referred to as "an unarmed black teenager." This quote, which is the opening sentence of the article, functions to immediately identify Trayvon Martin's race. However, George Zimmerman's race is not mentioned until the third page of the article, emphasizing that it is the race of Martin, the "unarmed black teenager," that ignited a "national debate on racial profiling and civil rights." Other probing questions that teachers can analyze for evidence are *What actions/events are taking place?*, which requires an analysis of verbs, and *When and how are these actions/events taking place?*, which involves analyzing prepositional phrases.

The use of negation under the language property of relationships (the second language property) throughout the article also provides linguistic evidence in answer to the question *How does race change the rules and norms of the case?* The use of negation can be seen in the following excerpts:

- "Mr. O'Mara disputed the notion that Mr. Zimmerman engaged in racial profiling. 'His history was *not* <u>as a racist</u>,' he said" (para. 21).

- "He added that if Mr. Zimmerman was <u>black</u>, he likely would *never* <u>have been charged</u>" (para. 22).

In these excerpts, the words "not" and "never" function to negate what follows. The first example displays how "racist" is negated by "not." This sheds even greater light on the issue of race, even though the attempt is to argue that race was not an issue. The second example compares Zimmerman's race with the act of being charged. However, race, represented as "black," is associated with the negated "never have been charged," thus underscoring the assertion that race did alter the events of the case.

By following the steps of the table, we were able to support our two themes (phrased as questions) with an analysis of text and the selection of particular language that provided evidence to answer the theme questions. Teachers can follow these steps to complete their own analysis in support of the themes they have chosen, which can enable students to engage in a critical text analysis. The table, and the questions within it, act as a scaffold in helping teachers to remain focused on identifying each theme's language features. This, in turn, becomes the activity through which teachers will lead students and which creates a safe space for an academic and text-based discussion of any social justice issue.

Discussion

Our purpose in this chapter is to showcase how teachers can use the presented steps to engage students in critical discourse analysis that facilitates discussions around racial issues and the public and political debate they generate. Using this approach, students' critical reading skills can be heightened as they use linguistic evidence to support their themes of discussion. The steps for analysis have the potential to give teachers a way to lead students to recognize the subjective nature of many articles and other forms of media. By illuminating social justice-oriented themes relating to race, class, gender, and the preservation of hegemonic power structures, our steps for analysis enable teachers to promote discussions of these prejudiced views with students and raise their awareness of the hidden biases that exist within

Theme	Property of Language	Supporting Excerpt or Example
Zimmerman is portrayed as the victim	Relationships	"In finding him not guilty of murder or manslaughter, the jury agreed that Mr. Zimmerman could have been justified in shooting Mr. Martin" (para. 3) "[Zimmerman's] GPS monitor would be cut off" (para. 10) "[Zimmerman] has no further business with the court" (para. 10) "George Zimmerman was never guilty of anything except firing the gun in self-defense" (para. 13) "while defense lawyers were elated with the verdict, they also expressed anger that Mr. Zimmerman spent 16 months filled with fear and trauma when all he was doing was defending himself" (para. 23) "Irrefutable evidence, photographs…indicated that there had been a fight and that Mr. Zimmerman had been harmed" (para. 36)
	Cohesion & Coherence	Introduction of the article presents information that primarily surrounds Zimmerman: "George Zimmerman, the neighborhood watch volunteer who fatally shot Trayvon Martin, an unarmed black teenager, igniting a national debate on racial profiling and civil rights, was found not guilty late Saturday night of second-degree murder. He was also acquitted of manslaughter, a lesser charge" (para. 1) "jury rejected the prosecution's contention that Mr. Zimmerman had deliberately pursued Mr. Martin because he assumed the hoodie-clad teenager was a criminal and instigated the fight that led to his death" (para. 2) "Mr. Zimmerman said he shot Mr. Martin on Feb. 26, 2012, in self-defense after the teenager knocked him to the ground, punched him and slammed his head repeatedly against the sidewalk. In finding him not guilty of murder or manslaughter, the jury agreed that Mr. Zimmerman could have been justified in shooting Mr. Martin because he feared great bodily harm or death" (para. 3)
Race changes the rules and norms of the case	People & Experiences	"George Zimmerman, the neighborhood watch volunteer who fatally shot Trayvon Martin, an unarmed black teenager" (para. 1) "After three weeks of testimony, the six-woman jury rejected the prosecution's contention that Mr. Zimmerman had deliberately pursued "Mr. Martin because he assumed the hoodie-clad teenager was a criminal and instigated the fight that led to his death" (para. 2) "Mr. O'Mara disputed the notion that Mr. Zimmerman engaged in racial profiling. 'His history was not as a racist,' he said" (para. 21) "The public outcry began after the police initially decided not to arrest Mr. Zimmerman, who is half-Peruvian" (para. 24)
	Relationships	"Even President Obama weighed in a month after the shooting, expressing sympathy for Mr. Martin's family and urging a thorough investigation. 'If I had a son,' Mr. Obama said, 'he'd look like Trayvon'" (para. 6) "His history was not as a racist" (para. 21) "He added that if Mr. Zimmerman was black, he likely would never have been charged" (para. 22)

TABLE 2. Themes of and Supporting Example from the Article

society. As well as introducing the steps for analysis, we have provided teachers with examples of how the steps could be used to expose and critically analyze controversial issues relating to social justice. It is our hope that this approach will be used by teachers to address inequality and to discuss it within their planned curriculum. It is important for educational researchers to continue creating new strategies in order to aid teachers in talking and teaching about these topics.

It is possible for discussions of racial issues to occur within classrooms without a critical text analysis. However, such discussions can lead to opinion-based arguments. The risks associated with engaging in opinion-based arguments cause teachers to avoid the topic altogether, as personal attacks and biased statements can be expected. By conducting critical text analyses using the presented steps, discussions become fueled by linguistic evidence. As teachers implement critical text analysis activities in their classrooms, they enable their students to read through a critical lens. Such a lens prevents students from simply accepting the written word in the newspaper, or any form of text, at face value. Rather, students can question texts by seeking a deeper understanding through the language features used, as opposed to justifying sometimes biased opinions.

Our steps for analysis allow teachers to facilitate critical dialogue that legitimizes the anger and frustration of all students, but especially those who are vulnerable to these issues, such as historically marginalized and culturally and linguistically diverse students, while creating a safe space for broaching these topics. Students are encouraged to become critical consumers of media, reading through a critical lens to identify, question, and discuss social injustices. This approach may help them feel comfortable discussing other controversial issues in class because they know that the teacher will approach the topic from a critical perspective. Once teachers have created a safe space in their classrooms for discussing critical issues such as those pertaining to race, teachers and students can begin to discuss ways to potentially destabilize dominant ideologies, like those that perpetuate racism. The steps that we have developed allow students to recognize how these representations contribute to shaping students' understanding of race (Brookes, 1995). Teachers may take solace in using this practical approach, which allows them to connect racial issues in and outside of schools with the realities and lived experiences of their students.

Additional Ideas for Classroom Application

A helpful aspect of the steps for analysis is that they align well with Common Core English Language Arts Standards (Common Core Standards Initiative, 2017), especially in the area of informational texts. Beyond having students identify the main topic and key details (aspects that Table 1 supports), this approach effectively helps students develop other skills that are related to their overall ability to analyze and make sense of text. For example, one 9th–10th grade standard states: "Analyze in detail how an author's ideas or claims are developed and refined by particular sentences, paragraphs, or larger portions of a text (e.g., a section or chapter)." Teachers can refer to the cohesion and coherence language property (in Table 1) that encourages students to consider how information is organized and connected throughout a text and how the use of language features such as "New/Given" or "Referents" functions to support this analysis of this language property. For the 4th-grade standard that states "Refer to details and examples in a text when explaining what the text says explicitly and when drawing inferences from the text," teachers can have students focus on who is being talked about by identifying the nouns and labels of the participants and the prepositional phrases that provide further information.

There is also a wide array of text types that can work well with the steps for analysis. While we demonstrated the application of the steps with a newspaper article (the informational genre), teachers can search for or ask students to bring in any type of text in any form that they want to discuss. Examples such as social media posts, articles, blogs, personal texts or emails, advertisements in any form, or even speech found in clips from movies/TV shows/song lyrics are all text types that students can select and analyze using some or all of the parts of the steps within the table. After defining the particular genre of the text (and therefore the reason it was written/developed), teachers can ask students to focus on one or more of the language properties and their guiding questions to find evidence for the major themes. In other words, we encourage teachers to use and adapt this approach to find ways that are meaningful and responsive to their students—their ages, experiences, interests, and backgrounds—by adhering to state standards that protect and encourage teachers' rights to integrate these topics and activities in their classrooms. Other important and relevant topics that a teacher may want to address in the classroom could be those that deal with racism (e.g., the school-to-prison pipeline, police brutality), environmental issues (climate change, the Dakota access pipeline), gender issues (LGBTQ rights, pay equity, reproductive freedom), immigration issues (the border wall, the Syrian refugee crisis), and other social issues (economic inequality, access to medical coverage, "English only" schooling laws). The classroom can serve as a welcoming space for students to reflect on such topics while learning how to critically engage with texts that treat contemporary issues.

References

Alvarez, L., & Buckley, C. (2013, July 13). Zimmerman is acquitted in Trayvon Martin killing. *The New York Times*. Retrieved from http://www.nytimes.com/2013/07/14/us/george-zimmerman-verdict-trayvon-martin.html? mcubz=2

Appiah, K.A. (1989). The conservation of "race." *Black American Literature Forum, 23*(1), 37–60.

Banks, J.A. (2015). *Cultural diversity and education: Foundations, curriculum and teaching* (6th ed.). Boston, MA: Pearson.

Beck, A. (2005). A place for critical literacy. *Journal of Adolescent and Adult Literacy, 48*(5), 392–400.

Bell, L. (2016). Theoretical foundations for social justice education. In M. Adams & L.A. Bell (Eds.), *Teaching for diversity and social justice* (pp. 3–26). New York, NY: Routledge.

Blackledge, A. (2000). *Literacy, power and social justice*. Staffordshire, UK: Trentham Books.

Bonilla-Silva, E. (1999). The essential social fact of race. *American Sociological Review, 64*(6), 899–906.

Bowen, M. (2017, July 3). Dedham High teacher alleges racist incidents in classroom. *Dedham Transcript*. Retrieved from http://dedham.wickedlocal.com/news/20170703/dedham-high-teacher-alleges-racist-incidents-in-classroom

Boyd, A. S., & Glazier, J. A. (2017). The choreography of conversation: An exploration of collaboration and difficult discussions in cross disciplinary teacher discourse communities. *The High School Journal, 100*(2), 130-145.

Brookes, H.J. (1995). "Suit, tie and a touch of juju"—the ideological construction of Africa: A critical discourse analysis of news on Africa in the British press. *Discourse & Society, 6*(4), 461–494.

Brown, L., Gutierrez, C., Okmin, J., & McCullough, S. (2017). Desegregating conversations about race and identity in culturally specific museums. *Journal of Museum Education, 42*(2), 120–131.

Capehart, J. (2015, February 27). From Trayvon Martin to "Black Lives Matter." *Washington Post.* Retrieved from https://www.washingtonpost.com/blogs/post-partisan/wp/2015/02/27/from-trayvon-martin-to-black-lives-matter/?utm_term=.67ebb8e7a787

Coles-Ritchie, M., & Smith, R.R. (2017). Taking the risk to engage in race talk: Professional development in elementary schools. *International Journal of Inclusive Education, 21*(2), 172–186.

Common Core State Standards (CCSS). (2017). *Common core state standards initiative.* Washington, DC: National Governors Association Center for Best Practices, Council of Chief State School Officers.

Delpit, L.D. (2006). *Other people's children: Cultural conflict in the classroom.* New York, NY: New Press.

Dewey, J. (1916). *Democracy and education.* New York, NY: The Free Press.

Eggins, S. (2004). *An introduction to systemic functional linguistics* (2nd ed.). New York, NY: Continuum.

Epstein, T. (2017). Turning a moment into a movement: Responding to racism in the classroom. *Critical Education, 8*(2), 41–47.

Fairclough, N. (1992). *Discourse and social change.* Cambridge: Polity Press.

Fairclough, N. (2013). Critical discourse analysis and critical policy studies. *Critical Policy Studies, 7*(2), 177–197.

Freire, P. (1970). *Pedagogy of the oppressed.* New York, NY: Continuum.

Garza, A. (2016). A herstory of the #BlackLivesMatter movement. *Black Lives Matter.* Retrieved from http://blacklivesmatter.com/herstory/

Gay, G. (2010). *Culturally responsive teaching: Theory, research, and practice.* New York, NY: Teachers College Press.

Gorski, P. (2008). What we're teaching teachers: An analysis of multicultural teacher education coursework syllabi. *Teaching and Teacher Education, 25*(1), 309–318.

Halliday, M., & Matthiessen, C. (2014). *An introduction to functional grammar* (4th ed.). London: Arnold.

Harwood, S.A., Mendenhall, R., Lee, S.S., Riopelle, C., & Browne Huntt, M. (2018). Everyday racism in integrated spaces: Mapping the experiences of students of color at a diversifying predominantly White institution. *Annals of the American Association of Geographers.* doi:10.1080/24694452. 2017.1419122

Justifiable Use of Force. FL § 776-013 (2017).

Ladson-Billings, G. (2009). *The dreamkeepers: Successful teachers of African-American children.* San Francisco, CA: Jossey-Bass.

Milner IV, H.R. (2017). Race, talk, opportunity aps, and curriculum shifts in (teacher) education. *Literacy Research: Theory, Method, and Practice, 66*(1), 73–94.

Noddings, N., & Brooks, L. (2017). *Teaching controversial issues.* New York, NY: Teachers College Press.

Provenzo, Jr., E.F. (2005). *Critical literacy: What every educated American ought to know.* Boulder, CO: Paradigm Publishing.

Schladebeck, J. (2017, April 6). Florida teacher fired over assignment asking students "how comfortable" they are around Black people, Arabs. *New York Daily News.* Retrieved from http://www.nydailynews.com/news/national/florida-teacher-fired-racist-offensive-assignment-article-1.3025267

Schleppegrell, M. J. (2011). Supporting disciplinary learning through language analysis: Developing historical literacy. In F. Christie & K. Maton (Eds.) *Disciplinarity: Functional linguistic and sociological perspectives* (pp. 197–215). New York, NY: Continuum.

Sembiante, S., Baxley, T., & Cavallaro, C. (2017). What's in a name? A critical literacy and functional linguistic analysis of immigrant acculturation in contemporary picture books. *Journal of Diaspora, Indigenous, and Minority Education*, 1–14. doi:10.1080/15595692.2017.1350640

Shields, C.M., & Mohan, E.J. (2008). High-quality education for all students: Putting social justice at its heart. *Teacher Development, 12*(4), 289–300.

Shor, I. (1992). *Empowering education: Critical teaching for social justice.* Chicago, IL: University of Chicago Press.

Shor, I. (1999). What is critical literacy? *Journal of Pedagogy, Pluralism, and Practice, 4*(1), 1–26.

Singleton, G. E. (2015). *Courageous conversations about race: A field guide for achieving equity in schools.* Thousand Oaks, CA: SAGE Publications

Sleeter, C. (2005). *Un-standardizing curriculum: Multicultural teaching in the standards-based classroom.* New York, NY: Teachers College Press.

Sleeter, C. (2008). Equity, democracy, and neoliberal assaults on teacher education. *Teaching and Teacher Education, 24*(1), 1947–1957.

Sleeter, C. (2016). Wrestling with problematics of whiteness in teacher education. *International Journal of Qualitative Studies in Education, 29*(8), 1065–1068. doi:10.1080/09518398.2016.1174904

Sniderman, P.M., Piazza, T., Tetlock, P.E., & Kendrick, A. (1991). The new racism. *Midwest Political Science Association, 35*(2), 423–447.

Teo, P. (2000). Racism in the news: A critical discourse analysis of news reporting in two Australian newspapers. *Discourse & Society, 11*(1), 7–49. doi:10.1177/0957926500011001002

van Dijk, T.A. (1993). Principles of critical discourse analysis. *Discourse & Society, 4*(2), 249–283.

Weaver, S. (2011). Jokes, rhetoric and embodied racism: A rhetorical discourse analysis of the logics of racist jokes on the internet. *Ethnicities, 11*(4), 413–435. doi:10.1177/1468796811407755

Wootson, Jr., C.R. (2016, October 21). "To be White is to be racist, period," a high school teacher told his class. *Washington Post*. Retrieved from https://www.washingtonpost.com/news/education/wp/2016/10/19/to-be-white-is-to-be-racist-period-a-high-school-teacher-told-his-class/

CHAPTER THREE

THE WORLD WITHOUT ART IS EH:

Aesthetic Engagement and Race in the Classroom

RITU RADHAKRISHNAN

THE ABOVE STATEMENT IS a bit misleading.[1] While art is an essential part of this conversation, the prevalent approach for generating constructive conversation about race lies in aesthetics. Engaging with aesthetics allows students to create meaning-making experiences and explore their own thinking about a topic. As a medium for social commentary and as a practice to empower social change (Medina, 2006; 2009; 2012), aesthetic engagement provides students with an opportunity to create meaningful experiences that address racial issues.

Maxine Greene (2001) describes the field of aesthetics as "concerned about perception, sensation, imagination, and how they relate to knowing, understanding, and feeling about the world" (p. 5). Sharing these processes and creations is often less polarizing than dialogues or debates and allows for inclusion of students with multiple modalities and talents. This curricular

---

1 Anonymous quote

approach involves more than simply creating an arts-integrated curriculum. Students should be creating, critiquing, and engaging with various forms of aesthetics (e.g., visual, drama, dance, music, etc.): "'Aesthetic'…is an adjective used to describe or single out the mode of experience brought into being by encounters with works of art" (Greene, 2001, p. 5). Greene reinforces John Dewey's (1934) idea that a "transaction" needs to occur between the individual and the aesthetic form. While both theorize that the engagement with aesthetic forms offers an opportunity to confront larger ideas about social justice, Greene suggests that a consciousness or awareness on the part of the individual is necessary for a full engagement or transaction. The individual interacting with the aesthetic form must be willing to engage with the form to create a transaction. This interaction can be transformed into social action and change (Beyerbach, Davis, & Ramalho, 2017; Dewey, 1934; Greene 2001; Medina, 2012).

A variety of artists ranging from South African singer-activist Miriam Makeba to American painter-activist Jean-Michel Basquiat have used their art to project their political and social voices. Introducing students to the work of powerful artist activists like these through aesthetic understanding and meaning-making presents an opportunity to engage in deeper discussions about the extent of racial discord. This chapter asserts that a powerful and underutilized way for public school teachers to generate and sustain effective conversations about issues of race, inside and outside of school, is to increase aesthetics and aesthetic understanding in the curriculum.

Students are very aware of the racial tensions that affect society, and societal issues manifest themselves in schools (Anyon, 1983; Giroux, 1983b). Ultimately, these tensions affect students' learning experiences and may result in frustration, anger, and, more specifically, higher dropout rates and a reproducing of systematic inequities in society. All students need an outlet, a space in which their voices can be cultivated and heard. Aesthetics offer a sustainable outlet to invoke voice and agency regarding the tensions that surround students inside and outside of the classroom. Students can make meaning and create critical narratives that reflect racial tensions depicted in photographs from news websites and social media.

Having aesthetic experiences will also present students with opportunities to explore new avenues for examining their own reactions to racial tensions. Students are aware that racial tensions manifest themselves in a society—including economically, emotionally, mentally, physically, politically, and socially—both in and out of schools. Instead of avoiding the issues, or leaving them outside of the classroom, teachers should embrace these conversations. Engaging in aesthetics creation as well as experiencing aesthetics as a captive observer offer opportunities for students to acknowledge their frustrations and feelings and to channel those emotions into peaceful but powerful political and critical statements.

Several studies have suggested positive effects that the arts and arts integration have on K–12 students' educational experiences (Leshnoff, 2003; Manzo, 2002; Reeves, 2007). Research has demonstrated how integrating art in various forms invokes creativity, imagination, and curiosity in students (Seidel, Tishman, Winner, Hetland, & Palmer, 2009). However, introducing K–12 students to aesthetics and the experience of art requires educators to look beyond the politics of standardized testing and the Common Core standards. Chris Higgins (2008) argues for the experience of arts and aesthetics in schools, asserting that if we remove the political and bureaucratic language of "improvement in student learning" or "achievement gains," we can recognize that art and aesthetics are a part of a rich human experience and meaningful life:

> If we want to evoke wonder and mystery and not merely name them, we must find a way of writing that somehow accomplishes what Shklovsky calls for in the epigraph: to make the stone stony. We must constantly search for fresh and subtle and pungent ways to articulate ideas that are always in danger of growing stale, simplistic, lifeless, or worse. (pp. 8–9)

Introducing what aesthetic understanding is and how to cultivate experiences with aesthetic forms to K–12 students should be part of both their learning experiences and their living experiences.

To reduce the wealth of art and aesthetics to catchphrases for educational policy diminishes the wonder and experience human beings receive from art alone. It is in this spirit that we find ways to introduce aesthetics in the classroom at the earliest of ages. Through this effort, we can help very young children to understand that there is more to humanity than simply what is taught or learned inside the classroom or the school. Children should understand at a young age that all human beings bring with them lived experiences that have the potential to invoke empathy and awareness. Introducing an awareness of aesthetics in schools for young children opens the door to a diversity of lived experiences. Whether those experiences derive from engagement with the works of established artists or through K–12 students creating aesthetic forms themselves, they are shared through the aesthetic interaction that an individual has with a form or work.

In 2008, Shepard Fairy's *Hope* poster (as well as the identical Change Poster) served as a rallying cry for Barack Obama's presidential platform and momentum (see Figure 1). Though the poster became a symbol of the presidential campaign, there is no denying the aesthetic power of the image. For many citizens who were frustrated with a failing economy and the ongoing violence and war in the Middle East, the image offered respite from their desperation. The colorful poster illuminated an idealistic African American man who did not represent the establishment. The word HOPE beckoned and suggested. At a time when hope was essentially lost as a result of economic and political tensions, one man inspired another to create a medium for—and of—hope and change. With all due respect to President Obama, it could be argued that the power of this aesthetic propelled almost 53% of voting citizens to participate in a societal movement. People voted for the feeling that the poster gave them; they voted for hope and change.

Similarly, for 47% of voters, the poster provoked an aesthetic response, most likely one of negativity or disbelief. This, in turn, led to satirical posters using the same aesthetic background but changing the text and the image to display anger or frustration to (see Figure 2). Regardless of the nature of the individual's experience, the aesthetic evoked a response. Individuals connected to the aesthetic and then manipulated the image to reflect their own frustrations and disappointments. Imagine the possibilities for rich learning experiences if this kind of awareness and responsiveness were available to students in educational spaces.

Offering aesthetics and aesthetic experiences as an outlet for the tensions that affect students' social and emotional learning is a form of critical pedagogy (Freire, 1970; Kincheloe, 2007). While the arts and aesthetics promote cognitive function, "they also celebrate the consummatory, non-instrumental aspects of human experience and provide the means through which meanings that are ineffable, but feelingful, can be expressed" (Eisner, 2002, p. 19). This approach encourages students to demonstrate agency and voice in their learning and to learn for social justice. The remainder

FIGURE 1. Barack Obama Hope Poster 1 by masterlord tango is licensed under CC By 2.0

FIGURE 2. Updated Obama Hope Poster 2—Hope You Find Work by Count to 10 is licensed under CC By 2.0

of this chapter will demonstrate the effectiveness of aesthetics and critical pedagogy in student learning and social action. The narrative will include connections to research and practical applications to classroom instruction.

Curriculum, Pedagogy, and Social Justice

Social issues manifest themselves in schools and are ultimately reflected in forms of curriculum (implicit, explicit, and null) (Eisner, 1985). To develop significant positive changes in students' learning experiences, curriculum must be examined: how it is theorized, how it is created, and how it is enacted (Radhakrishnan, 2014). A closer examination of various curricula reveals underlying philosophies that may range from didactic to critical in nature. Examining systems of curriculum reveals implicit and explicit norms, beliefs, values, behaviors, endeavors, and customs (Joseph, 2000; Radhakrishnan, 2014; Weis, McCarthy, & Dimitriadis, 2006). The examination of curriculum theory, research, and practice encourages us as educators to heighten our consciousness concerning curriculum and begin to critically consider the implications of curriculum on students' learning.

American education has consistently created curricula that ensure that students adhere to hegemonic principles that have helped lead to current societal inequities, emphasizing issues of race, class, gender, sexuality, and ability. As a result, our system of education continues to harm students from historically underrepresented and marginalized groups (Apple, 2006; Hursh, 2008; Sleeter, 2005). By implementing philosophies of curricula that develop critical understanding and consciousness, educational experiences would challenge students academically, creatively, and personally, fostering a sense of curiosity, agency, and voice in learning. This type of educational experience can be created through aesthetic education.

Today's "grammar of schooling" (Tyack & Cuban, 1995) is structured in ways that "train" students to emulate the existing culture. Students respond to the bell ringing and an official schedule as dictated by governing bodies such as administration and teachers. It is clear that American schools replicate institutional injustices toward marginalized groups As a result, "every student sits at the center of at least four nested structures of inequality and separation—states, districts, schools, and classes" (Hochschild, 2003, p. 825). Moreover, we know that the actual curriculum enacted differs vastly from school to school as a reflection of social class (Anyon, 1981). Students from affluent backgrounds are able to engage in activities that encourage creativity and critical thinking, while under resourced schools in high-poverty communities enact curricula that reproduce social inequities and encourage rote memorization in students' learning experiences.

Critical Pedagogy

Curriculum can be considered as a continuum. Two fields of philosophy (traditionalism and progressivism, or reconceptualism) created this continuum that different schools, districts, and states can choose to enact and implement. Traditionalists and reconceptualists appear to be at opposite ends of the spectrum. Current public school curriculum is determined by policymakers and bureaucratic actors working toward the goal of standardized academic achievement. However, if we widen the lens of achievement to include social action and change, students' learning experiences offer the possibility of replacing standardization as a way to "achieve." The goal of education becomes to learn as a way to live.

In 1968, Philip W. Jackson introduced the notion of the hidden curriculum, or the unwritten curriculum that teaches implicit lessons. These lessons may be learned through instruction and curriculum, as well as outside of the classroom, as a result of the transmission of norms, beliefs, and values not simply limited to the school culture. Since 1968, many researchers have found ways to expand upon the concept of the hidden curriculum. Eisner (1985) identified three forms of curricula (official, implicit, and null) that shape students' educational experiences in schools. The *official* curriculum represents what teachers are required to teach as mandated by federal, state, district, or administrative policies. The *implicit* curriculum is similar to the hidden curriculum, as it reveals the transmission of norms and expectations that reflect the ideas of larger society, in addition to expectations of the schooling. Finally, the *null* curriculum acknowledges that there are areas that are simply overlooked or not included in the curriculum for a variety of reasons. These forms of curricula reproduce societal inequities and transmit hegemonic educational, cultural, economic, social, and political forces. As a result, the opportunities for students—particularly students from historically underrepresented and marginalized groups—to receive a holistic education become limited, even altogether unavailable.

Implementation of critical pedagogy varies in how it is enacted by those who teach and those who receive the curriculum. The main purpose behind such a philosophy and implementation of critical approaches in curriculum and instruction is to disturb the hegemony of cultural influences. Such approaches to pedagogy encourage students and teachers to confront the dominant order of the curriculum (official, implicit, and null) and to enact discourse that is centered on morality and justice. The current state of our curriculum is considered to be one of resistance, embodying an inability to change. Further, there appears to be a lack of vision on the part of policy-makers and curriculum developers. "Change is difficult because educational practices are rarely subject to critical internal and public reflection beyond those related to efficiency in maintaining the status quo" (Windschitl & Joseph, 2000, p. 166). While the official curricula of the individual states are influenced by multiple political, economic, and social factors, critical approaches to curriculum provide an opportunity, despite standardized curriculum, to encourage diversity, equity, and agency in students' learning.

Paulo Freire (1970) is generally considered to be the foremost pioneer in critical theory and thought. A significant basis of Freire's beliefs about curriculum was grounded in his opposition to "banking education." "Banking education" is a curricular concept enforced by the oppressor to make the learner passive in his/her own learning. Learning is accumulated or "banked" by the learner, without acknowledgment of the learner's identity or background. Such approaches to curriculum reproduce existing inequalities and represent the traditional notions of curriculum that Freire opposed.

Freire encouraged activism in learning: an emancipatory curriculum that was enacted through lived experiences and engagement in learning for social justice. Based on his experiences with Brazilian adults who were illiterate and from impoverished backgrounds, Freire believed that teaching literacy to this group of individuals would represent an act of resistance. His notions of curriculum move past concepts of basic critical pedagogy to encourage emancipation and systematic social action. While it is impractical to implement a full emancipatory curriculum in the classroom, it is possible to encourage and draw from critical philosophies of curriculum and instruction—specifically, a way to develop curricula that represent Freire's ideals of confronting issues of equality, equity, justice, and compassion in connection to content-area learning standards. Employing a (somewhat subdued) emancipatory curriculum gives personal purpose to students' learning and creates a context in which they are encouraged to be agentic in their own learning.

In addressing racial tensions through aesthetic education, I believe that this type of critical pedagogy lends itself to the learner-enacting agency

(Giroux, 1983a) and voice (Giroux, 1983a).These terms offer non-standardized "outcomes," for lack of a better term, to gauge the effectiveness of the implementation of critical approaches to curriculum and pedagogy. I previously suggested (Radhakrishnan, 2014):

> Agency refers to the autonomous thinking by a learner and the way in which a learner can navigate standards and objectives that would empower him or her to make relevant connections to official standards and objectives dictated by the curriculum. Voice refers to a way in which the students demonstrated their agency in their learning by invoking voice or personal connections through various forms of text and discourse (i.e. visual art work, written artifacts, student reflections). (pp. 7–8)

Agency and voice are abilities that students can develop and improve upon over time. If an individual possesses these abilities, s/he will have the potential to learn to live long after their K–12 educational experiences are over.

The Aesthetic Connection
The connection between art and social justice can be traced through history from the political commentary of artists to the current support for social justice art through organizations such as Americans for the Arts and local community groups. However, aesthetics are generally understood in the traditional sense, as defined by the Oxford English Dictionary (2017): "concerned with beauty or the appreciation of beauty." John Dewey (1934) referred to aesthetics as "to experience as appreciative, perceiving, and enjoying" (p. 207). I would argue that in addition to the beauty and pleasure derived from aesthetics, there is also discomfort, pain, anxiety, and anger. Consider the 2008 *Hope* poster as an example. Aesthetics, and specifically art, have the power to create change and provide a commentary, either from the artist or the audience.

The field of aesthetics has a lengthy historical record stemming from philosophers such as Plato, Alexander Baumgarten, and Immanuel Kant. While Plato acknowledged the power of the arts to influence individuals, Baumgarten and Kant explored the idea of cognition developing through aesthetics (Kristeller, 1952; Shusterman, 1999). Educational theorists such as Dewey and, more recently, Maxine Greene (2001) and Elliot Eisner (2002), have examined the connection between aesthetics and cognition. I specifically used the works of Dewey, Greene, and Eisner in this chapter because of the imaginary conversation I expect they might have with one another. Their work complements and builds on each other in a way that acknowledges the student (or, as Dewey stated, "the Child") and recognizes the importance of student-centered learning through curriculum. This conversation is rich in its advocacy for aesthetics and, consequently, creativity and imagination in students' learning experiences.

Dewey (1934) suggested that the interaction between an individual (Dewey refers to this as a "live creature") and an object is an exchange—that is, "an experience is a product, one might almost say bi-product, of continuous and cumulative interaction of an organic self with the world. There is no other foundation upon which esthetic theory and criticism can build" (p. 220). Dewey's assertion suggests that significant meaning-making of aesthetic objects is a crucial step in developing skills to process and engage in an actual *experience* in which an individual develops an understanding to engage in learning. This occurs from the experience with the aesthetic alone.

Maxine Greene, in her many works on aesthetic education, suggests that the development of aesthetic education introduces a curriculum for humanity. Aesthetic education, at its core, is about "education here, not schooling" (2001, p. 7). Greene writes that aesthetic education offers students authentic experiences described as "situated encounters":

> That means that the perceivers of a given work of art apprehend that work in the light of their backgrounds, biographies, and experiences. We have to presume a multiplicity of perspectives, a plurality of interpretations. Clearly, this opens aesthetic educators to the likelihood of more than one interpretation of a poem, a dance, a play, a musical piece. (p. 174)

Greene's words suggest that aesthetic education involves a connection on the part of the learner with "actual live or authentic work" (instead of reproductions). Bose (2008) thoughtfully explains how different forms of aesthetic experience can initiate transactions in learning and living:

Whenever Greene speaks or writes about aesthetic education, the discourse is steeped in the visceral, emotional, and intellectual experiences of an array of works of art, the paintings of Cezanne, for example, the words of Toni Morrison, the movements of Martha Graham, and a vast array of other works. She, unlike Dewey, writes out of her own considered and eclectic experiences with specific works of art and with teaching artists; the ideas do not come abstractly about art, unattached to particular aesthetic experiences and works of art. (p. 65)

Greene and Dewey both introduce the concept of engagement with the aesthetic media. Greene introduces the "visceral, emotional, and intellectual experiences." This specification allows the experience of engagement to be less than "enjoying," as Dewey suggested; instead, the visceral, emotional, and intellectual experiences of the learner allow for a more developed and nuanced engagement and learning experience.

Elliot Eisner, one of the strongest advocates for art education, explored the connection between engagement in art and cognitive processes. He suggested (Eisner, 1996) that implementing arts and aesthetics in curricula and educational learning experiences will naturally encourage cognitive development. Eisner's belief in aesthetic education and the power of aesthetic experience as a cognitive process illustrates the possibility that aesthetics can help K–12 students to interpret and develop social thought and commentary, expression, and agency. Such abilities are necessary for learning, achievement, and life. Eisner's work emphasizes the connection between cognitive development and aesthetics. Cerveny (2001) outlined nine ways in which children's cognitive development is affected through arts and aesthetic education:

1. How to perceive and explore relationships. Human relationships. Cause and effect relationships. The relationship of parts to a whole.

2. How to think and express within the constraints and affordances of a medium. Or a set of rules. Or an existing set of conditions. How to choose when faced with a range of possibilities.

3. Nuance matters. How to pay attention to subtleties and be sensitive

to slight differences that can make very big differences to others, or to potential outcomes.

4. Form can express feeling. How the shape of the built environment or the elements within it affect our experience of place. How the forms we choose for communication affect the way we are heard.

5. Purposes are best held flexibly. Exploring opportunity is the essence of creativity, and being flexibly purposive is the key to solving problems.

6. Not all we know can take the form of language. Intelligence, awareness, and understanding are cultivated by developing the ability to think in images and symbols.

7. Surprise is the reward of imagination at work. Experiment and discovery are the rich pathways to ownership of learning. Measurement (as in "outcome measures" and "proficiency testing") measures little real learning.

8. There are many different and completely valid ways to be in the world. There is not always a single or even a right answer. Cultures, lifestyles, beliefs that are different can also be interesting—even exciting.

9. Some activities are self-justifying and important for their own reasons. The journey is the purpose. We do some things:

    • because we like the process
    • because we like the outcome
    • because there is a reward
    • because it is the right thing to do. (Cerveny, 2001, para. 8)

These theorists (Dewey, Greene, and Eisner) elaborate on how the cognition associated with engaging in aesthetic experiences can be integral to the education process and to enhancing students' experiences. Each theorist builds upon the others by strengthening and reinforcing the purposes for building aesthetic understanding and engagement into students' learning experiences.

Why Not Just "Art"?
While art is an integral part of an aesthetic experience, I cannot use the term

"art" interchangeably with aesthetics. The term "art" lends itself to the field of art education. Art educators have specifically developed skills and backgrounds that should not be minimized. Aesthetic education is a specialized field as well, and I do not want to minimize the extraordinary work that has and continues to be done. Within this framework, the term "art" is representative of a work or a product (finished or in progress); "aesthetics" is a term that describes the experience and the transaction that occurs with the work or product. Instead, I use the terms *aesthetics* and *aesthetic experiences* to help broaden students' educational experiences—specifically in addressing racial tensions in our public schools. Finding ways to help all classroom teachers be more engaged in aesthetic educational experiences allows for a spectrum of understanding. All individuals are capable of experiencing aesthetics. As a result, teachers do not need to have an extensive background or knowledge to implement aesthetic opportunities and to experience them along with their students. Aesthetic experiences have emotive, formative, and cognitive aspects that allow the learner to fully engage in an experience. Art is often an object or, more traditionally, a "work." It can exist alone or within a larger context. Aesthetics opens the discourse by offering "(1) A certain property, feature or aspect of things (e.g., beauty or grace), and (2) a certain kind of attitude, perception, or experience" (Levinson, 2003, p. 3).

Another reason for not using the term "art" is that I hope that this chapter helps classroom teachers to look beyond practices of art integration (Bresler, 1995). Bresler identified four ways in which classroom teachers have integrated arts into the curriculum: the subservient approach; the co-equal, cognitive integration style; the affective style, and the social integration style. While each of these approaches is helpful in integrating arts into the curriculum, Bresler acknowledges that art integration can still be problematic. He states:

> Advocates for integrating the arts with academic disciplines reflect a variety of perspectives, interests, and goals. Arts educators typically seek to establish, through integration, a more solid role for the arts within the academic curriculum. They envision arts specialists who collaborate with classroom teachers and, in the process, strengthen the links between the marginalized specialists and the institutions. Principals' vision of integration typically involves classroom teachers teaching the arts as part of the academic curriculum. (p. 1)

While I personally advocate for integrating the arts into academic disciplines as a pedagogical practice, it is often a long-term approach and, as mentioned above, requires skilled art educators to contribute to its development.

The concept of implementing aesthetics in the classroom to specifically address issues of race and racial tensions offers a different approach to exploring how racial tensions appear in the forms of curricula (official, hidden, and null). Teachers can draw from current events and students' backgrounds and knowledge. In this chapter, I suggest that the engagement and experience of aesthetics opens up the possibility that students can acknowledge the emotional jolts that may shudder through their bodies as they engage with a topic such as race.

Addressing Racial Tensions Through an Aesthetic Pedagogy

Research in aesthetic education has acknowledged a connection to morality and ethics that stems from Kant's (1790/2007) *Critique of Judgment*, in which he explored the link between judgment about aesthetics and its connection to morality (or lack thereof). Education cannot be moral if the same voices continue to be underrepresented and omitted. Attributing learning, agency, and voice through an integration of aesthetics into the curriculum suggests more than simply an integration of music, visual arts, dramatic arts, dance, and literature. It suggests that aesthetics present a way of addressing perspective and engagement, compelling the learner to develop skills of examination and criticism.

> The proper way to encounter another person is to be open to them, to be ready to see new dimensions, new facets of the other, to recognize the possibility of some fresh perception or understanding, so you may know the other better, appreciate that person more variously. This is, actually, how we ordinarily treat each other as persons. We do not treat each other as case histories, or instances of some psychological or sociological reality—not, that is, in personal encounters. Nor do we come up against each other as if the other were merely an inanimate object, incapable of reciprocation. There are analogues between this and encounters with works of art, especially in the readiness for fresh illumination, in the willingness to see something, to risk something unexpected and new. (Greene, 2001, pp. 53–54)

The foundation of aesthetic education encourages deeper understanding through an experience. This transaction can take many forms, including one between an individual and a work or product, or an aesthetic transaction between two individuals. The underlying principle requires the individual's readiness to deepen his or her understanding as a result of the transaction. This principle naturally lends itself to exploring students' voices through their engagement with and production of aesthetic experiences.

Medina's (2012) Critical Aesthetic Pedagogy (CAP) illustrates the natural intersection of critical pedagogy and aesthetic education. CAP is strategically grounded in critical pedagogy and aesthetic education. In Medina's model of CAP, she places an emphasis on "valuing students' voices and experiences in the classroom, enabling critical awareness, and challenging existing forms of schooling" (2006, p. 57). CAP explores the value of experiential knowledge through aesthetic experiences. Within this process, it is integral to provide students with a safe space in which they can share their own backgrounds, experiences, and understandings, in addition to being critical about their learning processes. Integral to Medina's CAP framework is the *soma* (body). Relying on her background as a dancer, Medina suggests that the soma brings memories and understandings that may be different for each individual. The somatic approach to aesthetic engagement, introduced as somaesthetics by Richard Shusterman (1999), presents a more dynamic approach to aesthetic engagement by involving the body, with its reactions and perceptions, in constructing knowledge. The somatic approach is often underutilized in many classrooms due to practical measures such as space and time limitations, as well as preventative measures such as behavior management and increased off-task behavior. However, it is important that the soma is included in students' aesthetic experiences and engagements, and not just through movement and dance. Students need to also be aware of their bodies' reactions to and perceptions of aesthetic processes and productions. In the same manner as the aesthetic transaction, students need to be aware of their interaction with their somas as well as the understanding that comes as a result of this specific interaction. The next section explores practical approaches to integrating instructional practices and activities into the classroom based on the above-mentioned theoretical principles.

Practical Approaches

Theoretical frameworks offer ideas and possibilities. Examining what past research has uncovered offers endless possibilities for building on these theoretical foundations. However, speculation about theories is not possible during the busy K–12 school day. In this section, I suggest opportunities for aesthetic implementation into *any* K–12 classroom. Many of these opportunities for aesthetic implementation are rooted in two theoretical foundations: the Visual Thinking Strategy (Housen, 1983); (Visual Understanding in Education, 1995) and literate practices (Gee, 2001; Moll, 1992; New London Group, 1996). Housen (1983) developed the idea of aesthetic experiences as a connection to constructivist experiences, where students create meaning through collaboration and drawing on their own experiences.

The Visual Thinking Strategy (VTS) engages the viewer in the aesthetic experience, often grounded in stages. In classroom use, Visual Understanding in Education (1995) offers a variety of instructional strategies, "provides a teaching methodology, a developmentally appropriate image curriculum, and a learner-centered professional development". Ultimately, VTS serves as a professional development tool to help teachers implement and support thoughtful aesthetic experiences in students' learning experiences.

The theories addressing literate practices include helping students draw from their "funds of knowledge" (Moll, 1992). The term "funds of knowledge" acknowledges that students bring cultural, historical, political, and social knowledge that is often shaped by their backgrounds. Gee (2001) introduces the idea of Discourse (capital D). Discourse refers to how language is conveyed through various social practices such as norms, taboos, customs, behaviors, and clothes, to name a few. Acknowledging the role of Discourse in an aesthetic engagement helps to support the visceral reaction a viewer may have while engaging with the aesthetic object. For instance, as an American student engages with unfamiliar food or clothes from an African or Asian country, s/he may experience confusion based on unfamiliarity alone. In 1996, the New London Group introduced the concept of multiliteracies, which highlighted the role of multimodal literacies (i.e. dance, music, gestures, etc.) and acknowledged the importance of multimodal literacies and linguistic diversity in developing and understanding literate practices. All three of these literacy frameworks offer a foundation for how students' aesthetic experiences may differ and may be processed differently. However, despite the differences, students engaging in an aesthetic experience are activating—*partially*—a literate practice.

While I draw from VTS and literate practices in this section, neither theoretical framework is stringently followed and applied, as they are both complex fields, and literacy is steeped in deep, philosophical context over history. Instead, I use both frameworks to help K–12 teachers think about how they can support students' aesthetic experiences about racial tensions in the classroom. Below I reference specific aesthetic mediums that can be used to help promote a discussion around issues of race and racial tensions. Though this list is by no means exhaustive, I hope it will serve as a starting point for considering aesthetics and possible mediums in our current society.

Art Work

This seems obvious, but it is important for teachers to realize the context of these many resources. Specifically, how do economic, historical, political, and social contexts help learners to make meaning? How does the engagement change as we help students to understand the artist's meaning? A crucial step in introducing and exploring aesthetic experiences is to provide context. This can occur before, during, or after the individual's experience with the piece. However, it is important to know how the artist conceptualized the piece as part of the overall aesthetic experience.

Graphic Design

As the field of graphic design advances and permeates art, advertising, merchandising, periodicals, and books (to name a few), it's important to help students understand the aesthetic power of graphic design. As a field new to the millennium and familiar to mostly millennials, K–12 students are aware of the power of text in such widespread spaces. These spaces offer an opportunity for students to engage with the piece critically in order to examine how issues of race, class, gender, sexuality, and ability are present and may or may not reinforce social inequities. Teachers should support students in their engagement by asking what they are seeing and feeling from their interaction, and how the experience has changed or reinforced their perceptions.

Photography

History has long highlighted the use of photography in understanding political situations, from Matthew Brady's *Scenes of the Civil War* to Lewis Hine's *Investigative Photos of Child Labor in America* to the Civil Rights Movement. This medium offers learners an opportunity to engage in a historical and/or political movement without words or sounds. The experience of engagement encourages the learner to recognize the context of the captured movement and allows for curiosity. Teachers should encourage students to consider what they are seeing and imagine the moments before and after this experience. They should also help students to imagine discourse and recreate dialogue and speech.

Sculpture

Sculpture is often overlooked when integrating aesthetics into the classroom, mainly because of the mechanics of the pieces. Sculptures are often two- and three-dimensional pieces and are frequently difficult to experience outside of the classroom. While I encourage field trips to art institutes and museums, sculpture gardens, and various community areas, this is not always a possibility. In these instances, photography, replicas, descriptions, and recreations are instrumental in helping the learner to engage in an authentic experience through alternative methods. Teachers should introduce students to samples of the materials used in such pieces and have them consider why such materials were used as a way for the artist to construct and convey meaning.

Paintings

While the most well-known paintings are generally in museums, there are a variety of replications accessible through venues such as Creative Commons and Google Images. These venues allow the learner to experience the work in a variety of contexts and instructional applications. An understanding of the artist's work is often strengthened by a collection or series that conveys meaning to the audience. However, as an instructional practice, do not underestimate the power that a single image can have when accompanied by strategic lighting and/or auditory accompaniment.

Children's Literature

The term "children's literature" covers a variety of texts. From using picture books to young adult novels, teachers have long understood how this medium engages children in a way that dry, lexile-based informational text does not. Specifically, recent forays into graphic novels and anime have extended the variety of genres available. Moreover, the implementation of literacy in all K–12 classrooms is crucial—and Common Core friendly. Most literacy strategies encourage aesthetic responses to the text. However, to further inspire authentic aesthetic experiences, teachers should allow students to communicate with characters and events beyond the traditional reader-response exercises by encouraging students to push beyond understanding to emotional engagement with the characters.

Community Murals (a.k.a. Graffiti)

In urban areas such as Chicago, Harlem, Los Angeles, and Philadelphia, it is not uncommon for political murals to appear. Figures such as Martin Luther King, Jr., Malcolm X, and Caesar Chavez, to name a few, often appear as symbols of hope, anger, fear, power, and resistance. Far less celebrated are "graffiti" representations, include tags, words, letters, wallpaper, and street art. While traditional perspectives often associate graffiti with acts of vandalism, it is important to understand that context matters in this situation. Tagging property that isn't yours and altering it without the owner's consent is vandalism. Street art, as well as social and political commentary that appears on public bridges and buildings that belong to a community, is art. These works are saying something and speaking to a large audience. Teachers should allow students to engage with these works and to receive what is being conveyed. Engage with graffiti as the work of art that it is, and acknowledge the emotions that it may stir up.

Dance and Movement

Dance is a choreographed representation of semiotics. Specifically, dance conveys meaning through movement as symbols and signs. As a result, dance may also be political. Alvin Ailey was one of first well-known African American choreographers and is often identified as an activist. Ailey's dance company brought attention and popularity to modern dance through African American dancers. Using dance and movement creates an opportunity for students to interpret meaning and to convey meaning through connections to historical, political, and social events.

Memes & GIFs (and yes, Emojis)

Today's K–12 students have grown up in the age of technology, and it is crucial for teachers find ways to integrate technology into social media. Memes, GIFs, and Emojis are ubiquitous and are purposely used to convey meaning to other individuals. These media forms are a popular and normal part of historical, political, and social culture. Students can interpret memes in ways that help them to understand how information from current events is interpreted. These interpretations are created by millions of people through Twitter, Instagram, and Facebook. Such forms of social media also identify crucial events in real time and offer a way for students to process issues that deal with and exude racial tension.

Many teachers may be afraid to use social media because of the unfiltered nature of these forms of media, and the threat of distraction is always present. However, social media is the world in which our students live. Currently, millions of people are employed in some form of social media, and employers are seeking employees whose role is specifically to navigate social media in strategic ways. Our K–12 students need to be aware of this and to learn how to use social media tactically as a way to progress successfully in society, and also as a form of social action.

Music

Music has long been a way for musicians to convey their emotions and ideas. From Mariam Makeba's anti-apartheid lyrics to Taylor Swift's anguished pop, lyrics convey the artists' thoughts and feelings vocally. Artists use specific instruments and cadences to fully communicate emotions. Music has also served as an instructional strategy for teachers. There are many ways to integrate music in the classroom, from examining lyrics for meaning to using them in vocabulary and grammar lessons. Ideally, part of the process needs to include simply letting students engage with the sounds, including beats, instruments, and voices. Let the aesthetic experience of the music envelop the student.

Poetry/Spoken Word

Much like lyrics, poetry and the spoken word possess literate power. That is, poetry and the spoken word provide opportunities for literacy strategy and instruction. However, much like music, poetry and the spoken word involve an auditory process. Cadence, verse, and voice communicate ideas and meaning that allows the individual to interpret this experience in a variety of ways. Often poetry and the spoken word make people uncomfortable; this is part of the aesthetic experience.

Political Cartoons/Comic Strips

Much like the forms of social media, political cartoons and comic strips comprise a medium that enables students to engage in political understanding through multiple forms of representation. Cartoonists often exaggerate physical characteristics (think of Barack Obama's ears) as a way to convey their ideas about a political figure or event. These mediums, to repeat, offer an opportunity to utilize visual thinking skills and to apply analysis and interpretation by highlighting the aesthetic awareness students may gain through their engagement.

Propaganda Posters (including Campaign Posters)

Propaganda posters and campaign posters can be viewed in a similar manner as memes, political cartoons, and other representations. This medium offers the viewer the opportunity to aesthetically engage with a clear message and to respond to the strength and power the piece may or may not have. Using the aesthetic experience, students can consider how these pieces might help or hinder racial tensions. Helping students to examine the affective response from such pieces can lead to more thoughtful conversations surrounding race.

Speeches

In this medium, students should be able to understand the role of discourse. Examining the context of a speech provides a partial understanding of the medium. A significant part of the aesthetic experience of a speech acknowledges the discourse that surrounds the speech and affects the speaker. Behaviors, customs, and dress often play a role in how the viewer experiences the speech.

The above suggestions for practical aesthetic applications in the classroom involve mediums that have often reflected racial tensions within a community. Racial tensions cover a variety of issues and beliefs. From implicit bias to oppression to outright violence, issues of race are complex and layered. Each classroom, school, and community will incorporate different mediums in different ways. The goals of including aesthetic responses in K–12 classrooms to address racial tensions are (a) to find an open and safe space to acknowledge and discuss race as individual students may have experienced it, and (b) to identify a positive, significant, and meaning-making outlet for the emotions that students may be subjected to as a result of experiences with race.

Conclusion

In our current societal climate, in which issues of social justice are constantly addressed and debated, it is crucial that we help students at every level and from a very young age. The current discourse surrounding racial tensions outside of school is fraught with frustration, misunderstanding, and, all too often, anger and hatred. This cycle needs to end. Children are aware of race at a young age. Early on, it is simply a matter of physical characteristics, and their observations often are unaccompanied by stereotypes or background knowledge. It is not until children grow and are exposed to belief systems that the issue of race becomes muddy and misconstrued. The concept of race is complicated; respect is not.

Teachers, administrators, and the curriculum itself are often reluctant to confront this muddiness in K–12 classrooms. There is no section of most curricula, or even the Common Core, to address students' emotions and inquiries about Black Lives Matter or the fear of deportation. When these issues are ignored, the lack of knowledge shapes the muddiness, and the muddiness becomes the foundation for misunderstanding and unaware-ness. Implementing aesthetics in K–12 classrooms and exposing children to difficult *but constructive* conversations about race offer an opportunity to change the political landscape in revolutionary ways.

In this chapter I have attempted to extend the purpose of aesthetics in the classroom beyond the concept of engagement and achievement. Students who experience aesthetic engagement and production in the class-room have the opportunity to develop agency and choice for social action, social change, and for themselves. Implementing aesthetics in the classroom presents more than a learning experience for students; it presents a lifestyle experience. It's difficult to find more appropriate words than Dewey's to illustrate the importance of art and aesthetics and our ability as human beings to fully experience them. I refer to Dewey's *Art as Experience* (1934):

> When artistic objects are separated from both conditions of origin and operation in experience, a wall is built around them that ren-ders almost opaque their general significance, with which esthetic theory deals. Art is remitted to a separate realm, where it is cut off from that association with the materials and aims of every other form of human effort, undergoing and achievement. A primary task is thus imposed upon one who undertakes to write upon the phi-losophy of fine arts. This task is to restore continuity between the

refined and intensified forms of experience that are works of art and the everyday events, doings, and sufferings that are universally recognized to constitute experience.... (pp. 204–205)

Incorporating aesthetics into an official curriculum (and, subsequently, the hidden curriculum) allows students to connect their lived experiences in constructive ways and in original spaces. A critical aesthetic instructional approach acknowledges the variety of backgrounds every student brings to the classroom and encourages connection and reflection. "The test, finally, is in the aesthetic experiences we can make possible, the privileged moments through which we can enable our students to live" (Greene, 1988, p. 294). Aesthetics presents an opportunity for future generations to live in ways that may encourage society's understanding of issues of social justice. Life deserves to be lived as more than just "eh."

Appendix: Additional Resources
Aesthetic Understanding & Arts Integration

The Maxine Greene Institute
    https://maxinegreene.org/index
Scholastic
    https://www.scholastic.com/teachers/collections/teaching-content/
    strategies-arts-integration/
Edutopia
    https://www.edutopia.org/arts-integration-resources
Education Closet
    https://educationcloset.com/classroom-strategies/
    https://educationcloset.com/arts-integration-and-steam-strategies/

References

Anyon, J. (1981). Social class and school knowledge. *Curriculum Inquiry, 11*(1), 3–42.

Anyon, J. (1983). Social class and the hidden curriculum of work. In H. Giroux & D. Purpel (Eds.), *The hidden curriculum and moral education: Deception or Discovery?* (pp. 143–167). Berkeley, CA: McCutchan Publishing.

Apple, M.W. (2006). Afterword. In L. Weis, C. McCarthy, & G. Dimitriadis

(Eds.), *Ideology, curriculum, and the new sociology of education: Revisiting the work of Michael Apple* (pp. 203–219). New York, NY: Routledge.

Beyerbach, B., Davis, R.D., & Ramalho, T. (Eds.). (2017). *Activist art and social justice pedagogy* (rev. ed.). New York, NY: Peter Lang.

Bose, J.H. (2008). *Aesthetic education: Philosophy and teaching artist practice at Lincoln Center Institute.* Unpublished doctoral dissertation, City University of New York, New York, NY.

Bresler, L. (1995). The subservient, co-equal, affective, and social integration and their implications for the arts. *Arts Education Policy Review, 96*(5), 31–37

Cerveny, K. (2001). Elliot W. Eisner, the role of the arts in educating the whole child: A Cleveland area presentation. *GIA Reader, 12*(3). Retrieved from https://www.giarts.org/article/elliot-w-eisner-role-arts-educating-whole-child

Dewey, J. (1934). *Art as experience.* New York, NY: Perigee Books.

Eisner, E.W. (1985). *The educational imagination: On the design and evaluation of school programs.* New York, NY: Macmillan.

Eisner, E.W. (1996). *Cognition and curriculum reconsidered* (2nd ed.). London: Chapman.

Eisner, E.W. (2002). *The arts and the creation of mind.* New Haven, CT: Yale University Press.

Freire, P. (1970). *Pedagogy of the oppressed.* New York, NY: Continuum.

Gee, J. P. (2001b). Reading as situated language: A sociocognitive perspective. *Journal of Adolescent & Adult Literacy, 44*, 714–725.

Giroux, H.A. (1983a). *Theory and resistance for education: A pedagogy for the opposition.* Westport, CT: Bergin & Garvey.

Giroux, H.A. (1983b). Theories of reproduction and resistance in the new sociology of education: A critical analysis. *Harvard Educational Review, 53*(3), 257–293.

Greene, M. (1988). The artistic aesthetic curriculum. *Curriculum Inquiry,*

6(4), 283–296.

Greene, M. (2001). *Variations on a blue guitar*. New York, NY: Teachers College Press.

Higgins, C. (2008). Instrumentalism and clichés of aesthetic education: A Deweyan corrective. *Education and Culture, 24*(1), 7–20.

Hochschild, J.L. (2003). Social class in public schools. *Journal of Social Issues, 59*(4), 821–840.

Housen, A. (1983). *The eye of the beholder: Measuring aesthetic development*. Ed.D. thesis, Harvard University Graduate School of Education, Cambridge, MA. UMI no. 8320170.

Hursh, D. (2008). *High-stakes testing and the decline of teaching and learning: The real crisis in education*. Lanham, MD: Rowman & Littlefield.

Jackson, P.W. (1968). *Life in classrooms*. Austin, TX: Holt, Rinehart and Winston.

Joseph, P.B. (Ed.). (2000). *Cultures of curriculum*. Mahwah, NJ: Lawrence Erlbaum Associates.

Kant, I. (1790/2007). *Critique of judgment*, Trans. by J. H. Bernard. London: Camp Press.

Kincheloe, J. (2007). *Critical pedagogy*. New York, NY: Peter Lang

Kristeller, P.O. (1952). The modern system of the arts: A study in the history of aesthetics. *Journal of the History of Ideas, 13*(1), 17–46.

Leshnoff, S.K. (2003). Teaching art, moral conduct, and John Dewey for today. *Art Education, 56*(6), 33–39.

Levinson, J. (2003). *The Oxford handbook of aesthetics*. Oxford: Oxford University Press.

Manzo, K.K. (2002). Study identifies the benefits of art curriculum. *Education Week, 22*(1), 10.

Medina, Y. (2006). *Critical aesthetic pedagogy: Toward a theory of self and social understanding*. Unpublished doctoral dissertation, University of North Carolina at Greensboro, Greensboro, NC.

Medina, Y. (2009). Art education programs: Empowering social change. *Perspectives on Urban Education*, 58–61.

Medina, Y. (2012). *Critical aesthetic pedagogy*. New York, NY: Peter Lang.

Moll, L. (1992). Funds of knowledge for teaching: Using a qualitative approach to connect homes and classrooms. *Theory into Practice, 31*(2), 132–141.

New London Group. (1996). A pedagogy of multiliteracies: Designing social futures. *Harvard Educational Review, 66*(1), 60–93.

Oxford English Dictionary. (2017). *Aesthetics*. Retrieved from http://www.oed.com/view/Entry/3237

Radhakrishnan, R. (2014). *Painting the lily: An examination of 5th grade students' learning experiences in an art-infused curriculum*. Unpublished doctoral dissertation, University of Illinois, Urbana-Champaign, IL.

Reeves, D. (2007). Academics and the arts. *Educational Leadership, 64*(5), 80–81.

Seidel, S., Tishman, S., Winner, E., Hetland, L., & Palmer, P. (2009). *The qualities of quality: Understanding excellence in art education*. Cambridge, MA: Project Zero, Harvard Graduate School of Education.

Shusterman, R. (1999). Somaesthetics: A disciplinary proposal. *Journal of Aesthetics and Art Criticism, 57*(3), 299–313.

Sleeter, C.E. (2005). *Un-standardizing curriculum: Multicultural teaching in the standards-based classroom*. New York, NY: Teachers College Press.

Tyack, D., & Cuban, L. (1995). Why the grammar of schooling persists. In D. Tyack & L. Cuban (Eds.), *Tinkering toward utopia: A century of public school reform* (pp. 85–109). Cambridge, MA: Harvard University Press.

Visual Understanding in Education. (1995). *VTS: Visual Thinking Strategies*. Retrieved from: https://vtshome.org

Weis, L., McCarthy, C., & Dimitriadis, G. (Eds.). (2006). *Ideology, curriculum, and the new sociology of education: Revisiting the work of Michael Apple*. New York, NY: Routledge.

Windschitl, M.A., & Joseph, P.B. (2000) Confronting the dominant order. In P.B. Joseph, S.L. Bravmann, M.A. Windschitl, E.R. Mikel, & N.S. Green (Eds.), *Cultures of curriculum* (pp. 137–160). Mahwah, NJ: Lawrence Erlbaum Associates.

CHAPTER FOUR

IGNORANCE IS NOT BLISS:
Why Early Childhood Educators Need to Teach Young Children About Race and Racism

TERRY HUSBAND

MRS. JACKSON IS A second-grade teacher at Cedarwood Elementary School. She is enjoying her leftover chili in the teacher's lounge while the television in the background plays miscellaneous national and local news updates. Mrs. Williams is a first-grade teacher at Cedarwood Elementary. She enters the lounge, and the two women begin to engage for several minutes in a friendly conversation about a range of topics. Suddenly, their conversation is interrupted by the all-too-familiar words from the news reporter on the television: "This just in...." The reporter begins discussing new updates in the case involving the police officer who shot Philando Castile, a 32-year-old Black Minnesota resident whom he had pulled over. The two women listen intently as the commentator begins discussing the salience of race and racism in an allegedly "post-racial" society. As the news show goes to commercial, the two women begin discussing the details of the verdict and their perspectives and positions as teachers. "I cannot believe the officer was found not guilty," states Mrs. Jackson in an angry voice. "This just goes to show us that we still have so much more work to do in this area," Mrs. Jackson adds. "What do you mean we?" asks Mrs. Williams. "I mean us as U.S. citizens and us as teachers in particular," responds Mrs. Jackson. "In fact, I already started brainstorming how I might potentially discuss this issue in my class this week. What about you?" asks Mrs. Jackson. "Well, I don't want to talk about that stuff in my classroom!" responds Mrs. Williams. "I don't want to offend anyone or cause any problems, so I prefer to simply avoid stuff like that. Also, I really don't see color in my classroom. I try to treat all of my students the same," she states. "Refusing to deal with the issue will not make the issue go away," argues Mrs. Jackson. "In fact, I believe that particular approach actually makes things worse!" she adds. "Well, I guess we'll just have to agree to disagree on this one," replies Mrs. Williams. "I guess so," Mrs. Jackson says in a disappointed voice. The clanging sound of a bell marking the end of the recess period begins. The two women quickly gather up their belongings and begin making their way toward the exit to pick up their students from recess.

Much like the teachers in this vignette, many early childhood educators (preschool–Grade 2) assume that children should not be taught about issues of race and racism in society. Teachers who subscribe to this school of thought often argue that early childhood students are "too young" to learn about racism and that introducing young children to this topic has the potential to cause more harm than good. Notably, a growing body of research (i.e., Boutte, Lopez-Robertson, & Powers-Costello, 2011; Husband, 2016; Ramsey, 2004) suggests that this line of thinking is somewhat problematic. More specifically, several studies point out that children begin to recognize race as early as age two or three (Bigler & Liben, 2007; Kelly et al., 2005, 2007). Further, studies suggest that children begin developing racial biases and in-group favoritism as early as three to five years of age that may or may not be consistent with the racial perspectives of the adults in their lives (Aboud & Amato, 2001; Kinzler, Shutts, DeJesus, & Spelke, 2009; Kinzler & Spelke, 2011). Based on the premise that young children tend to develop racial biases toward various groups in society, it is important for early childhood teachers to reconsider ignoring issues of race and racism in the curriculum. The purpose of this chapter is to identify reasons why early childhood teachers should instruct children about race and racism in the curriculum. The topics that I discuss here include implicit racial bias, lack of diversity in texts and curriculum, racial socialization, and racial identity development. In addition, a framework of different approaches is provided to assist early childhood teachers in teaching children about race and racism. Finally, important political and ethical considerations are discussed for teachers who engage in this form of teaching and learning.

Teaching Young Children About Race and Racism

Why talk about race and racism with young children? Many early childhood teachers, motivated by both political and developmental concerns, assume that children are too young to learn about race and racism (Husband, 2016). In essence, many early childhood teachers believe that "colorblind" approaches to race and racism in the classroom will lead to positive outcomes for children. However, several studies (e.g., Aboud & Amato, 2001; Hirschfeld, 2008; Patterson & Bigler, 2006; Van Ausdale & Feagin, 2001) suggest that early childhood teachers should, indeed, teach children about race and racism for a number of reasons. First, young children often hold implicit racial biases toward people who do not share their in-group racial identities (Aboud & Amato, 2001; Kinzler, Shutts, DeJesus, & Spelke, 2009; Kinzler & Spelke, 2011). For example, Kelly and colleagues (2007) found evidence that infants often show a preference for own-race faces and are more adept at recognizing adults of their own race than adults with other-race faces. Their study involved a total of 192 infants ranging from 3 to 9 months of age. The participants were individually presented 24 images of adults from four racial groups (African, Asian, Middle Eastern, or Caucasian) on a projection screen, while two researchers observed and recorded each infant's eye movements. The amount of time each infant looked at the various images was recorded and analyzed. Essentially, the 3-month-old infants recognized all of the faces from the four different racial groups. In contrast, the 6-month-old infants were only able to recognize Caucasian and Chinese faces. Finally, the 9-month-old infants only recognized faces that were similar to their own race. These findings suggest that racial preferences begin to develop in children who are 6–9 months of age.

Much like the study involving infants, Dunham, Chen, and Banaji (2013) found that children as young as 3 years old begin to show implicit racial biases as well. The researchers conducted four different experiments on a total of 883 children ranging in age from 3 to 14 years. The children in the first experiment were White and were asked to view a series of faces on a computer screen and to categorize each face as Black or White. Some of the faces had visibly angry expressions, while the others had neutral expressions. The children in the second experiment were White and were asked to categorize each face they saw on the computer screen as White or Asian. The children in the third experiment were Taiwanese and were asked to categorize each face they saw as White or Asian. The children in the fourth experiment were Black and were asked to categorize the faces they saw as Black or White. Findings indicate that the White children were more likely to categorize the angry faces they saw on the screen as Black than White. In a similar manner, the Taiwanese children in the study tended to categorize the angry faces as Black more often than the non-angry faces. What this study ultimately suggests is that children frequently hold implicit racial biases toward various groups in society. Hence there is a need for early childhood educators to identify, resist, and counter these biases in their classrooms.

In a more recent study, Dore, Hoffman, Lillard, and Trawalter (2014) found that young children have a racial bias related to perceptions of pain between Black and White people. The researchers examined the implicit bias in 159 children ranging in age from 5 to 10 years. Of the participants in the study, approximately 90% of the children were identified as White. Four of the participants were identified as Asian, one as Hispanic, and one as African American. Nine of the parents chose the "other" response option to identify their child's race or chose more than one response option. In short, the participants were shown a series of faces and asked to rate the level of pain the person in each photograph was experiencing. Each child saw only one photograph of a Black child and one photograph of a White child (both of their own gender) throughout the procedure. In addition, the researchers used three photographs of each gender and race across the sample to guard against the possibility that any effects observed were specific to a particular photograph. Two important findings emerged from the data analysis. First, bias was detected in and among the 7-year-olds in the study. Further, the 10-year-olds demonstrated a significant degree of bias as well. More specifically, the 10-year-old children rated the pain of a Black target as lower than the pain of a White target. Not only do these findings suggest that bias develops early in a child's life; they also indicate that this bias may increase as the child gets older. It is therefore imperative for early childhood teachers to deal with these biases during the initial years of a child's schooling.

Another reason why early childhood teachers should discuss issues of race and racism with their students concerns the texts that are used and the curriculum that is taught in many classrooms. Unfortunately, many of the texts used in early education minimize and marginalize the voices and perspectives of people of color (Derman-Sparks, Ramsey, & Edwards, 2011). For example, a recent study conducted by the Cooperative Children's Book Center (CCBC) in 2015 found that a strikingly large number of the characters in children's books published during that year were White. Of approximately 3,400 children's books published that year in the United States, 7.6% depicted African American characters, 3.3% depicted Asian Pacific and Asian Pacific American characters, 3.3% depicted Latinx characters, and 0.9% depicted American Indian characters. At the same time, it is important to note that approximately 12.5% of the books published that year featured animals, trucks, or other non-human creatures or objects as the main characters. Ultimately, as a result of early childhood teachers using books that neglect the voices, experiences, and contributions of people of color in the classroom, young children often develop a view that White people and Whiteness are superior to the views and ideologies of people of color in society (Aronson, Callahan, & O'Brien, 2018; Hughes-Hassell & Cox, 2010; Mabbott, 2017). Even more important, the lack of exposure to—or, indeed, the sheer absence of—positive images and knowledge related to people of color can lead children to construct negative and stereotypical views about such people. Hence, as a means of combatting and countering the development of these racial biases in and among students, early childhood teachers should engage them in discussions of race and racism during the early childhood years.

Much like the books that are used in many early childhood classrooms in the United States, the experiences, perspectives, and contributions of people of color are often excluded from the formal curriculum that is taught in many schools (Brown & Brown, 2010; Heilig, Brown, & Brown, 2012; Pollock, 2004). For example, based on a textual analysis of the social studies standards in the state of Texas, Heilig and colleagues (2012) found that the narratives of people of color were discussed very minimally within the larger narrative of U.S. history. This was especially true for the narratives of Asian American and Native American people. In addition, notions of race and racism were missing from the larger discussion of U.S. history. In fact, the term "racism" was excluded completely from the formal state standards document. Ultimately, what this study suggests is that the experiences and perspectives of people of color are not being examined in many classrooms and schools across the United States. Thus, early childhood teachers should discuss issues of race and racism in an open and forthright manner in order to remedy the lack of representation of people of color within school curricula and classroom texts.

A third reason why early childhood teachers should instruct children about race and racism deals with racial socialization. Frequently, children receive and are socialized by the racist stereotypes and messages they are exposed to from the media (Bigler & Liben, 2007). Whether we want to admit it or not, children spend a considerable amount of time engaging in various forms of media outside of school (Roberts & Foehr, 2004). For many children, television is the way they learn about things in life in which they have little or no personal experience (Barcus, 1983; Graves, 1999). Unfortunately, however, television often perpetuates racist stereotypes and messages about people of color in society. While older children frequently have the ability to identify and counter these racist stereotypes and messages, young children are more likely to accept these messages as truth (McKenna & Ossoff, 1998). For example, in a study examining racial representation and role portrayal, Maher, Herbst, Childs, and Finn (2008) found that minorities are disproportionately underrepresented in many of the commercials that children watch. Of the 155 commercials examined in their study, the researchers found that Caucasians made up approximately 82% of the characters in these commercials. By contrast, African Americans constituted approximately 14% of the characters; Hispanics represented approximately 1.5% of the characters; and Asian Americans represented approximately 2.7% of the characters in the commercials. With regard to role portrayal, African Americans and Hispanics were underrepresented in major roles and overrepresented in minor roles in these commercials. At the same time, the African American and Hispanic characters were largely overrepresented in restaurant advertisements, while White and Asian characters were overrepresented in toy advertisements. The study concludes that that many of the television shows children watch either neglect to portray the experiences of people of color or communicate fixed or oversimplified messages related to them. To this end, these messages often work to cultivate negative racial stereotypes—for example, Mexicans are lazy, and Blacks are aggressive (Brown-Givens & Monahan, 2005; Children Now, 2004; Graves, 1999). Early childhood educators can work toward disrupting and countering these messages by teaching children about race and racism in an open, honest, and explicit manner in their classrooms.

Much like television, parents serve as significant socializing agents in a child's life. When it comes to racial attitudes and perspectives, parents can have a positive or negative impact on a child's racial attitudes (Vittrup & Holden, 2011). In many instances, children accurately identify and interpret their parents' implicit, subtle, nonverbal cues (related to race) as they interact with people from different racial backgrounds (Castelli, De Dea, & Nesdale, 2008). For example, Castelli, Zogmaister, and Tomelleri (2009) found that mothers' implicit racial attitudes were significant predictors of children's racial attitudes. Seventy-two middle-class, White children participated in this study. The children ranged in age from 3 to 6 years old. They were shown drawings that portrayed a White and a Black preschool-age male. The children were required to choose which of the two children they would prefer as a playmate. Next, the researcher introduced eight cards with one trait written on each card. Four traits were positive (i.e., nice, happy, clean, and likable) and four traits were negative (i.e., ugly, sad, dirty, and bad). The researcher read aloud the trait written on the card and asked each child to assign it to the drawing that it matched. Four response options were allowed. Each trait could be given to the White child, to the Black child, to both of them, or to neither of them. The parents of these children were given a computerized Implicit Association Test (Greenwald, McGhee, & Schwartz, 1998) to evaluate their racial attitudes and to compare those attitudes with the attitudes of the children who participated in the study. Data analysis revealed that the racial attitudes of the children who participated in the study were somewhat inconsistent with the *explicit* racial attitudes of the parents who participated. Nevertheless, the *implicit* racial attitudes of the children in the study were directly consistent with the implicit racial attitudes of the parents who participated. Ultimately, what this study suggests is that if a parent has an implicit racial bias toward a particular group of people in society, it is likely that his or her child will develop a similar bias toward that same group. Early childhood teachers can combat this bias by discussing issues of race and racism in the classroom.

A fourth reason why early childhood teachers should teach children about race and racism deals with children developing an acute awareness of racial injustice in society. As mentioned previously, many early childhood teachers prefer teaching a colorblind perspective on race and racism in their classrooms (Ramsey, 2004). In short, a colorblind approach to race and racism minimizes and or completely avoids discussions of racial difference and racial injustice and oppression in the classroom (Boutte et al., 2011). Instead, a colorblind approach emphasizes commonalities across various racial groups in society. Many early childhood teachers assume that avoiding discussions of race and racism is the most effective means of not communicating negative and or stereotypical messages about people of color to young children. Interestingly, there is evidence to suggest that a colorblind approach to race and racism actually makes it difficult for children to recognize and identify acts of racial injustice in the world (Boutte et al., 2011). For example, in a study involving 60 children (51 White and 9 Asian) ranging in age from 8 to 11 years, Apfelbaum, Pauker, Sommers, and Ambady (2010) found that children who participated in lessons where racial diversity was ignored were less likely to identify racial injustice than children who participated in lessons where racial diversity was emphasized. The children in the study reviewed different versions of a multimedia storybook. Half of the children received a colorblind version of the storybook and the other half received a value-diversity version. In both versions the narrator championed racial justice, but the colorblind version of the storybook encouraged and minimized race-based distinctions. In contrast, the value-diversity version of the storybook encouraged and embraced racial differences and distinctions. After the storybooks were read, the children listened to three stories containing varying degrees of racial bias. In the control story, a White child was marginalized by his White schoolmates' contribution to a school science project. In the neutral story, a White student excluded a Black student from his birthday party. In the explicitly biased story, a White student assaulted a Black student in a soccer game. After the stories were read, the children were asked to describe the three events, and their responses were video recorded. Data analysis revealed that the children who had read the value-diversity version of the storybook were more likely to detect evidence of racial discrimination than the children who read the colorblind version of the storybook. Approximately 43% of these children recognized racial discrimination in the ambiguous story. In addition, approximately 77% of these children recognized racial discrimination in the explicitly biased story. In contrast, the frequency with which children recognized discrimination dropped significantly among the children who read the colorblind storybook. Approximately 10% of these children recognized racial discrimination in the ambiguous story. To this end, only about 50% of these children recognized racial discrimination in the story that portrayed an overt example of racist behavior. Ultimately, the study suggests that avoiding discussions of race and racism in the classroom can anesthetize children in terms of their ability to identify racial injustice in the world around them. Early childhood teachers can combat this issue by teaching their students about race and racism in an explicit manner.

A fifth reason why early childhood teachers should teach children about race and racism deals with racial identity development. In short, racial identity development is defined as the process of developing a positive sense of one's race/ethnicity that does not involve an inferior or superior view of other races/ethnicities in society (Cross, 1995; Tatum, 1992). Children who develop positive racial identities tend to experience fewer social, emotional, and academic challenges at school than children who develop negative views of their own racial/ethnic identities. For example, in a study aimed at examining the relationship between racial/ethnic identity development and child functioning among 4- and 5-year-old Latino children at school, Serrano-Villar and Calzada (2016) found that children who had a considerable knowledge of their racial/ethnic identity had fewer external and internal problems at school than children who had limited knowledge about their racial/ethnic identity. Notably, the researchers point out that the children who felt more secure in their understanding of their racial/ethnic identity were more self-confident at school and less susceptible to the stressors related to navigating between home and school than children who did not have a secure understanding of their racial/ethnic identity. As the researchers further point out, children with positive racial/ethnic identities used these identities to "protect" themselves from many of the adversities and negative messages they often experienced at school. Ultimately, this study suggests that developing a positive racial/ethnic identity can help students navigate the challenges inherent in schools more effectively than students who do not have a positive racial/ethnic identity.

Is discussing issues of race and racism beneficial for White and non-White children alike? Theories of racial identity development assert that it is necessary for *all* children to engage in meaningful and critical discussions about race and racism to develop a positive racial identity. In many instances, the process of racial identity development may be different for White children and children of color. For example, Cross (1991) explains that Black Americans and other people of color tend to evolve through a series of five stages as they develop positive racial identities. These stages are known as

(1) Pre-encounter; (2) Encounter; (3) Immersion/Emersion; (4) Internalization; and (5) Internalization-Commitment. In the first stage, Pre-Encounter, people of color absorb and internalize messages and values from the broader society that "White is right" and "Black is wrong." Essentially, Whiteness is seen as having more value and status than non-Whiteness. In the second stage, Encounter, people of color experience racism and are forced to realize that it exists in the world. In the third stage, Immersion/Emersion, people of color seek to surround themselves with symbols and personal interactions that predominantly or exclusively involve other people of color. This is done primarily as a means of countering the dominant messages communicated by the broader society. In the fourth stage, Internalization, people of color develop a secure sense of self as they establish meaningful relationships with Whites, while simultaneously maintaining positive attitudes about their own racial identity. The final stage, Internalization-Commitment, involves developing a commitment toward combatting racial injustice in the world. Cross further points out that the Internalization and Internalization-Commitment stages are achieved through sustained and positive educational experiences and interactions that celebrate and value people of color. In this vein, it is vital for early childhood teachers to incorporate positive and affirming discussions of the experiences, perspectives, and histories of various non-White racial groups in their classrooms.

In contrast to Cross's theory of positive racial identity development for people of color, Helms (1992) identifies the six stages involved in positive racial identity development for Whites in society. These stages are: (1) Contact; (2) Disintegration; (3) Reintegration; (4) Pseudo-Independence; (5) Immersion/Emersion; and (6) Autonomy. The first stage, Contact, involves seeing the world through a colorblind lens. White people who are at this stage in their racial identity development do not see race or racism as significant issues in the world. In the second stage, Disintegration, White people are confronted with experiences that cause them to identify issues of racial privilege and marginalization in their personal lives and the broader society. It is common during this stage for White people to experience feelings of guilt and shame related to being benefactors of racial privilege. The third stage, Reintegration, typically involves White people blaming people of color for negative experiences related to race and racism. For example, a White person at this stage in their identity development might rationalize racial profiling as law enforcers simply taking steps to make a neighborhood safe for the citizens who live there. The fourth stage, Pseudo-Independence, begins when Whites start to acknowledge and validate the experiences of people of color related to race and racism. In other words, Whites who are at this stage in their racial identity development are willing to admit that racism does exist in the world and is something that needs to be addressed. In the fifth stage, Immersion/Emersion, White people begin to consider themselves to be anti-racist—that is, they begin to take a proactive stance against racism in the world. The final stage, Autonomy, involves White people engaging in ongoing social action to combat racism in the world. Essentially, the goal at this stage is to move beyond simply identifying themselves as anti-racist persons to taking action (in an open and explicit manner) to combat racial injustice in their everyday lives and in the world around them. Helms further points out that progress through these stages is a direct result of ongoing, non-deficit, and equal-status educational and personal experiences and interactions with people of color. Hence, early childhood teachers can help contribute to the positive identity development process in White children by teaching about race and racism in an open and forthright manner (Neblett, Rivas-Drake, & Umaña-Taylor, 2012).

A Framework for Teaching Children About Race and Racism

The dynamics, demographics, and experiences of early childhood students will inevitably vary from classroom to classroom and context to context. Consequently, there are multiple ways of engaging children in critical discussions of race and racism that lead to fruitful outcomes. Critical multicultural educators and theorists argue that multicultural children's literature can serve as a valuable tool for engaging children in critical discussions of race and racism (Chaudhri, 2017; Hollingsworth, 2009; Moya & Hamedani, 2017). In the next section, I provide a framework of four distinct approaches (see Figure 1) to teaching children about race and racism through the use of multicultural children's literature. It is important to note here that each approach can be implemented individually or in conjunction with the other approaches.

The first approach is what is known as the *Reader Response* approach (Brooks & Browne, 2012; Rosenblatt, 1985; Sipe, 2008). In keeping with this approach, readers are positioned in ways that encourage them to actively construct meaning as they interact with various texts. Moreover, readers are asked to use their own experiences, knowledge base, and frames of reference to negotiate meaning as they interact with the information presented in a particular text. In this sense, reading becomes a transactional experience (Rosenblatt, 1985). For instance, a second-grade teacher who is implementing this particular approach to teaching children about race and racism might begin her lesson by asking the students to share what they have heard about race and racial prejudice and discrimination. The teacher might then record the responses on chart paper and refer back to them as she reads a multicultural picture book entitled *Amazing Grace* by Mary Hoffman (1991). This particular book tells the story of a young Black girl named Grace who is prejudged by her classmates on the basis of her race and gender. In short, her classmates tell her that she can't play the role of Peter Pan in the play because she is Black and a girl. Ultimately, Grace is given the opportunity to play the role and performs it exceptionally well. Using a Reader Response approach, the teacher would engage her students in dialogue and activities that allow them to draw from their personal experiences, knowledge base, and references related to racial discrimination as well as the experiences and information presented in the text to construct new interpretations of racial- and gender-based discrimination. Furthermore, instead of seeking to uncover a singular meaning related to race and racism, a Reader Response approach seeks to equip children with the tools, skills, and dispositions needed to construct multiple meanings of race and racism as they interact with various texts on this topic.

Another approach to teaching children about race and racism in early childhood classrooms is what is commonly known as the *Critical Literacy* approach (Lewison, Flint, & Van Sluys, 2002; McLaughlin & DeVoogd, 2010; Vasquez & Felderman, 2012). In short, Critical Literacy is a reflective, dialogic, and problem-based approach to literacy that seeks to reveal various forms of injustice in the world through the use of specific literacy tools and texts. The four dimensions of Critical Literacy include:

1. disrupting a common situation or understanding (seeking to understand the text or situation in more or less detail in order to gain perspective;

2. interrogating multiple viewpoints (examining the events in the text from the perspectives of the people there as well as those who are missing);

3. focusing on sociopolitical issues (thinking about power in relationships between and among people and exploring how power relationships shape perceptions, responses, and actions); and

4. taking action and promoting social justice (reflecting and acting to change an inappropriate, unequal power relationship between people) (Lewison et al., 2002).

Essentially, the goal of a Critical Literacy approach to race and racism is to use texts and other literacy tools and processes to identify, resist, and combat racial injustices in society. For example, a first-grade teacher who is applying this approach in his or her classroom might read and discuss the book *Rosa* by Nikki Giovanni (2005) to prompt a discussion related to the Jim Crow era and the Civil Rights Movement. Next, the teacher might engage her students in a series of small-group activities that provide opportunities for them to examine this topic from a wide range of multiple perspectives such as the bus driver, the passengers on the bus, the people outside of the bus, and so on. Then, the teacher might instruct her students to write a "Letter to Rosa" to communicate their personal stance on this issue. The teacher might follow with a discussion of the ways in which protests are being used in modern-day contexts to combat issues of racial injustice. Finally, the teacher might work with the students in her classroom to develop and implement a plan of action for combatting racial injustice in everyday life.

A third approach to teaching children about race and racism through the use of multicultural children's literature is known as the *Inquiry-Based Learning* approach (Barron & Darling-Hammond, 2008; Callison, 2015; Edelsky, Smith, & Faltis, 2008). In short, an Inquiry-Based Learning (IBL) approach provides an opportunity for students to learn about race and racism by investigating authentic and organic questions related to race and racism. Typically, an IBL approach involves the following five steps: (1) asking questions; (2) planning and researching answers; (3) creating and experimenting; (4) sharing and presenting findings and conclusions; and (5) reflecting on the product and process and developing new questions. In keeping with this approach, an early childhood teacher might read a multicultural picture book related to race and racial justice. Next, the teacher might engage students in a critical dialogue related to this issue. During this dialogue, the teacher works to solicit questions from the students that could be used as a basis for future study. Then the teacher and the students decide how they plan to research this topic in depth and how they plan to present the information they find. After providing ample time complete the project and present the information, the teacher and students then develop new questions that might be explored in the future. This approach provides opportunities for teachers to work alongside students to explore issues of race and racism in ways that are contextually specific and driven by students' natural interests and curiosities.

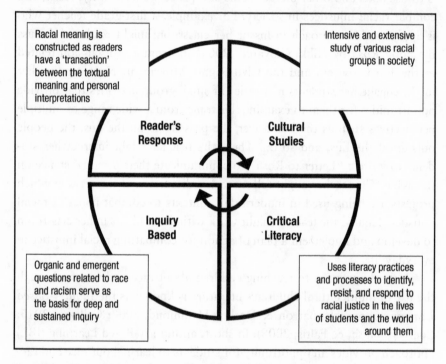

FIGURE 1. Four Approaches to Teaching Children About Race and Racism

A final approach to teaching children about race and racism through the use of multicultural children's literature is known as the *Cultural Studies* approach (Banks, 2016; Sleeter, & Flores Carmona, 2017; Vittrup, 2016). Using this approach, an early childhood teacher identifies a particular racial group that she and the students can learn about over an extended period of time. The goal of this approach is for students to gain a rich, deep, and nuanced knowledge base of particular racial groups in society. For instance, a kindergarten teacher applying this approach might decide to develop and implement a month-long unit on the historical and contemporary experiences of Native American people in the United States. Throughout this unit, students have an opportunity to read and explore myriad texts written by and about Native American people. Ultimately, this approach helps children develop a deeper understanding of some of the historical and contextual complexities and conflicts associated with being a member of a non-White racial group in today's society.

Table 1 provides a brief list of multicultural picture books that might be used to teach children about race and racism. It is important to note here that all multicultural picture books are not the same in terms of literary quality and/or the ways in which they represent the historical and contemporary experiences of people of color. That said, it is important for early childhood teachers to carefully and thoughtfully scrutinize the content of these books prior to introducing them in the classroom. Factors to be weighed in evaluating multicultural picture books for use in the classroom include, but are not limited to, the following: accuracy of events; cultural/racial authenticity; language; stereotypes; literary elements; illustrations; and the voices/perspectives that are present and missing (2009).

Cautions and Considerations

Throughout this chapter I have argued in favor of teaching young children about race and racism in critical and meaningful ways. While this endeavor is certainly important, given the current social and political context of race and racism in the United States, it is not without potential personal and professional consequences. In this sense, engaging in racial dialogue with children is often what I deem a form of "dangerous pedagogy." To successfully navigate and overcome many of the potential and perceived dangers associated with this form of critical praxis with young children, teachers must first be willing to consider and embrace several important factors related to race and racial dialogue. First, early childhood teachers must come to terms with the notion that race and racial dialogue are deeply personal. In other words, teachers cannot fully, honestly, and critically discuss issues of racism in the world and in the lives of their students without first critically reflecting on the role of racial privilege and marginalization in their own lives (Milner, 2010). Therefore, teachers should engage in critical self-reflection related to issues of race and racism prior to teaching children about race and racism. In short, critical self-reflection involves thinking about the ways in which race, racial privilege, and racial marginalization exist and operate in one's own life and within various institutions in society at large (Milner, 2010).

Title	Author	Copyright Date	Brief Summary
The Soccer Fence: A Story of Friendship, Hope and Apartheid in South Africa	Phil Bildner	2014	Tells the story of a young boy named Hector who is not allowed to play soccer with White children because of apartheid in South Africa. After Nelson Mandela is elected President and apartheid is ended, Hector is permitted to play soccer and develops many cross-racial friendships.
Amazing Grace	Mary Hoffman	1991	A young Black girl named Grace is discouraged from playing the role of Peter Pan because of her race and gender by her White classmates. She is encouraged by her grandmother to overcome this prejudice.
Last Stop on Market Street	Matt de la Peña		Tells the story of a young boy who interacts with people from diverse racial and socioeconomic backgrounds as he rides the bus each week.
A is for Activist	Innosanto Nagara		This board book uses rhyme and alliteration to discuss various forms of justice and activism.
The Story Of Ruby Bridges: Special Anniversary Edition	Robert Coles	2010	Tells the story of the first African American child to integrate the public school system in New Orleans.
Separate Is Never Equal: Sylvia Mendez and Her Family's Fight for Desegregation	Duncan Tonatiuh	2014	Tells the story of a child of Mexican and Puerto Rican heritage who was denied entrance to a Whites-only school in California.
Sonia Sotomayor: A Judge Grows in the Bronx / La juez que crecio en el Bronx	Jonah Winter	2009	Tells the story of Sonia Sotomayor, who rose up from a childhood of poverty and prejudice to become the first Latina to serve on the U.S. Supreme Court.
A Picture Book of Cesar Chavez	David A. Adler Michael S. Adler	2001	Tells the story of a Hispanic California farmworker who fought for economic justice and fair pay.
The Name Jar	Yangsook Choi	2003	Tells the story of an Asian girl who is self-conscious about her name as she enters a new school.
D Is for Drum: A Native American Alphabet	Michael Shoulders Debbie Shoulders	2006	This book uses the alphabet to introduce readers to Native American culture and customs.

TABLE 1. Sample Picture Books that May Be Used to Teach Children About Race and Racism

The primary goal of the form of critical self-reflection is for teachers to identify ways in which they may have benefitted (consciously or unconsciously)
from racist acts, processes, and institutions in their personal and professional lives. The secondary goal, then, is for teachers to use this information to
implement curriculum, teaching, learning, and assessment practices that are
more racially just in nature (Derman-Sparks, 2015).

In addition to critically reflecting on the role of race in their personal
and professional lives, early childhood teachers who endeavor to engage
children in critical discussions of race and racism must also recognize that
racial dialogue is deeply and explicitly political in nature (Ohito, 2016).
That is, teachers must realize that engaging in discussions of racial privilege
and marginalization cannot be carried out in a seemingly politically neutral
manner (Ladson-Billings, 2009). Discussing issues of race and racism with
children will likely position teachers in ways that contrast to the traditional,
status quo, and "safe" ways of being an early childhood teacher in most
classrooms (Doucet & Keys Adair, 2013). In other words, teachers who
engage their students in discussions of racism or other forms of injustice in
the world are often seen by their colleagues as being "radical" or in conflict
with the status quo (Fergus, 2017). Thus, teachers must be willing to fully
embrace this political positionality within their respective teaching contexts.

Inevitably, children will bring to the classroom different experiences,
frames of reference, and knowledge bases related to race and racism. Consequently, teachers should consider teaching children about race and racism
in a developmental or progressive manner (Derman-Sparks, 2015). That is,
teachers should make an effort to assess children's prior knowledge related
to historical and contemporary racial events, figures, and groups in society
and then make long-range plans to contribute to their current knowledge
base. Instead of thinking about racial dialogue as a short-term curriculum
objective, teachers should think about teaching children about race in a
manner that potentially spans months or even years, if possible. As a result,
children will be able to develop a broader and more comprehensive understanding of race and racism in the world.

Extensive exposure to people from different racial backgrounds can significantly reduce implicit racial bias (McGlothlin & Killen, 2010). In other
words, children who are exposed to and interact with people from racially
diverse backgrounds tend to exhibit less implicit racial bias than children
who interact solely with people who share their racial identity. Therefore,

to the degree that it is feasible, early childhood teachers should provide opportunities for other people of color to share their firsthand experiences and narratives related to race and racism. This will help children develop a more nuanced understanding of those factors that is frequently missing from traditional textbooks and other curriculum materials.

How should discussions of race proceed in early childhood classrooms where the vast majority of the children are White? Interestingly, early childhood teachers who work in such classrooms tend to be especially reluctant to discuss issues of race and racism with their students (Derman-Sparks et al., 2011). Many of these teachers assume that discussions of race and racism are irrelevant, since most of the students in their classrooms are White. The effects of racism within the broader society have negative consequences for all racial segments of that society (Wise, 2010). Therefore, early childhood teachers who work in predominately White settings must also be willing to discuss issues of race, racism, and racial justice with their students. Notwithstanding, these discussions of race and racism are likely to be different in predominately White classrooms than in classrooms that are more racially diverse. Derman-Sparks and colleagues (2011) point out that early childhood educators, who work in predominately White classrooms, should make a special effort to help White children accomplish the following goals as they discuss issues of race and racism:

1. develop authentic racial identities that do not rest on notions of White superiority;

2. explore the differences and similarities between Whites and other racial groups in society;

3. explore the nuances that exist within and across various racial groups;

4. develop the capacity to empathize with various racial groups who have been and continue to be marginalized in society;

5. develop the perspective that all human beings (regardless of race) deserve the right to a healthy, comfortable, and sustainable life;

6. identify and challenge stereotypes and prejudice as they appear in the world around them; and

7. make connections to and with other White people who have fought and continue to fight for racial justice in the world.

On the whole, it will likely take years for many early childhood educators to abandon colorblind perspectives and approaches to teaching and learning in the classroom and to fully embrace race-conscious perspectives and approaches. As difficult, uneasy, and emotionally taxing as this form of pedagogy may appear to be, it is nonetheless a necessary first step in making the world a more racially just place. Children cannot respond to issues of racial injustice and oppression in the world in an effective manner without first being taught when, where, and how racism exists and functions explicitly and implicitly in many of the taken-for-granted practices and systems in society. Hence, teaching children about race and racism in today's classrooms is an essential component to ensuring that children become citizens who are committed to creating and sustaining a more racially just society in the future.

References

Aboud, F.E., & Amato, M. (2001). Developmental and socialization influences on intergroup bias. In R. Brown & S. Gaertner (Eds.), *Intergroup processes* (pp. 65–89). Oxford: Blackwell.

Apfelbaum, E.P., Pauker, K., Sommers, S.R., & Ambady, N. (2010). In blind pursuit of racial equality? *Psychological Science, 21*(11), 1587–1592. doi:10.1177/0956797610384741

Aronson, K.M., Callahan, B.D., & O'Brien, A.S. (2018). Messages matter: Investigating the thematic content of picture books portraying underrepresented racial and cultural groups. *Sociological Forum, 33*(1), 165–185. doi:10.1111/socf.12404

Banks, J.A. (2016). *Cultural diversity and education: Foundations, curriculum, and teaching.* New York, NY: Routledge.

Barcus, F.E. (1983). *Images of life on children's television: Sex roles, minorities, and families.* New York, NY: Praeger.

Barron, B., & Darling-Hammond, L. (2008). *Teaching for meaningful learning: A review of inquiry-based and cooperative learning. Powerful learning: what we know about teaching for understanding.* San Francisco, CA: Jossey-Bass.

Bigler, R.S., & Liben, L.S. (2007). Developmental intergroup theory: Explaining and reducing children's social stereotyping and prejudice. *Current Directions in Psychological Science, 16*, 162–166.

Boutte, G.S., Lopez-Robertson, J., & Powers-Costello, E. (2011). Moving beyond colorblindness in early childhood classrooms. *Early Childhood Education Journal, 39*(5), 335–342.

Brooks, W., & Browne, S. (2012). Towards a culturally situated reader response theory. *Children's Literature in Education, 43*(1), 74–85. doi:10.1007/s10583-011-9154-z

Brown, A., & Brown, K. (2010). "A spectacular secret": Understanding the cultural memory of racial violence in K–12 official school textbooks in the era of Obama. *Race, Gender & Class, 17*(3), 111–125.

Brown-Givens, S., & Monahan, J. (2005). Priming mammies, jezebels, and other controlling images: An examination of the influence of mediated stereotypes on perceptions of an African American woman. *Media Psychology, 7*, 87–106.

Callison, D. (2015). *The evolution of inquiry: Controlled, guided, modeled, and free.* Santa Barbara, CA: Libraries Unlimited.

Castelli, L., De Dea, C., & Nesdale, D. (2008). Learning social attitudes: Children's sensitivity to the nonverbal behaviors of adult models during interracial interactions. *Personality & Social Psychology Bulletin, 34*, 1504–1513.

Castelli, L., Zogmaister, C., & Tomelleri, S. (2009). The transmission of racial attitudes within the family. *Developmental Psychology, 45*, 586–591.

Chaudhri, A. (2017). *Multiracial identity in children's literature: Reading diversity in the classroom.* New York, NY: Routledge.

Children Now. (2004). *Fall colors: Prime time diversity report 2003–04.* Oakland, CA: Children Now.

Cooperative Children's Book Center. (2015). Children's books by and about people of color and first/native nations. Retrieved from http://ccbc.education. wisc.edu/books/multicultural.asp

Cross, W. (1991). *Shades of Black: Diversity in African-American identity.* Philadelphia, PA: Temple University Press.

Cross, Jr., W.E. (1995). The psychology of nigrescence: Revising the Cross model. In J. Ponterotto, J. Casas, J. Manuel, L. Suzuki, & C. Alexander (Eds.), *Handbook of multicultural counseling* (pp. 93–122). Thousand Oaks, CA: Sage.

Derman-Sparks, L. (2015). *Leading anti-bias early childhood programs: A guide for change.* New York, NY: Teachers College Press.

Derman-Sparks, L., Ramsey, P.G., & Edwards, J.O. (2011). *What if all the kids are White? Anti-bias multicultural education with young children and families.* New York, NY: Teachers College Press.

Dore, R.A., Hoffman, K.M., Lillard, A.S., & Trawalter, S. (2014). Children's racial bias in perceptions of others' pain. *British Journal of Developmental Psychology, 32*(2), 218–231. doi:10.1111/bjdp.12038

Doucet, F., & Keys Adair, J. (2013). Addressing race and inequity in the classroom. *Young Children, 68*(5), 88–97.

Dunham, Y., Chen, E.E., & Banaji, M.R. (2013). Two signatures of implicit intergroup attitudes: Developmental invariance and early enculturation. *Psychological Science, 24,* 860–868.

Edelsky, C., Smith, K., & Faltis, C. (2008). *Side-by-side learning: Exemplary literacy practices for English language learners and English speakers in the mainstream classroom.* New York, NY: Scholastic.

Fergus, E. (2017). Confronting colorblindness. *Phi Delta Kappan, 98*(5), 30–35.

Giovanni, N. (2005). *Rosa.* New York, NY: Henry Holt.

Graves, S.B. (1999). Television and prejudice reduction: When does television as a vicarious experience make a difference? *Journal of Social Issues, 55,* 707–727.

Greenwald, A.G., McGhee, D.E., & Schwartz, J.L.K. (1998). Measuring individual differences in implicit cognition: The Implicit Association Test. *Journal of Personality and Social Psychology, 74,* 1464–1480.

Heilig, J.V., Brown, K.D., & Brown, A.L. (2012). The illusion of inclusion: A critical race theory textual analysis of race and standards. *Harvard Educational Review, 82*(3), 403–424.

Helms, J.E. (1992). *A race is a nice thing to have: A guide to being a White person or understanding the White persons in your life.* Alexandria, VA: Alexander Street Press.

Hirschfeld, L.A. (2008). Children's developing conceptions of race. In S.M. Quintana & C. McKown (Eds.), *Handbook of race, racism, and the developing child* (pp. 37–54). Hoboken, NJ: John Wiley & Sons.

Hoffman, M. (1991). *Amazing grace.* New York, NY: Dial Books for Young Readers.

Hollingworth, L. (2009). Complicated conversations: Exploring race and ideology in an elementary classroom. *Urban Education, 44*(1), 30–58.

Hughes–Hassell, S., & Cox, E.J. (2010). Inside board books: Representations of people of color. *Library Quarterly, 80*(3), 211–230.

Husband, T. (2016). *But I don't see color: The perils, practices, and possibilities of antiracist education.* Rotterdam, Netherlands: Sense Publishers.

Kelly, D.J., Quinn, P.C., Slater, A.M., Lee, K., Ge, L., & Pascalis, O. (2007). The other-race effect develops during infancy: Evidence of perceptual narrowing. *Psychological Science, 18,* 1084–1089. doi:10.1111/j.1467-9280.2007.02029.x

Kelly, D.J., Quinn, P.C., Slater, A.M., Lee, K., Gibson, A., Smith, M., & Pascalis, O. (2005). Three-month-olds, but not newborns, prefer own-race faces. *Developmental Science,* 8(6), 31–37. doi:10.1111/j.1467-7687.2005.0434a.x

Kinzler, K.D., Shutts, K., DeJesus, J., & Spelke, E.S. (2009). Accent trumps race in guiding children's social preferences. *Social Cognition, 27,* 623–634.

Kinzler, K.D., & Spelke, E.S. (2011). Do infants show social preferences for people differing in race? *Cognition, 119,* 1–9.

Ladson-Billings, G. (2009). *The dreamkeeper: Successful teachers of African American children.* San Francisco, CA: Jossey-Bass.

Lewison, M., Flint, A.S., & Van Sluys, K. (2002). Taking on critical literacy: The journey of newcomers and novices. *Language Arts, 79*(5), 382–392.

Mabbott, C. (2017). The We Need Diverse Books campaign and critical race theory: Charlemae Rollins and the call for diverse children's books. *Library Trends, 65*(4), 508–522.

Maher, K.J., Herbst, C.H., Childs, N.M., & Finn, S. (2008). Racial stereotypes in children's television commercials. *Journal of Advertising Research, 48*(1), 80–93.

McGlothlin, H., & Killen, M. (2010). How social experience is related to children's intergroup attitudes. *European Journal of Social Psychology, 40*(4), 625–634.

McKenna, M., & Ossoff, E. (1998). Age differences in children's comprehension of a popular television program. *Child Study Journal, 28,* 53–68.

McLaughlin, M., & DeVoogd, G. (2010). Critical literacy as comprehension: Understanding at deeper levels. In D. Lapp & D. Fisher (Eds.), *Handbook of research on teaching the English language arts* (pp. 278–282). New York: Routledge.

Milner, H.R. (2010). *Start where you are, but don't stay there: Understanding diversity, opportunity gaps, and teaching in today's classrooms.* Cambridge, MA: Harvard Education Press.

Moya, P.L., & Hamedani, M.G. (2017). Learning to read race: Multicultural literature can foster racial literacy and empower students. *California English, 22*(4), 10–13.

Neblett, E.W., Rivas-Drake, D., & Umaña-Taylor, A.J. (2012). The promise of racial and ethnic protective factors in promoting ethnic minority youth development. *Child Development Perspectives, 6,* 295–303. doi:10.1111/

j.1750-8606.2012.00239.x

Norton, D.E. (2009). *Multicultural children's literature: Through the eyes of many children.* Boston, MA: Allyn & Bacon/Pearson.

Ohito, E.O. (2016). Making the emperor's new clothes visible in anti-racist teacher education: Enacting a pedagogy of discomfort with White preservice teachers. *Equity & Excellence in Education, 49*(4), 454–467. doi:10.1080/10665684.2016.1226104

Patterson, M.M., & Bigler, R.S. (2006). Preschool children's attention to environmental messages about groups: Social categorization and the origins of intergroup bias. *Child Development, 77*, 847–860.

Pollock, M. (2004). *Colormute: Race talk dilemmas in an American school.* Princeton, NJ: Princeton University Press.

Ramsey, P.G. (2004). *Teaching and learning in a diverse world* (3rd ed.). New York, NY: Teachers College Press.

Roberts, D., & Foehr, U. (2004). *Kids and media in America.* Cambridge, UK: Cambridge University Press.

Rosenblatt, L. (1985). Viewpoints: Transaction versus interaction—A terminological rescue operation. *Research in the Teaching of English, 19*, 96–107.

Serrano-Villar, M., & Calzada, E.J. (2016). Ethnic identity: Evidence of protective effects for young, Latino children. *Journal of Applied Developmental Psychology*, 4221–4230. doi:10.1016/j.appdev.2015.11.002

Sipe, L. (2008). *Storytime: Young children's literary understanding in the classroom.* New York, NY: Teachers College Press.

Sleeter, C.E., & Flores Carmona, J. (2017). *Un-standardizing curriculum: Multicultural teaching in the standards-based classroom.* New York, NY: Teachers College Press.

Tatum, B. (1992). Talking about race, learning about racism: The application of racial identity development theory in the classroom. *Harvard Educational Review, 62*(1), 1–25.

Van Ausdale, D., & Feagin, J.R. (2001). *The first R: How children learn race and racism.* Lanham, MD: Rowman & Littlefield.

Vasquez, V.M., & Felderman, C.B. (2012). *Technology and critical literacy in early childhood.* New York, NY: Routledge

Vittrup, B. (2016). Early childhood teachers' approaches to multicultural education & perceived barriers to disseminating anti-bias messages. *Multicultural Education, 23*(3/4), 37–41.

Vittrup, B., & Holden, G.W. (2011). Exploring the impact of educational television and parent-child discussions on children's racial attitudes. *Analyses of Social Issues & Public Policy, 11*(1), 82–104. doi:10.1111/j.1530-2415.2010.01223.x

Wise, T.J. (2010). *Colorblind: The rise of post-racial politics and the retreat from racial equity.* San Francisco, CA: City Lights Books.

CHAPTER FIVE

THE PEDAGOGICAL DILEMMAS OF ADDRESSING BLACKFACE AND WHITE PRIVILEGE IN THE CLASSROOM

Mary Beth Hines

T HIS CHAPTER HIGHLIGHTS A pedagogical predicament, a potentially "teachable moment" about race, that occurred in a ninth-grade English class in Last Chance High School (LCHS), an alternative school in the Midwest. For the past five years, I have conducted a study of engagement and resistance in Molly's English 9–10 classroom. As a researcher with a strong commitment to social justice, I wanted to work with an exemplary teacher who shared such priorities, and Molly was just that person. A National Board-certified veteran teacher who had 15 years of teaching at alternative schools, Molly embraced culturally relevant education (Aronson & Laughter, 2016; Gay, 2010; Ladson-Billings, 1995), sometimes referred to as culturally sustaining pedagogies (Ladson-Billings, 2017; Paris & Alim, 2017). She was passionately committed to enacting social justice in the English classroom (Boyd, 2017) and to teaching marginalized students who had fallen through the cracks (Nygreen, 2013). She was an inspirational force who walked her talk and frequently joined me as a co-investigator of the complex array of social justice factors and forces needed to support literacy instruction for the non-mainstream students who entered her classroom.

This chapter focuses on an experience we had in her class, one in which we—both White in a school that served predominantly White, low-income, and non-mainstream students— encountered a racist image in the form of a virtual and actual student painted in blackface. The student was painted to look like the stereotypical "Blackie" figure frequently featured in early nineteenth-century minstrel shows for a role in a student video project. Blackface has recently made a comeback in social media with the emergence of White nationalism and the Black Lives Matter movement (*Blackface!*, n.d.; Dubois, 2014; Heim, 2014). Then and now, blackface images are perceived to be racist—a catalyst for, quite literally, incendiary actions and reactions. When Molly and I discovered the first blackface image in a student-made video, we looked at each other in disbelief, unable to string together words to communicate the magnitude of the image's visual impact on us. In other words, we were stunned into silence, face-to-face with the students who had created the blackface. This chapter explores the pedagogical possibilities and the ethical implications of addressing a blackface incident within the context of a predominantly White population whose privilege was offset by generational poverty, academic marginalization, and an array of social, economic, familial, and legal issues associated with precarity. "Doing school" at LCHS included a consideration of the volatility of social relations and the fragility of success within this context, complicating discussions of race and privilege in and out of the classroom. Before unpacking that moment of alternatives to the stunned silence, the only reaction we could muster, the next section provides an overview of the larger study from which this chapter was taken and a brief history of blackface. The question at the heart of this chapter is this: In light of the situated context of LCHS, how should Molly and I have responded to the blackface?

Engagement and Resistance at Last Chance High

The data for this chapter are culled from a 5-year qualitative study of engagement and resistance in Molly's English class. She taught at Last Chance High School (LCHS), an alternative school informally known as an "alternative to expulsion" school— that is, a school site populated by students who were mandated to attend or opted to attend instead of facing suspension, expulsion, or incarceration. Using critical sociocultural perspectives (Lewis, Enciso,

& Moje, 2007), the study explores the dynamic, systemic interplay of power and privilege as it informs literacy practices and plays out in patterns of engagement and resistance in English. Because blackface resurrects legacies of racism that inform the contemporary moment, I draw on Whiteness studies (Alcoff, 2015; Shannon, 2017) and critical race theory (Ladson-Billings, 1998) to amplify systems of racial oppression and privilege, adding additional layers to the situated context of the English classroom. In addition, I draw from that scholarship to consider my own positionality as a White, middle-class researcher working with a White, middle-class teacher in a school that is predominantly White and low-income (Ladson-Billings, 1998; Shannon, 2017). Finally, I use Judith Butler's work (Butler, 2009, 2015; Butler & Athanasiou, 2013) on precarity and dispossession to illuminate the impact of marginalization and transience on students sent to Molly's school, Last Chance High School. In order to understand the blackface incident, the next section traces the history of blackface in American culture.

Blackface in the White Cultural Imaginary

Blackface refers to a stereotypical image of a Black person with over-exaggerated comedic features issuing from nineteenth-century traveling minstrel shows. Blackface or "Blackie" images represent dehumanizing caricatures of African American facial features and carry a racist legacy. (For examples and history, see Ikachina, n.d.). Blackface became popular during the era of minstrel troupes, circa 1830–1890. Blackface paint was made with a layer of cocoa butter or burned cork, and facial features were exaggerated for comedic effect. Lips were painted white or red, and eyes were circled in white or black paint. Blackface characters wore outlandish costumes, also intended to produce laughter from audiences. While the popularity of minstrel shows and blackface declined after the 1920s (Lensmire & Snaza, 2010), blackface images persisted through cartoons, movies, radio, and theater productions, crystallizing in dehumanizing and racist stereotypes that persist today. Spike Lee's "blackface montage" in *Bamboozled* (https://www.youtube.com/watch?v=C45g3YP7JOk&t=30s) offers examples and invites critical inquiry of the racist stereotype. More recently, blackface has been re-inserted into American debates about race because of its resurgence in social media, serving not only as a historical signifier of racism but also as a contemporary one. To suggest the ubiquitous and controversial nature of the racist image today, a Google search conducted on February 28, 2018, listed 3,900,000 sources on the topic. From that perspective, perhaps it should come as no surprise that blackface surfaced even as Molly promoted equity and justice in her classroom. The next section describes LCHS and explains why and how that context is so important to understanding the blackface incident.

The "Socially Assigned Disposability" of Students at Last Chance High School

Last Chance High School, as one teacher said, serves as "a dumping ground" for students who were largely unsuccessful at mainstream high schools. According to several LCHS teachers, district administrators routinely mandated that unruly students transfer there, although it should be acknowledged that some students voluntarily enrolled after enduring uncomfortable experiences at the mainstream schools. The issues compelling students to voluntarily turn away from the mainstream schools ran the gamut—learning challenges; bullying; family issues; transience; legal, psychological, social, and emotional issues—and the 15 students interviewed for this study each told a different tale, though all shared the common denominator of their being "not a good fit" with the mainstream schools, as one student said. Students who did not fit the student profile preferred by the mainstream schools were shipped off to LCHS, ostensibly relegated to positions of "socially assigned disposability" (Butler & Athanasiou, 2013). In short, such students were at odds with the "normative and normalizing powers" of mainstream schools (p. 2).

Complicating matters, as if LCHS students and teachers did not have enough social challenges to deal with, many students entered with learning issues that complicated pedagogy in the "dumping ground." Twenty percent of the school's 44 students had special needs; 68% of ninth- and tenth-graders had reading scores below grade level; and only 20% of students passed English and math end-of-course assessments. In short, students in the school could be characterized as having histories of academic struggle and/or failure. Reflecting the demographics of the neighborhood, 78% of students received free/reduced lunch, and 88% were White. With a predominantly White, low-income population of students who were, as one student explained, "not a good fit" with the mainstream schools, issues of marginalization, equity, and difference were everywhere apparent. With a 44% graduation rate, Molly was keenly aware of the complex array of factors impeding success for her students and reproducing their status of "socially assigned disposability" (Butler & Athanasiou, 2013, p. x).

In spite of the many obstacles facing teachers and students, Molly remained determined to work at LCHS because the alternative school offered an opportunity for success to students who were not functioning effectively at the mainstream schools. Working with non-mainstream students meant putting into practice her commitment to social justice in culturally relevant pedagogy (Aronson & Laughter, 2016; Boyd, 2017; Gay, 2010)—that is, by throwing a lifeline to linguistically and culturally diverse students cast off from the mainstream schools. She was keenly aware that many LCHS students experienced untenable or precarious living situations, and several were homeless at any given point in the school year. Many experienced poverty, food insecurity, negative relationships with school administrators and teachers, and struggles in academic, legal, familial, and/or psychological/social realms. The challenges students faced on a daily basis formed key issues in their backstories, what Zipin (2009) refers to as students' "dark funds of knowledge." According to Zipin, this term refers to the domain of antisocial, negative and/or resistant affect, norms, practices usually affiliated with histories of unethical, illicit, illegal, or unconventional activities, resources that these nonmainstream students galvanized for negotiating the "dark lifeworlds" (p. 317) they inhabited. Molly negotiated relationships with students mindful of their dark funds of knowledge, recognizing that a stressful encounter with a student could trigger a blowup or be a catalyst for a student to shut down. She recognized that the accumulation of negative schooling experiences contributed to students' dark funds of knowledge, informing an array of students' performed identities from indifference to resistance to schooling. As the next section will show, she consciously avoided igniting students' dark funds of knowledge as she constructed her response to the blackface incident.

The Video Trailer Project for *Monster*

The incident in question occurred in a unit based on Walter Dean Myers' *Monster* (2004), a popular young adult text about an incarcerated African American young adult who shares his anticipation and anxiety while awaiting trial, written in diary format. Students were highly engaged in reading the novel and were excited about planning the culminating activity— multimodal projects that would serve as trailers for the book. The day the videos were due, the activity level became frenzied. Several groups left the class-room to film their productions, and two other groups remained in class to work. Molly and I were unable to talk to a group that consisted of two new-comers, Gary and Josey, and another LCHS student, John. Gary and Josey were White. Josey was very talkative, but Gary was not, continually pulling his head inside his hoodie during discussions. John had been at the school for several years. He was biracial; his mother was White, and his father was African American. John, like Gay, was quiet.

Over the past several days, the trio did not seem to be actively engaged in the small group project. However, on the last day, they worked feverishly in a back corner of the room. We did not notice that midway through class they had moved into the hall to film. Toward the end of class, Josey came back into the classroom, interrupting students working with Molly, and waved me over. She proudly handed her iPad to Molly, proclaiming that the group's "AWESOME" video was finished. She begged Molly and me to view the video right then and there. We were not prepared for what we saw next.

The first image was of Gary, a blonde White student, painted in black-face. John, whose mother was White and whose father was African Amer-ican, most closely resembled the *Monster*'s African American protagonist depicted on the book cover. In spite of that, the students never explained why the group opted to make Gary, a blonde, the central character. Josey proudly pointed to Gary's face as evidence of her aptitude for cosmetol-ogy, as she hoped to enter cosmetology school the following year. She had intended Gary's skin tone to match John's, although neither was as dark as the book's cover illustration of the protagonist. As if on cue, Gary, still in blackface, appeared in class. In the flash of seconds it took for Molly and me to process the fact that there was an actual blackface character in Molly's classroom, all either of us could do was to blink, as we were both rendered speechless. As he came closer, we could see that Gary's make-up had dried into a mottled layer of caked-on foundation that was tawny, not black. He had big, white, glue-like circles around his eyes and bunches of blonde hair sprouting around the face. I tried to find words but failed, and so did Molly; but the bell rang before either of us could say anything to the students.

When Molly and I were able to talk about this, she said she did not think the students were aware of the history of blackface. I was skeptical, thinking that everybody must have some knowledge of it, given its place in history, the Civil Rights Movement, and Black Lives Matter. Together, in retrospect, we wondered what we should have said and done at that moment when we first registered the appearance of the blackface in a 2018 classroom. As a reviewer of this chapter commented, Gadamer's notion of being "pulled up short" (as cited in Kerdemen, 2003) speaks to our shared experience of that moment:

> When we are pulled up short, events we neither want nor foresee and to which we may believe we are immune interrupt our lives and challenge our self-understanding in ways that are painful but transforming (p. 294).... [B]eing pulled up short invariably catches us off-guard...a blind spot that diminishes or distorts who we are in the world. (p. 303)

I wondered if my stammering inability to address the matter at hand illuminated a "blind spot," given that I was caught completely off guard. I was worried for Molly, who literally taught the pre-service education course on linguistic and cultural diversity, and the irony of this event occurring in her classroom did not escape me. Did our inability to rise to the occasion "diminish or distort who we are in this world"? Did our faltering response mean we were complicit in an act of racism, a "painful" question we now had to consider? As Lensmire and Snaza (2010) argue, "The scholarship on blackface ministrelsy emphasizes that this racial history is still with us, in us" (p. 417). In light of that history, what should Molly and I have done? Perplexed, we brought our questions to other staff members who shared our commitments to students and social justice. The next section features commentary from faculty and staff, focusing on how they would have addressed the blackface incident.

"Your Engagement Is Cool, But It's All Wrong"

Charles was the principal during the incident in question, and he had spent most of his career as a teacher or administrator in alternative schools by choice, intentionally working with students who were "not a good fit" for the usual public school building. He weighed in:

> For the first time in the school year, she [Molly] had three previously much disengaged students actively participating in an as-

signment.... Although these students were finally engaged in a class activity, the activity itself may have crossed the lines of good taste, social consciousness, racial bigotry. The dilemma was balancing the fact that students were engaged in an activity when they have never been engaged before against the "teachable moment" that might need to let them know what they were doing was potentially highly culturally and/or socially unacceptable. Additionally, the three students were seeing firsthand how participating in academics can enhance their social standings when other students began surrounding them and encouraging them to continue their efforts. If the teacher confronts them (the "teachable moment") about the impropriety of the blackface piece of their project, is she risking quashing their enthusiasm? Such a comment would sound to them something like, "Your engagement is cool but it's all wrong." And no matter how she says it, she runs the risk of now sabotaging the fact that for the first time in three months those students are doing something in the class that is benefiting them. Furthermore, if Molly had gone forward with a discussion of the inappropriateness of their actions, the three students could have been made examples of lewd behavior, and it would have further dispossessed them from the culture of academics and school.

Charles weighs the value of "the teachable moment" against the importance of the engagement of students who had been theretofore indifferent. To Charles, pursuing the teachable moment about a racially charged image would have led students to believe that Molly was finding fault with them and their work, "risking quashing their enthusiasm." In other words, at that time, the students would have perceived any historical clarification as correction, making them "wrong" and potentially compelling them to quit engaging in class. The alternative approach would involve taking time to create the conditions for trust to flourish so that the students would be open to learning, engaging, and succeeding in the class. Once students trusted that Molly had their best interests at heart and respected them, the teacher could approach an array of controversial social justice issues without fear of students shutting down.

Charles placed a premium on building solid relationships with LCHS students, seeing adult affirmation and trust with students as crucial to their success. That said, not every professional in the building, as in the profession, would agree with Charles on this issue. The next section explores how Maura, another English teacher with a strong commitment to social justice, declared a different perspective on the blackface incident. She emphasized the importance of declaring a position on issues of social justice and "drawing a line" against racism, thus taking up opportunities for improvising in teachable moments.

Should the Teacher "Quell Enthusiasm" or Embrace "the Teachable Moment"?

Maura, the other English teacher in the building, expressed empathy for Molly and me by recognizing our dilemma, although she would have acted differently. On the one hand, a group of students who had not been participating in class suddenly engaged with fervor. "When teachers see students who resist the routine of the classroom become engaged and excited about learning...it's not a time to quell students' enthusiasm." On the one hand, Maura acknowledged that talking about the blackface image as racist could "quell students' enthusiasm" for class activities. On the other, the group did indeed create a racist image, and that had to be addressed directly, she said. Additionally, Maura did not know how comfortable she would have been with allowing the other students in the classroom to see the blackface video. "My educational background and experience as a teacher motivate me toward the teachable moment here," Maura related, "perhaps leading the class in an investigation of the comment on race and identity that surfaced due to the application of makeup on Gary's face." She viewed the face painting as an opportunity to create a teachable moment in spite of how it might dampen enthusiasm for the class or adversely affect her relationship with students.

While Maura cautioned against accusing the students of doing something intentionally racist, she did not think the students' actions in creating the blackface could be considered acceptable and insisted that the classroom teacher had to directly address the situation, uncomfortable as it might be:

I do not deny the trickiness of the situation. At some point, though, one must draw a line and say, "Here's my view, and I cannot allow that," and then follow with a class discussion of the very

themes involved regarding racial depictions and representations....
I would want to respond...by taking my students to places of questioning and reflection and guide them to a place of understanding and acceptance.

Maura problematizes the notion of pluralism (i.e., that all perspectives are relative and should be accepted) in the classroom. Maura commented that if she observed the students applying makeup on Gary, she would have wanted to say, "That is so racist. That's so wrong in so many ways." Although Maura understood why Molly and I faltered, tongue-tied in response to the blackface incident, she would have addressed the situation immediately and directly, identifying blackface as a problematic and iconic racist image.

Maura's and Charles's competing perspectives on classroom practice signal different processes and priorities while working toward the shared goal of sensitizing students to social justice issues at LCHS. For me, this raises questions about which social justice priorities should prevail in this setting. Should teachers place a premium on fostering student engagement, moving disenfranchised students incrementally closer to academic success so that they can be productive citizens? Alternatively, is it more important to alert students to social justice issues in the making by pointing out the racist image, thereby placing a premium on developing socially responsible students? Is it possible to do both? If the teacher opts for student engagement, is she providing tacit approval of blackface and collusion with racism? If the teacher takes up the teachable moment, is she inadvertently signaling to Josey, Gary, and John that their approach to this project was wrong, as Charles argues, thereby possibly shutting down their involvement with the class and reproducing the tenuous teacher-student relationships that drove them to LCHS in the first place? These are the questions that Molly and I considered after interviews with Charles and Maura. We wanted to bring them to the students in the blackface group, too. While staff members provided rich and thoughtful feedback, we also wanted to hear from the students themselves. The next section explains student perceptions of what happened.

Student Perspectives: "I'm White"
A week after the video was made, Molly asked Josey, Gary, and John if

they knew what blackface was, said they all said no. Rephrasing, she asked the students why they wanted to paint Gary's face, and Josey said it was truer to the book's cover image, featuring the face of an African American male, presumably the protagonist. Besides, then she could display her cosmetology skills for the video. When prompted, John, generally a quiet student, just shrugged. Gary explained, "I'm White trying to play a Black dude. It just don't seem right" to have a White person in the movie trailer. Apparently Gary, who was biracial, did not want to take the lead role of the protagonist. Molly's hypothesis—that the blackface was not an intentionally racist act—was validated by students' disclosures. In Molly's interviews with students, they said that they were oblivious to the social and historical significance of blackface. Even so, if Molly and I were to remain silent and not educate students about the history of blackface, we would be complicit in reproducing the status quo, thereby contradicting our expressed commitment to social justice. Our next step was to consider how we could sponsor a conversation about blackface without damaging our relationships with students or without seeming to accuse students of racism. The next section illuminates Molly's approach to doing just that.

Molly: Building a "Safe and Inclusive Community"

Using Charles's and Maura's feedback as a springboard, Molly, with the benefit of hindsight, articulated a new strategy that sidestepped the teachable moment of the blackface incident:

> In retrospect, I think I acted in the best way possible at that time and in that situation. I didn't want to shut down their creativity, even for a moment. It was that fragile. It is also true that if other students, Black or White, had taken offense at their video, we would have had to talk about the issue as a class. I was prepared to do that, but glad I didn't have to. At that point, early in the year, I was still attempting to build a safe and inclusive community, and such a conversation might have been volatile. I don't believe there is necessarily a right or wrong choice here. Much depends on the teacher's point of view and priority. Helping me to make such a decision would be whether I believed there was intent to "cross lines," as Maura said, or whether this was done more so out of lack of

knowledge and understanding. Knowing the ages of these students, their educational backgrounds, and their relative understanding of social justice issues would help in any decisions about challenging their work at the risk of dampening their newfound work ethic. In the case of these particular students, I do not believe there was any malicious intent in their focus. I believe they most likely really had no clue that what they were doing might be offensive.

Molly makes several key points here that are supported by educational research of the last few decades. First, she underscores the emphasis on cultivating a "safe and inclusive" space, a theme reverberating through many educational studies and considered foundational to "reaching and teaching" all LCHS students. In addition, the safe and inclusive classroom is a cornerstone of research on culturally sustaining/culturally relevant/and culturally sensitive teaching invoked in discussions of effectively engaging linguistic and culturally diverse classrooms.

This perspective has been most succinctly noted in a review of mainstream "best practice" literature on building community in the classroom. Helm (2009) synthesizes key perspectives in the literature reviewed:

> Educators should remember that setting a safe classroom environment begins with building good relationships with students. If the instructor does not have a supportive relationship with his or her students, effective learning will be compromised.... Students will not discuss sensitive issues in a classroom that feels unsafe to them or with a teacher whom they do not trust. (p. 48)

Helm (2009) cites a wide variety of studies supporting Molly's position on the importance of establishing strong relationships and building community with her students before sponsoring difficult conversations.

In addition, the literature on pedagogies that support linguistically and culturally diverse students—culturally relevant education (CRE)—also emphasizes the importance of the "safe and inclusive" classroom community, validating Molly's priorities. In their recent literature review of culturally relevant education across disciplines, Aronson and Laughter (2016) mention the value of "inclusive" classrooms in which "teachers created spaces where students learned to value their own and others' perspectives" (p. 197). In other words, as Molly said, before the work of understanding and critiquing inequities can begin, teachers and students need to trust one another, and classroom "spaces" must be deemed safe for speaking out without fear of reprisal.

Another key feature of Molly's approach that was validated in the research literature was that she leveraged her knowledge of LCHS students in crafting her instructional strategies for blackface. As her statement indicated, she articulated several distinguishing features of students' backgrounds as salient: (1) age, (2) educational experiences, (3) understanding of social justice issues, (4) incipient work ethic, and (5) presumed lack of malice. In other words, Molly argued that the gravity of the blackface incident was tempered by an understanding of students' relative unfamiliarity with the racist legacy of blackface, so she would temper her discourse accordingly.

The "inclusive and safe space" that was foundational for Molly and many other researchers has also been a source of concern for some scholars working in the arena of social justice. Such scholars claim that "safe" classrooms offer "false promises of comfort and uncritical acceptance in the classroom" (Barrett, 2010, p. 9), especially for students from under-represented groups. In a review of the literature on safe spaces, Barrett divides the critiques into four categories: "(a) the impact of safety on student intellectual development; (b) the impossibility of safety for students in marginalized and oppressed populations, indeed, for all students; (c) the challenges of assessing student learning in safe environments; and (d) ambiguity in defining safety for students" (p. 5).

Because power relations outside the classroom are often reflected inside the classroom, the notion of safety for students from marginalized groups is elusory. Another line of inquiry interrogates the political/social construction of what counts as "safe," and other scholars problematize safety by examining its limits on learning, diluting risk-taking and engagement.

From Molly's perspective, every student at LCHS could be described as a member of a marginalized group; as such, all deserved safety and acceptance, especially given the negative experiences at other schools that compelled them to enroll at LCHS. Most were White students living in poverty and dealing with housing/food insecurities, but some were African American or Latinx; others had psychological, social, and/or learning issues that impacted their school performance. Given the predominantly White, working-class student population and the Confederate flags flying from trucks in the parking lot, Molly recognized how "fragile" the community was early in the year, when "volatile" emotions quickly ramped up to acts of violence. Molly's sensitivity to the lived experiences of LCHS students and the racial politics of the surrounding community led her to believe that creating the conditions for mutual trust and respect for the general good needed to occur before any authentic dialogue about race could take place. Maura insisted that such conversations needed to occur when opportunities presented themselves, but they needed to occur in non-confrontational ways.

Molly cited other contextual factors as motives for building community before addressing potentially "volatile" issues. She pointed out that Josey and Gary, the White students, were newcomers to the school and, as such, needed to experience positive social relationships with teachers, unlike those they had formed in their prior schooling. Whether publicly or privately, Molly explained, calling attention to the images of blackface in the classroom and on the video would have repositioned her relationships with them onto tenuous ground and would have reinforced the message that each of these students had long ago internalized: "You are not a good fit" with the school, as one of their classmates characterized the LCHS student body.

While teachers from mainstream schools might have opted for more academic alternatives for dealing with blackface, such as encouraging inquiry about the history of blackface or tracing the recent resurgence of the image in social media, Molly believed that such routes would not be productive with her students at this point in the school year. Her students' checkered histories with schooling, their myriad dark funds of knowledge, and the "socially assigned disposability" of students at LCHS created trust issues that needed to be resolved before serious learning could occur, Molly believed. Within the corridors of LCHS, those trust issues were magnified, as low graduation and high dropout rates suggested that many LCHS students teetered on the brink of dropping out, failing, or withdrawing at any point in the year, reinforcing the possibilities of "volatile" social dynamics.

Race Matters: "Messy and Fragile"

At a later point in the semester, I asked Molly to reflect back on the blackface incident. In an email, she wrote:

Teaching and learning are simultaneously messy and fragile. What I wish I would have done was to have had a subsequent lesson, one not in any way connected with the *Monster* module, one much later in the year when our classroom community was such that difficult issues could respectfully be discussed. I would have focused this lesson on language, on the current Black and White appropriation of the "N-word" and on its racist uses in history. I would tie into the lesson the related history of blackface. At some point during the lesson, I would have taken Gary, Josie, and John aside privately and I would have gently reminded them of their video and of the ways it might have been viewed by others as offensive, but I would be clear to point out that I had faith they had not intended that sort of offense.

With the added benefit of hindsight, Molly articulated her version of a best-possible scenario for addressing the blackface incident. She would have scaled up discussions of race and other sensitive topics in proportion to the sense of safety and acceptance fostered in the classroom community, which was increasing over time. In so doing, she would have sidestepped difficult conversations about race that would have interfered with building relationships with students, which she deemed "fragile." She would have directly addressed the blackface issue within the context of a broader discussion of race, but only at a later date and only with the three students involved, in an attempt to decrease flammability. She believed that a broader discussion about racial politics would create an occasion to converse with Josey, John, and Gary about the blackface incident. In that conversation she could provide information about the iconic image without indicting them for possible complicity in perpetuating racism. While shutting down the group project to avoid potential controversy would have been an option for some teachers, Molly, Maura, and Charles vigorously opposed it. They unanimously agreed that such a move would have run the risk of completely alienating the three students, who would have chalked that up to typical mainstream teacher behavior.

Molly, Maura, and Charles generated an array of productive ideas for addressing blackface as a racist icon. While the processes that each proposed varied, they shared the same outcome—educating students about the racist nature of the icon. Interestingly, all three staff members foregrounded the importance of the collective histories of students who had migrated to the school and how their prior experiences shaped present and future social practices and the culture of LCHS. Those three staff members and I concurred on the value of demonstrating and contextualizing culturally relevant pedagogical practices, being mindful of the predominantly White student and teacher population as well. While we all recognized that White privilege had to be a factor in framing the blackface incident, all four of us failed to consider how our ideas and practices were disturbingly embodied in the research on studies of White teachers. The next section situates LCHS and its predominantly White, low-income, non-mainstream population against the backdrop of research and theory dedicated to the cultural politics of predominantly White schools, teachers, and communities, drawing upon critical Whiteness studies.

White Gaze, White Privilege, and Blackface Pop-Ups

Critical White teacher studies need to be viewed against the larger backdrop of critical Whiteness scholarship. That body of work is dedicated to unpacking the deeply entrenched dominant and pervasive circulation of Whitenesss in our culture, exposing "white as normative invisibility" (Jupp, Berry, & Lensmire, 2016, p. 1158), a force dominating power relations and shaping social norms and practices. Drawing from critical race theory and culturally humanizing pedagogical theory, other scholars trace the ways in which Whiteness materializes in "the listening and framing practices of 'Whitestream institutions'" (Paris & Alim, 2017, p. 3). Obscuring the norms and practices of linguistically and culturally diverse peoples, "the panoptic White gaze" tacitly surveys and regulates the lives of linguistically and culturally diverse peoples who see themselves through the double vision of White supremacy and diversity (Morrison, 1998; Paris & Alim, 2017).

Drawing on these perspectives, first-wave critical White teacher studies of the 1990s painted a bleak, deficit portrait of White teachers who were unaware of their own privilege and power, and inadvertently complicit in racist practices (Crowley, 2016). One key distinguishing feature of these studies is the pre-service/in-service teachers' use of "race evasive strategies" (Jupp et al., 2016, p. 1159) to avoid, obscure, and diminish discussions of race (Borsheim-Black, 2018; Crowley, 2016; Lensmire & Snaza, 2010). Haviland (2008) refers to these deferral tactics as "white educational discourse," defined as a "constellation of ways of speaking, interacting, and thinking in which white teachers gloss over issues of race, racism, and white supremacy in ways that reinforce the status quo, even when they have a stated desire to do the opposite" (p. 41). She draws upon earlier research by McIntyre (1997), who identified White pre-service teachers' strategies of denying, subverting, and diminishing awareness of racial issues through "white talk." Additional tactics that McIntyre observed included stammering, joking, invoking silence, encouraging student voice, failing/refusing to talk, and/or cultivating a "culture of niceness" (McIntyre, 1997, p. 46). Taken together, the first wave of White-teacher studies illuminated the deficit thinking of White teachers and their efforts to avoid discussions of race, oblivious to the needs of linguistically and culturally diverse students in their classrooms and to their own privilege.

The second-wave studies (2004–2014) reflected not only the persistence of race-evasive discourses, but also more complex and anti-essentialist profiles of White teachers (Jupp et al., 2016; Johnson, 2013). These studies illuminated teachers' contradictory impulses in working toward (and against) anti-racist pedagogy. Second-wave White teachers began seeing themselves embodied in the research of earlier studies, and that recognition propelled them toward self-reflexive critiques of their own privilege and greater sensitivities to "race-visible" teachers/students of other races/ethnicities. In short, second-wave studies forwarded "racially conscientizing teacher education" (Jupp et al., 2016, p. 1177).

I wonder if the hypothetical choices that Maura, Molly, Charles, and I explored need to be unpacked from the standpoint of critical Whiteness studies. What is disturbing is that the race-evasive discursive practices of first- and second-wave studies—especially the White talk strategies of stammering, failing to talk, deferring racial awareness—were traits that Molly and I demonstrated in the moments we registered recognition of the blackface and failed to find words. As we fit the profile of race-evasive teachers, I wondered as well if those discursive practices were also symptomatic of what Lensmire and Snaza (2010) describe in their research on White teachers, and the history of blackface minstrelsy, as a "profound ambivalence... at the core of white selves" (p. 413). Did the potential discomfort of talking about blackface with students materialize in race-evasive strategies, or were we just startled and momentarily tongue-tied while processing the (horrifying) appearance of an actual blackface in Molly's classroom? In addition, did a predominantly White setting make such a conversation about racism more or less urgent, but all the easier to defer (Haviland, 2008)? In addition, did my mumblings, silence, and deferral in the moment signal my own racial anxieties (Alcoff, 2015) in sponsoring difficult conversations about race with youth, despite my commitments to social justice and to advocating for LCHS students?

I think what's missing from the literature on White teachers is a recognition that culturally responsive education is, by definition, well, responsive—an improvisation borne of a fleeting moment, shaped in a particular institutional context, and drawn from a teacher's deep knowledge of students, the community, the school, and the subject matter—all of which come into play in the improvisational moment. In this improvisation, Molly isn't let off the hook for deferring the discussion but is given additional opportunities for it, working in pedagogically appropriate and culturally responsive ways. For Molly, Maura, and Charles, it was the intersectionality of race, class, prior schooling, and lived experiences that informed their variegated responses to addressing the blackface incident with students. Race was a determining factor, but it was not the only factor they considered. LCHS students faced multiple inequities even as they enjoyed White privilege, keenly aware of their "socially assigned disposability" (Butler & Athanasiou, 2013, p. 20).

The blackface incident could have created the occasion for problematizing the notion of White privilege among predominantly low-income students. That is, the low-income White students of LCHS do not benefit from the full scale of White privilege because they are poor, yet at the same time, they acquire some benefits because of their skin color. The blackface incident could have become a catalyst for students to consider their own positionality as low-income White students, nuancing White privilege with a status (Shannon, 2017, p. 178) referred to as "white priority." She explains: "It is middle and upper class white people who count as normal, even superior, in the United States, not poor whites" (p. 178). My sense is that Molly read the situation through the lens of heightened sensitivity to the intersecting oppressions that LCHS students experienced, as her final strategy for addressing blackface also demonstrated understanding of students' socioeconomic status and their academic histories as struggling/failing/problematic students. That said, it is in the locus between White privilege and White priority that we can begin the campaign of sensitizing students and teachers to their own agency, privilege, and oppression within larger systems of power and privilege, leveraging the precarity inherent in White priority as an epistemic resource for community building and social action. Therein lies the hope.

References

Alcoff, L. (2015). *The future of Whiteness*. Cambridge, UK: Polity Press.

Aronson, B., & Laughter, J. (2016). The theory and practice of culturally relevant education: A synthesis of research across content areas. *Review of Educational Research, 86*(1), 163–206.

Barrett, B. (2010). Is "safety" dangerous? A critical examination of the classroom as safe space. *Canadian Journal for the Scholarship of Teaching and Learning, 1*(1). http://dx.doi.org/10.5206/cjsotl-rcacea. 2010.1.9

Blackface! (n.d.). *History of blackface*. Retrieved from http://www.black-face.com/

Borsheim-Black, C. (2018). "You could argue it either way": Ambivalent White teacher racial identity and teaching about racism in literature study. *English Education, 50*(3), 228–254.

Boyd, A. (2017). *Social justice literacies in the English classroom*. New York, NY: Teachers College Press.

Butler, J. (2009). *Frames of war: When is life grievable?* Brooklyn, NY: Verso Press.

Butler, J. (2015). *Notes toward a performative theory of assembly*. Cambridge, MA: Harvard University Press.

Butler, J., & Athanasiou, A. (2013). *Dispossession: The performative in the political*. Malden, MA: Polity Press.

Crowley, R. (2016). Transgressive and negotiated White racial knowledge. *International Journal of Qualitative Studies in Education, 29*(8), 1016–1029.

Dubois, L. (2014, June 25). Why are these fans showing up in blackface?

And what is FIFA going to do about it? *The New Republic.* Retrieved from http://www.newrepublic.com/article/118382/why-are-these-fans-showing-world-cup-Fox News

Gay, G. (2010). *Culturally responsive teaching: Theory, research, and practice.* New York, NY: Teachers College Press.

Haviland, V. (2008). "Things get glossed over": Rearticulating the silencing power of Whiteness in education. *Journal of Teacher Education, 59*(1), 40–54.

Heim, M. (2014, June 27). *Selma native takes viral pic in Brazil of fans in blackface, compares SEC and Kick Six to World Cup.* Retrieved from http://www.al.com/sports/index.ssf/2014/06/selma_native_took_viral_pic_in.html

Helm, K. (2009). Creating a safe learning space for the discussion of multicultural issues in the classroom. *Ethnicity and Race in a Changing World: A Review Journal, 1*(1), 47–50.

Ikachina. (n.d.). Black–Face! [YouTube Channel]. Retrieved from https://www.youtube.com/user/ikachina

Johnson, E. (2013). Embodying English: Performing and positioning the White teacher in the high school English class. *English Education, 46*(1), 5–33.

Jupp, J., Berry, T., & Lensmire, T. (2016). A review of second-wave White teacher identity studies, 2010–2014. *Review of Educational Research, 86*(4), 1151–1191.

Kerdemen, D. (2003). Pulled up short: Challenging self-understanding as a focus of teaching and learning. *Journal of Philosophy of Education, 37*(2), 293–308.

Ladson-Billings, G. (1995). Toward a theory of culturally relevant pedagogy. *American Educational Research Journal, 32*(3), 465–491.

Ladson-Billings, G. (1998). Just what is critical race theory, and what is it doing in a nice field like education? *International Journal of Qualitative Studies in Education, 11*(1), 7–24.

Ladson-Billings, G. (2017). The (R)evolution will not be standardized: Teacher education, hip hop pedagogy, and culturally relevant pedagogy 2.0. In D. Paris & S. Alim (Eds.), *Culturally sustaining pedagogies: Teaching and learning for justice in a changing world* (pp. 141–156). New York, NY: Teachers College Press.

Lensmire, T.J., & Snaza, N. (2010). What teacher education can learn from blackface minstrelsy. *Educational Researcher, 39*(5), 413–422.

Lewis, C., Enciso, P., & Moje, E. (2007). *Reframing sociocultural research on literacy: Identity, agency, and power.* New York, NY: Routledge.

McIntyre, A. (1997). *Making meaning of Whiteness: Exploring racial identities with White teachers.* Albany, NY: SUNY Press.

Morrison, T. (1998). *From an interview on Charlie Rose.* Public Broadcasting System. Retrieved from https://www.youtube.com/watch?v=-Kgq3F8wbYA

Myers, W. (2004). *Monster.* New York, NY: Amistad/HarperCollins Publications.

Nygreen, K. (2013). *These kids: Identity, agency, and social justice at a last chance high school.* Chicago, IL: University of Chicago Press.

Paris, D., & Alim, H.S. (Eds.). (2017). *Culturally sustaining pedagogies: Teaching and learning for justice in a changing world.* New York, NY: Teachers College Press.

Shannon, S. (2017). White priority. *Critical Philosophy of Race, 5*(2), 171–182.

Zipin, L. (2009). Dark funds of knowledge, deep funds of pedagogy: Exploring boundaries between lifeworlds and schools. *Discourse: Studies in the Cultural Politics of Education, 30*(3), 317–331.

CHAPTER SIX

IT'S MESSY: YOU CAN'T *JUST* TALK ABOUT RACE

MICHAEL HERNANDEZ, PAUL MARKSON III, KATHRYN YOUNG

Introduction

THREE TEACHING PROFESSIONALS RECENTLY met for a series of conversations on teaching about race in schools. One is a biracial, male teacher who is phenotypically White, is of Caucasian and Mexican lineage, but self-identifies as neither and teaches about race in a high school sociology class. Another is a biracial male teacher who is phenotypically Black but self-identifies as Korean/Black and teaches about race in a high school African American history class. The third is a White, female professor who teaches about race to college students, many of whom are training to become teachers.

It is important to talk about race in schools for a variety of reasons. Perhaps most importantly, conversations about race enable school professionals to discuss issues of race as they relate to student achievement, discipline, and learning. These conversations enable teachers to examine their own beliefs about students' abilities and possibilities and how they overlap with race (Sleeter, 2007). These conversations permeate the classrooms as well. Classroom conversations on race "contribute to students' and educators' understandings of a racialized society, their construction of and reflection on relationships among students, as well as to their learning of academic content knowledge" (Brown, Bloome, Morris, Power-Carter,

& Willis, 2017, p. 453). Students actually do better academically when they feel good about their own race (Milner, 2015). One way for students to feel good about their race is to be able to talk about race in school—to not feel as though they must be silent about race. Teachers who create purposeful *welcoming* interactions between students of different backgrounds increase student achievement (Pittinsky, 2012). The opposite matters as well: not talking about race has deleterious effects. Silence about race in schools "leaves students misinformed and curious and contributes to the ongoing tensions that exist in our country" (Howard, 2017, para. 3).

Talking about race in schools is often a controversial topic (see, e.g., Crowe & Mooney, 2015), but the teachers in this chapter do not shy away from the controversy or the conversation. Our conversations were sparked by Chandler's (2015) challenge to explore race and controversy in the social sciences. She notes: "Race is controversial and emotional—it has been this way for our entire history as a nation" (p. 6). We decided that the only way to begin our collaborative exploration of teaching about race was for each person to share some thoughts about his/her racial/ethnic background in the first person. I, the White, woman academic, act as scribe due to my role at the university. The male teachers and their pedagogies are the focus of this article. The teachers maintain that talking about race is messy in that the "messy, contradictory nature of human experiences and behaviors...[and] conflicting actions" (Chapman, 2007, p. 160) are so complex and often ambiguous as a result of contextual conditions that there is no easy way to *just* talk about race.

This chapter situates each of the author's identities, provides background on the prevalence of teaching about race in the district, and then focuses on the ways in which the two high school teachers talk about race in their classrooms. They model ways of teaching such as embracing intersectionality, investigating implicit bias, modeling honesty, evoking citizenship and moral responsibility, and working on building empathy to normalize talking about race.

Who We Are

Michael Hernandez

On my mom's side, I am part English and Irish. Culturally there was not much influence on me growing up, as my maternal grandfather died when my mom was six and my grandmother died when I was five. My mom was an only child and had no other living family members.

On my father's side, both of my grandparents were born in Zacatecas, Mexico, and migrated to the United States in the early 1900s during the Mexican Revolution. My father had five brothers. (One died when he was young.) I had 29 cousins on my dad's side, and 25 of them lived in the same small neighborhood in Pueblo, Colorado, where my dad grew up. I spent most of my weekends there as a child and thus grew up in a very vibrant, culturally Mexican environment. It was also very challenging because I look very White, and as I got older (middle school age), I experienced a lot of discrimination from other Mexican kids in Pueblo because of my appearance. As I transitioned to high school, I began to lose my identity as Mexican. I guess you can say that I do not identify as White or Mexican; I exist somewhat outside of a specific identity.

Paul Markson III

My personal racial history is one of confusion. I say confusion because of the personal struggles with who I am. I was born in Korea to a Korean mother and an unknown father. However, I can assume that my father was in the military and was an African American G.I. In Korea, society dictates that you are your father. Being Black, I was an outcast for the first seven years of my life. I didn't fit into that society. As society rejected me, so did my mother. She no longer could take care of my sister and me, and, as a result, we were taken to an orphanage.

In the orphanage, I would dream and pray that someone from America would adopt me, because people there looked like me and I would no longer bear the scars of being an outsider. That dream became a reality when a family in America adopted my sister and me. I remember feeling a sense of relief and joy in knowing that I would come to a place where people looked like me.

Once I arrived in the United States, society would once again reject me. I was a foreigner, "a chink," and due to the language barrier, I was often pulled out of class and made to feel different. I hated feeling different. As the years went by and I became fluent in English, I began to deny my Asian heritage. I associated being Asian with a disease, and because I could pass as African American, I did. I would deny my Asian heritage as my birth mother had denied me.

I was no longer Asian. But what did it mean to be African American, with Caucasian parents? As I began to identify as African American, I was conflicted—conflicted because the media told me that being African American made one a detriment to society. African Americans were a drain on society. We were drug addicts, gang members, prisoners, affirmative action cases, and a disease. As the negative stereotypes flashed on my television set, I became ashamed. Not only was I *ashamed* of being Black. I *hated* being Black. Why couldn't I be like my parents? I wanted to be White. The benefits of being White are many. Because of my parents' social standing in our community, I was able to escape incarceration and becoming another statistic for the African American community. I recognize now society is changing, and now that I have children of my own, my own personal racial history will continue to evolve.

Kathryn Young

I am a White, middle-class, cisgender female whose identity characteristics map onto the characteristics of most public school teachers today. I grew up not talking about race, but talking about countries of the world and how they were similar or different. My family had lived in South Africa and Ghana before I was born. My mother gave birth to me in India, moved to the Philippines, and returned to India before moving to the United States when I was six. We moved in ex-pat circles rather than live with people from each of these countries, but we went to school and the store and engaged in other daily experiences within the surrounding community. When we moved to the United States, all the kids in our family "acted funny" because everyone respected the teachers and were very obedient in school. Living abroad surely affected my siblings more than it did me, as I was only six when we moved to suburban Ohio. We continued to move between the South and North through high school. Issues of culture were always of interest to me—but in the sense of looking out at culture, not knowingly being a part of it. I did not think much about my cultural identity until late in my twenties, when a multicultural class in a master's program asked us to think about these issues. Since that time I have been reworking the narrative of my youth to better understand how omissions in learning about my own race, class, ability, and other identity issues are actually a very strong form of learning about those issues.

Who Teaches About Race in Denver?

In the Denver Public Schools (DPS), there are 22,410 students enrolled in high school social studies courses, from basic geography to concurrent enrollment and Advanced Placement (AP)-level courses in Denver's district-run schools (non-charters). Six percent of students take Sociology, African American History, Black Experience Today, Chicano Studies/Latino American History, Native American History, Social Problems, or Minority Cultures as a social studies class (DPS Social Studies Curriculum Specialist personal communication, Spring 2018).

East High School, the school at which Paul Markson and Michael Hernandez teach, offers classes both in African American history and sociology, and each teacher is the only instructor for that class in his school. This is a comprehensive high school of almost 2,500 students. The school is a highly sought-after, racially diverse high school in Denver, Colorado (Denver Public Schools School Finder, 2018). In 2017–2018, 32.4% of the students qualified for free or reduced lunches (all terminology is school district terminology), 6.8% have special education designation, 14.6% are considered to be English Language Learners, and 52.9% are classified as minority. Both teachers have been teaching at the school for over 10 years, and both teach a variety of other social studies classes in addition to the classes considered in this chapter.

How Hernandez and Markson Teach About Race

This section of the chapter provides an overview of the big ideas that Hernandez and Markson rely on to enter into deep and meaningful conversations with their students. It then offers examples of lessons and activities that the teachers use to engage in conversations about race with their students. Both embrace intersectionality, investigate implicit bias, model honesty, evoke citizenship and moral responsibility, and work on building empathy to normalize talking about race. They take controversy as a given, not as a negative in their classrooms.

Embracing intersectionality. Given these two teachers with personal identities that do not fit cleanly into any one racial narrative (Renn, 2008; Root, 1990), it is no surprise that they have similar goals in teaching about race—that is, to show that race is multifaceted and situationally variable. Intersectionality is well encompassed in the research about biracial identity development, where people who experience multiple identities come to see race as fluid and contextual (Renn, 2008; Root, 1990). Both teachers seek to share the fluidity and contextuality of race with their students through the way they talk about and teach about race.

Although neither teacher calls it intersectionality, both teach from an intersectional perspective. This means they help students examine how socially and culturally constructed identities interact in a variety of ways (Crenshaw, 2015). Talking about race also necessitates bringing students' own backgrounds (race, class, gender identity, etc.) into the conversation (Levinson, 2012), which adds to the intersectional nature of these conversations.

Investigating implicit bias. Students are challenged to understand that people have different experiences in our society because of their racial appearance. For example, both teachers find that many students begin the year with an "I'm not racist" ideology. Quickly, the teachers ask students to understand that everyone has implicit biases related to race, since we exist in a stratified society and within a racialized history embedded in the very structure of our nation. The teachers ask students, "Why did this happen, and what part did I have in making this happen?" For example, when students come into class talking about "All Lives Matter" rather than "Black Lives Matter," Hernandez challenges them by saying, "Well, of course all lives matter, that goes without saying, but there is a reason we specify. There is something that is happening here. How would I feel if I were disenfranchised, discriminated against, targeted?"

The teachers reiterate to students continually that "we all have biases; it is okay; racism is a part of everyday life. It is not going away. It is not like one day you realize wow, I am kind of racist, I need to work on that and then it is gone." Hernandez and Markson often focus conversations about race on personal responsibility rather than "outsourcing responsibility," which to them means "avoiding the practice of looking at someone who is obviously racist, labeling them as racist and therefore rationalizing that you yourself are not racist" (Hernandez). These conversations intertwine with conversations about systems of oppression and the history of race in the United States so that students can move between the micro and the macro as they learn how to talk about race in school.

Modeling honesty. Before undertaking any lessons about race, both teachers talk about the importance of modeling honesty and vulnerability in classes. They do "think-aloud" strategies with students and each other about how talking about race can be difficult. Similar to Ellsworth (1989), they talk with the students about needing "high levels of trust and personal commitment to individuals" in their classes (p. 316). They agree that what is usually missing in discussions about race when other people teach it is that teachers are often unwilling to be honest with themselves in talking about race. Both teachers use opportunities that come up in the course of the semester organically to model their own personal struggles in talking about the complexity of race, their personal biases, and how to break down stereotypes. For example, in 2015, high school students across the nation were staging walk-outs in support of protests in Ferguson, Missouri. Students at East High School led some of the student walk-outs in Denver. Markson and Hernandez used these events to talk about race in the United States and race in Colorado. This foundational modeling of talking about race openly and honestly in both classes helps students talk freely when it is time to address race in the curriculum.

Evoking citizenship and moral responsibility. For both teachers, conversations about race are intricately tied to conversations about citizenship and moral responsibility. They push students to see that their personal responsibility to learn about and talk openly about race is part of their responsibility as citizens. They must imagine not just their own experiences in this nation, but the experiences of disenfranchised groups and marginalized groups as well. Students from disenfranchised groups also learn that not all those in the majority group think the same way. And everyone realizes that whatever group you may be in now may shift with the political and cultural tides.

Building empathy. Both teachers extol the importance of empathy as part of citizenship. Teaching students to break down stereotypes leads to empathy across groups of people. Denying the race experience denies personal introspection regarding different perspectives and halts the goal of becoming a strong citizen. Both teachers use the debate format to build listening skills and to cultivate empathy. A debate allows students to learn that "I do not have to agree with you, I do not have to integrate your world view into mine, but I do have to listen to you and to the merit of your argument" (Hernandez). Debate allows for practicing empathy and listening skills. It allows social studies to become active and uncomfortable while students listen to one another's points of view.

Hernandez's Sociology Class

Hernandez's sociology class is about one-third White, one-third Black, and one-third Latino/a (Hernandez's terminology). He teaches race as part of a unit on social inequality, along with social class and gender, and also allows space in the unit for students to address other groups impacted by the topic. They define social inequality in the class as the existence of unequal opportunities and rewards for different social positions or statuses within a group or society. The reason why the class studies race under the umbrella of social inequality is that it allows them to examine the intersectionality of systems of oppression. They begin the unit by learning about social class and then move on to gender and, finally, race. By building up to race, students become more open to sharing, which allows for some of the "uncomfortable" conversations about race to be more productive. Hernandez believes that employing a systemic approach leads to a deeper understanding of the topic of social inequality and ultimately to a deeper understanding of the complexity of race.

This unit begins with an examination of implicit bias. Students view a TED Talk from Vernā Myers (2014). Hernandez then leads a discussion centered on the following principles: Everyone has implicit bias. To address your biases you must (a) create a filter and identify your biases, (b) move toward groups you have a bias against, and (c) seek disconfirming data that dispel your bias. Students also take the Harvard Implicit Association test on race and discuss the results. Hernandez adds: "Clearly, implicit bias shapes our perspective of all groups victimized by social inequality, and this common understanding strengthens our understanding of intersectionality."

With implicit bias as a foundation, the class moves forward more comfortably. As a class, they acknowledge that conscious racism is a negative quality that should be examined in depth; however, most racism encountered on a daily basis is implicit and not intentional. This perspective allows students to be less defensive and results in deep, powerful conversations about race.

Hernandez shares that he believes:

that as a result of the binary nature of our cultural perspective, most people come to believe that you are either racist, or you're not. Most people identify with the latter and live in denial about their implicit biases around race. By expanding the complexity and ownership of racial bias, my students are able to walk away with a personal connection to the subject which allows for a deeper investigation into traditional types of racism. One of my core beliefs as an educator is that if you can facilitate a strong connection between the content and a student's daily experience, they are going to be more likely to retain the information for a longer period of time.

A few days before he addresses race head-on in class, he groups students into pairs differentiated by gender and race. He does not tell them that this activity is related to the work they will be doing on stereotypes in a few days. He asks each pair to come up with a list of ten things they have in common and ten things that are different. Students quickly come up with things they have in common: they like pizza, they both went to the same middle school, they both have divorced parents, and so on. Even though the pairings were based on differences (girl/boy, Latino/ Black), they struggle to come up with ways in which they differ. Eventually, they come up with differences in the type of music they prefer, the number of siblings they have, or where they live.

Several days later, Hernandez takes the students out to the hallway and asks them to agree or disagree with a series of statements, such as "It is OK for White people to say 'the N-word'?"; "It is OK for Black people to say 'the N-word'?"; and "Black people are better at sports." Then the students form groups according to whether they agree or disagree. Hernandez cold calls on students to explain their positions. The goal of this activity is to allow students to orally, kinesthetically, and visually share their opinions with their classmates.

Hernandez moves the students from a similarities and differences exercise to one where they openly share their positions on stereotypes. The class is finally ready to examine definitions of racism. Hernandez places students in groups that are different than the groups from the prior day and hands out a sheet that lists ten definitions of racism (Appendix A). He asks each group to decide on the strongest definition and to explain why. This activity helps students develop a shared understanding of what they, as a class, mean when they say and hear "racism." The definition exercise helps students understand the contextual factors that influence any learning about race and racism.

Markson's African American History Class

Markson's class is one-third male; two-thirds female; more than one-half Black, non-Hispanic; one-fourth White, non-Hispanic, and one-seventh Hispanic (Markson's terminology). In this class he asks students to complete the prompt, "What does it mean to be Black?" Everyone in the class is asked to answer the prompt in writing. In prior years he used the written answers to help him learn about students, their perspectives, and their backgrounds. With the help of student teacher Brent Dysart, Markson decided to read the responses back to the students—with permission. The response from the class regarding sharing with and learning from each other was overwhelmingly positive. Students learned that they each had more complex racial histories and identities than a quick stereotype allowed. Some students had non-White parents, even though they appeared to be White; others were multiracial, though they had never shared their identity in class before.

Another strategy Markson uses is that of sharing his reading list with students. He brings in books he is reading to share with his class in order to build empathy, to broaden perspectives, and to demonstrate the structural aspects of racism through the written word. The books he chooses are often ones that rely on understanding racism in different parts of the world or at different points in time. His choices reflect a desire to illustrate for students the long-term impact of structural racism and the varied forms it takes in society. For example, Markson has shared James Ciment's *Another Liberia: The Story of Liberia and the Former Slaves Who Ruled It* (2013) with his students. He states: "This book is fascinating because it allows students to see how racism is learned. We discuss plantation life for slaves in the Americas and, after gaining their freedom, what the freed slaves did to the indigenous people in Liberia. We compare and contrast the plantation systems of Liberia and America and the impact it has on the enslaved."

Markson has also taught students using Tom Burrell's *Brainwashed: Challenging the Myth of Black Inferiority* (2010). For Markson, "This book is insightful because it touches on many aspects of African-American culture and how we have been brainwashed into thinking we are inferior. The nice thing about this is it allows students solutions to problems and it makes one really take a look at their behavior and take ownership." His continual flow between macro historical and economic influences on race today and micro impacts of those macro forces on students' daily lived experiences and the choices they make within their own personal spheres of influence work in tandem to encourage agency in students while acknowledging systemic inequalities. In Todd Boyd's *The New H.N.I.C.: The Death of Civil Rights and the Reign of Hip Hop* (2004), students closely examine the Civil Rights Movement (CRM) through hip-hop music. They have even read books about higher education such as Craig Steven Wilder's *Ebony and Ivy: Race, Slavery, and the Troubled History of America's Universities* (2013) and its relationship to race in the United States. Through this book, Markson focuses on helping students examine the impact of slavery on America's Ivy League colleges. Students use Wilder's ideas along with added information from Markson to write papers discussing whether or not they support Reparations and Affirmative Action in higher education. The breadth and the variety of the books that Markson chooses help students see race not only from their own personal perspectives, but also from the wider lens of society.

Markson shares his own journey in continually learning about race as he reads new books right along with his students. He hopes that by sharing his continuing journey toward understanding his own biases he can model for students how understanding the concept of race and our personal interactions with it is a lifelong experience.

Conclusion

Even though both teachers approach teaching about race in different ways to different groups of students, they both seek to instill in students the messiness, the complexity, and the ambiguity of race and talking about race, and further, that talking about race means talking about everything related to race, such as gender, social class, family idiosyncrasies, and so on. These honest conversations help students to dive into deep and meaningful learning about race in a sociology and an African American history course.

Interestingly, these teachers—perhaps unknowingly—make talking about race acceptable. The social studies literature evokes many cases of race being a controversial topic (see, e.g., Crowe & Mooney, 2015) that leads teachers and students to shy away from talking about this important issue. Both Hernandez and Markson embrace intersectionality, investigate implicit bias, model honesty, evoke citizenship and moral responsibility, and work on building empathy with their students as they discuss race in high school classrooms.

Having sat in on both of their classes, I have been personally impressed with the depth and humility students bring to talking about race with these teachers and with one another. I have also witnessed other classes attempt to engage in racial dialogue—attempts that fall flat or lead to the reinforcement of stereotypes or platitudes about race while still adhering to "colorblindness" as the preferred way to talk about race in schools.

Hernandez and Markson use organically produced, student-driven conversations about race as their base pedagogy, then inject intersections with gender, location, and family dynamics to delve deeper into race, racism, and intersectionality. These classes examine discrimination on multiple levels and help students understand how overlapping oppressions contribute to systematic structural, political, and social inequality (Crenshaw, 1989). Both teachers help students see "where certain modes of oppression become visible and/or invisible" (Mitchell, 2006, p. 138) in their own lives, in the lives of other students, and in the lives of (non)citizens more broadly.

The teachers rely on being honest about the messiness of race in order to help students break down barriers across racial groups, to help them understand each other's different experiences in the same school, and to make them accustomed to talking openly about race. Both teachers hope that modeling these honest conversations early in their adolescent students' lives will help these pupils to be better equipped to continue the conversations later on. They will serve as models for others students and adults, and their future conversations about race can be honest, productive, and generative. The students will know—and be able to talk about—how you can't *just* talk about race.

References

Boyd, T. (2004). *The new H.N.I.C.: The death of civil rights and the reign of hip hop.* New York, NY: New York University Press.

Brown, A.F., Bloome, D., Morris, J.E., Power-Carter, S., & Willis, A.I. (2017). Classroom conversations in the study of race and the disruption of social and educational inequalities: A review of research. *Review of Research in Education, 41,* 453–476. doi:10.3102/0091732X16687522

Burrell, T. (2010). *Brainwashed: Challenging the myth of Black inferiority.* New York, NY: Smiley Books.

Chandler, P.T. (2015). Knowing where we started: Race and controversy in social studies. *Ohio Social Studies Review, 52*(1), 4–7.

Chapman, T. (2007). Interrogating classroom relationships and events: Using portraiture and critical race theory in education research. *Educational Researcher, 36*(3), 156–162.

Ciment, J. (2013). *Another Liberia: The story of Liberia and the former slaves who ruled it.* New York, NY: Hill and Wang.

Crenshaw, K. (1989). Demarginalizing the intersection of race and sex: A Black feminist critique of antidiscrimination doctrine, feminist theory, and antiracist politics. *University of Chicago Legal Forum, 140,* 139–167.

Crenshaw, K. (2015, September 24). Why intersectionality can't wait. *Washington Post.* Retrieved from http://www.washingtonpost.com/news/in-theory/wp/2015/09/24/why-intersectionality-cant-wait/

Crowe, A., & Mooney, E. (2015). Come together, right now over science issues and citizenship in social studies education. *Ohio Social Studies Review, 52*(1), 14–20.

Denver Public Schools. (2018). *School finder.* Retrieved from https://dps.schoolmint.net/school-finder/schools/74/east-high-school

Ellsworth, E. (1989). Why doesn't this feel empowering? Working through the repressive myths of critical pedagogy. *Harvard Educational Review, 59*(3), 297–324.

Howard, T.C. (2017). *When we talk about race, let's be honest: Four ways educators can address race with students.* Retrieved from https://www.edweek.org/ew/articles/2017/08/18/when-we-talk-about-race-lets-be.html

Levinson, M. (2012). *No citizen left behind.* Cambridge, MA: Harvard University Press.

Milner, H.R. (2015). *Rac(e)ing to class: Confronting poverty and race in schools and classrooms.* Cambridge, MA: Harvard Education Press.

Mitchell, D.D. (2006). Flashcard: Alternating between visible and invisible identities. *Equity and Excellence in Education, 39*(2), 137–145.

Myers, V. (2014, November). *How to overcome our biases? Walk boldly toward them.* Retrieved from https://www.ted.com/talks/verna_myers_how_

to_overcome_our_biases_walk_boldly_toward_them

Pittinsky, T.L. (2012). *Us plus them: Tapping the positive power of difference*. Boston, MA: Harvard Business Review Press.

Renn, K.A. (2008). Research on biracial and multiracial identity development: Overview and synthesis. *New Directions for Student Services, 123,* 13–21. doi:10.1002/ss.282//

Root, M.P.P., & Brown, L. (1990). *Diversity and complexity in feminist therapy*. New York, NY: Routledge.

Sleeter, C.E. (2007). *Facing accountability in education: Democracy and equity at risk*. New York, NY: Teachers College Press.

Wilder, C.S. (2013). *Ebony and ivy: Race, slavery, and the troubled history of America's universities*. New York, NY: Bloomsbury Press.

Appendix A

This list was compiled for educational purposes from a variety of websites a few years ago. It uses and adapts definitions found across many sources.

Name_____
Social Problems

Definitions of Racism

There are many definitions of racism. Here are a few:

1. **Racism** = Prejudice + Power

2. **Racism** is something someone does or says that offends someone else in connection with their color, background, culture or religion.

3. **Racism** is when a person is teased or called names because of their culture or the color of their skin, their religion, the country they come from, their language and the way they talk, the food they eat, the clothes they wear, or their background.

4. **Racism** is when people are stereotyped because of their color or religion.

5. **Racism** is when a person is rejected or excluded from a group because of their color or religion.

6. **Racism** is when an organization does not provide equal services to some people because of their background.

7. **Racism** is the systematic denial of rights and exclusion from power of one group by another, based on prejudice about skin color, ethnic origin, or culture.

8. **Racism** is based on the belief that certain "races" are superior to others. It demeans all cultures by suggesting that there is an "ordinary" or "normal" way to be. Its purpose is to cause all of us to be afraid of differences.

9. **Racism** is the belief that "races" have distinctive cultural characteristics determined by hereditary factors and that this endows some "races" with an intrinsic superiority over others

10. **Institutional Racism** is the collective failure of an organization to provide an appropriate and professional service to people because of their color, culture, or ethnic origin. It can be seen or detected in processes, attitudes, and behaviors that amount to discrimination through unwitting prejudice, ignorance, thoughtlessness, or racist stereotyping that disadvantages minority ethnic people.

11. **Other:**

    Six Different Types of Racism:
    - **Pre-reflective Gut Racism**
    - **Post-reflective Gut Racism**
    - **Cultural Racism**
    - **Institutional Racism**
    - **Paternalistic Racism**
    - **Color-Blind Racism**

    1. **Pre-reflective Gut Racism:** This name is being used instead of the now-redundant term "racialism," implying racial hatred. Its name suggests that it has emotional rather than rational origins and con-

tent. It can be observed in both individuals and groups. Its deep psychological roots can be traced to three main factors. First, there is a tendency to feel fear, anxiety, insecurity and suspicion in the presence of any persons or groups who are perceived as strange, foreign or unfamiliar.... Second, there are certain motivational dispositions such as rejection, aggression, dominance and superiority which some psychologists consider fundamental to human personality.... The third factor is ignorance of racial minorities, which leaves people open to the too-ready acceptance of myths, stereotypes and other fear-arousing communications.

Examples/notes:

2. **Post-reflective Gut Racism:** This type of racism is concerned with providing a justification for the continuation of racial privilege, and this may involve the creation of an ideology of racial superiority and domination. Whereas pre-reflective gut racism may be attacked for making arbitrary distinctions between people on the basis of irrelevant differences, post-reflective gut racism counterattacks by claiming that the differences are not irrelevant. Post-reflective gut racism therefore involves the post-hoc rationalization of practices emanating from racial prejudice, such as social avoidance, scapegoating and overt acts of racism. This rationalization may take two forms: first, the establishment and acceptance of an unfounded system of beliefs which would, if it were true, justify racial discrimination; and second, the misapplication of well-founded scientific theories to provide support for racist ideology. Both forms of rationalization may ultimately be the product either of conspiracy or self-deception.

Examples/notes:

3. **Cultural Racism:** This term is being used with increasing frequently to draw attention to a shift in the focal point of racism from physical characteristics such as color of skin, type of hair, or bodily features to cultural characteristics such as social customs, manners and behavior, religious and moral beliefs and practices, language, aesthetic values and leisure activities. Whereas post-reflective gut racism seeks to explain and justify racist attitudes in religious or

scientific terms, cultural racism attempts the same thing in cultural terms. It involves prejudice against individuals because of their culture. The culture of minority groups is seen as flawed in some way and thus as standing in the way of their progress. Unlike post-reflective gut racism, however, cultural racism does not involve belief in the existence of any biological incapacity to change. On the contrary, change is exactly what is sought. Minorities are encouraged to turn their backs on their own culture and to become absorbed by the majority culture.

Examples/notes:

4. **Institutional Racism:** In one sense, this type is closely linked to type three, for the institutions of a society are a product of, and a part of, its culture. But whereas cultural racism focuses attention on the differences or supposed flaws in the culture of minority groups, which are said to justify their treatment as inferiors, institutional racism generally refers to the way that the institutional arrangements and the distribution of resources in our society serve to reinforce the advantages of the White majority.... The standard analysis of institutional racism involves four steps:

    a. The historical creation of an institution which is non-racist in intent because it is designed for a homogenous society. If it contains any elements of racism, these must not be conscious, because if they were, the institution would exemplify type two racism.

    b. A change in the context within which the institution exists, so that new minority groups are disadvantaged by the continued existence of the institution. For example, giving preference to the employment of the "lads of the dads" may make it more difficult for new racial minorities to get jobs; and seeing exclusively White faces in school textbook illustrations might give Black children a poor self-image.

    c. The power of the White majority over the institution. The institution may be perpetuated intentionally for racist reasons (because the Whites perceive it to be to their advantage to do so), intentionally for non-racist reasons (because, for example, tradition and normal procedures are highly valued), or unintentionally (in that customary procedures are adhered to unreflectively).

d. The moral judgment that once the discriminatory consequences of the institutional practices are raised to consciousness, anyone seeking to perpetuate them is guilty of racism. A stronger version of institutional racism involves the claim that merely going about business as usual in such a context makes one an "accomplice in racism."

The main difficulties with this analysis are its oversimplified view of White individuals as the source of institutional power and its assumption that the raising of individual consciousness is sufficient to bring about institutional change....

Institutional racism, which I am referring to as type four, refers to the long-established organizational practices that disadvantage members of racial or ethnic minorities for no other reason than that they are members of those minorities.
Examples/notes:

5. **Paternalistic Racism:** This type of racism refers to the process whereby the freedom of Black people is defined or restricted by generally well-intentioned regulations that are drawn up by Whites.... It differs in two ways from institutional racism. First, it involves the initiation of new practices and procedures in response to the presence of racial minorities in the country, whereas institutional racism involves the failure to adapt longstanding practices and procedures to new needs. Second, it involves a more clear-cut wielding of power by White people, whereas it was argued above that in institutional racism it is a mistake to oversimplify the power that any individuals can wield in established institutions. Paternalistic racism implies that White people have the right to interfere in the lives of Blacks for their own good and the power to define that good.
Examples/notes:

6. **Color-Blind Racism:** Color-blind racism is the type which most closely corresponds to what is commonly called "unintentional racism...." What is it that makes color-blindness a type of racism rather than merely a misguided form of action? I want to argue that color-blindness not only leads to undesirable outcomes (the disadvantaging of Black people by ignoring or marginalizing their distinctive needs, experiences, and identity), but may also involve racial injustice. It is not a new idea (indeed it can be traced back to Aristotle) that there can be injustice in treating people the same when in relevant respects they are different, just as much as there can be in treating them differently when in relevant respects they are the same.... When a color-blind approach is adopted to any social policy in this country, White people are usually able to dominate because the common experiences are defined in terms that White people can more easily relate to than Blacks, and which tend to bolster the White self-image at the expense of the Black.... Color-blindness falls down because it is based on an idealistic principle (that all people are equal), which may be valid but which fails to take into account the contingent facts of racial inequality and disadvantage in our present society.

Examples/notes:

CHAPTER SEVEN

PROCESSES AND PROTOCOLS FOR CREATING AND SUSTAINING CROSS-RACIAL DIALOGUE AMONG K-12 EDUCATORS

SUSAN ADAMS & JAMIE BUFFINGTON-ADAMS

Introduction

THIS CHAPTER DESCRIBES THE necessary conditions for sustaining cross-racial dialogue that strengthens and prepares educators to excavate and bring to the surface their own personal biases and prejudices in order to transform classroom conditions into equitable learning spaces for all students, but particularly for Black and Brown K–12 students. Like the work of one such group (Lewin, 1948), these spaces and conversations are structured by protocols and group agreements that can provide needed experiences for teachers to later take these practices into K–12 classrooms and engage students in thoughtful dialogue across diverse racial identities. We recommend and describe the use of agreements, shared leadership, and specific discussion protocols to facilitate the creation of safe spaces for these conversations for both K–12 educators and their students.

The/Our Study Group

Throughout this chapter, we, the authors and members of the study group, will reference "our study group" as we describe processes and techniques that support teachers in creating and sustaining cross-racial dialogue and enacting more equitable practices in their classrooms. The study group we mention consisted of six teachers, ourselves included, who lived in the same geographical location but worked across differences in race, gender, age, teaching expertise, and teaching location and who met on a monthly basis for two years to grapple with issues of racial inequity as it existed in each of their schools. The group formed during a week-long, intensive Teaching for Educational Equity seminar when a facilitator challenged them to continue the work of the seminar in their own contexts. The experiences and work of the study group are the foundation of the practices included in this chapter.

Conceptual Framework: Adult Learning

When educators talk about learning in school settings, it is too often talked about as an activity in which only students engage. Yet teachers, too, must continue to learn if we hope to have robust curricula, effective pedagogy, and critical consciousness in our nation's schools. One might imagine that *professional development* would be the term for, or means by which, teachers would continue to add to their knowledge of the field and hone their classroom practices. Unfortunately, most professional development offerings in schools run contrary to the research on adult learning. While traditional professional development sessions, often set in what are sometimes euphemistically called professional learning communities or PLCs (Dufour, 2004, 2011; Dufour & Eaker, 1998), tend toward what is commonly referred to as a "sit-and-get model," adult learning theory demonstrates that, like their students, teachers need moments of cognitive dissonance and opportunities to engage with new learning and to grapple personally with new ideas in order to experience *transformational adult learning* (Mezirow, 1991; 2000).

The processes we describe in this chapter are founded on an understanding of adult learning as that which is transformative, or self-actualizing in nature, and is rooted primarily in the work of Jack Mezirow (1991; 2000), Robert Kegan (2000), and Kegan and Lisa Lahey (2001). These theorists employ a series of stages in their work that explain how adult minds change and grow over time. In both cases, these stages begin with adult learners who largely accept transmitted knowledge as truth and move toward stages in which adults test or question new experiences and knowledge in ongoing cycles of reflection, which leads to the revision or transformation of previously held truths. Additionally, Mezirow's work includes descriptions of the reflexive cycle in which adults who are engaged in transformative learning first grapple with new and dissonant experiences, internally leading to shifts in perspectives that manifest themselves externally in changed words and actions.

According to both Mezirow (1991) and Kegan (2000), adults who remain at stages where learning constitutes little more than being the recipient of transmitted knowledge cannot engage in the reflexivity that affects change. The implications then are clear: professional development providers cannot furnish teachers with an endless stream of sit-and-get professional development and expect transformation to take place in our schools. This is particularly true when that which needs changing requires teachers to address critical issues and systemic inequalities. What is needed instead are spaces in which teachers are encouraged to take charge of their own learning, to grapple with tough topics, to listen to others' truths, to question their own beliefs and practices, and to feel supported in attempting to effect change in their own contexts.

Principles of Critical Friendship and Intentional Learning Communities

In order to create conditions in which all members of the group feel safe and supported enough to sustain cross-racial dialogue and transformational learning, our study group utilized principles and approaches associated with what are variously known as critical friendship or intentional learning communities.[1] As we and other critical friendship practitioners[2] have written elsewhere (Adams & Buffington-Adams, 2016; Adams & Peterson-Veatch, 2012; McDonald, Mohr, Dichter, & McDonald, 2007), critical friendship, unlike a PLC (Dufour, 2004; 2011; Dufour & Eaker, 1998), which is a top-down model used in many educational settings, is organized, planned for, and facilitated by the members themselves. This model is built on the assumption that the members know what needs to be accomplished and are capable of building individual and collective

---

1 To learn more about these learning communities, see School Reform Initiative (n.d.): http://www.schoolreforminitiative.org

2 To learn more about the use of protocols and to see a large selection, see School Reform Initiative (n.d.): http://www.schoolreforminitiative.org/protocols/

capacities for creating, maintaining, and sustaining a rich community of professional practice over time.

Three foundational approaches provide structure, equitable opportunity, and buy-in over time: the creation of shared agreements or norms; co-created and negotiated meeting agendas; and the consistent use of structured protocols with fidelity. Next we will analyze each of these approaches and indicate how each supports cross-racial professional dialogue over time.

Agreements

Critical friendship most often begins with the group explicitly naming the conditions necessary to ensure that each member of the group is safe and comfortable enough to speak honestly and to share vulnerable components of professional practice. Rather than simply assuming that each member knows what is expected in terms of behaviors, talk time, contributions, and so forth, critical friendship and intentional learning communities state them explicitly and revisit them regularly to fine-tune or revise them as needed. Our study group took these agreements seriously and insisted that creating and maintaining agreements was an essential component of building the level of trust necessary for professional cross-racial dialogue (Adams & Buffington-Adams, 2016).

Groups use a variety of approaches for creating norms or agreements, depending upon how much time is available and how long the group plans to be together. A short-term work group may want to simply borrow a "typical" list of agreements we have found most groups need in order to be successful, such as these:

- Be fully present.

- Support each other's learning.

- Take responsibility for your own learning.

- Take care of your own needs.

- Content of the meetings is anonymous, not confidential.

- Give "gentle reminders" when we stray from these agreements. (Adams & Peterson-Veatch, 2012, p. 41)

While the ways in which each group states its agreements is as unique as the group itself, most effective groups have some variation of each of these agreements in their agreement list. Groups that expect to work together indefinitely will find the process of co-negotiating and crafting agreements worth the investment of time necessary to come to a consensus.

In the case of our study group, we began by adopting Singleton and Linton's (2006) *Courageous Conversations About Race* agreements and simply added the proviso, "Anonymous, not confidential" to the list. Singleton and Linton's list is simple, yet elegant:

- Stay engaged.

- Speak your truth.

- Experience discomfort.

- Expect and accept non-closure.[3]

We found that these statements formed parameters which named and framed the challenging space we hoped to create and provided guidance for times in which we grew weary, frustrated, or overwhelmed by working across racial identities. Agreeing that each of us would speak our own truth authorized each member to tell their own individual stories as the rest of us simply listened with compassion and with respect. As simple as this approach sounds, the three members of the group who identify as Black repeatedly insisted that being listened to in this way was a rare occurrence for them. Staying engaged, even when we were busy or tired, and agreeing to experience discomfort together meant we were able to speak freely and to broach topics often considered off-limits or too inflammatory in cross-racial groups. Expecting and accepting non-closure kept us humble as we recognized the depth and complexity of the history of racial identity in U.S. schools. We understood that while what we were doing was significant, on our own we were not going to singlehandedly "fix" American K–12 schools or eradicate systemic racism even from our own schools.

---

3   Adapted from Singleton & Linton (2006, pp. 58–65).

Shared Agendas

In our experience, the use of co-created and negotiated agendas is strikingly and sadly rare. Too often educators are simply told what the focus of a meeting will be. We have found that co-constructing an agenda, or even offering a draft agenda for feedback and quick revision, generates trust, good will, shared ownership, and buy-in from the members. Having some say in the content and flow of an agenda empowers the members to take responsibility for adhering to and working through the agenda once it has been established.

A co-constructed agenda can be built prior to a meeting and crafted by the group through the use of email or other electronic communication, or it can be drafted or revised on-site at the beginning of a meeting. Either way, the entire group is always invited to make suggestions for adding, replacing, or re-ordering the content and/or processes suggested in the agenda draft. While this process may sound taxing or time-consuming, in reality it seldom takes long and is a valuable investment in nurturing shared ownership of the group's work and its ways of being. In addition, sharing responsibility for agenda building prevents any individual voice, role, or perspective from taking control of the content and purpose of meetings and ensures that all voices are heard regularly.

Use of Protocols

Of the three elements, the use of protocols, or turn-taking mechanisms for talking, listening, meaning-making, and sharing work, is perhaps most significant for meaningful cross-racial dialogue. As stated in the literature (Adams & Buffington-Adams, 2016; Adams & Peterson-Veatch, 2012; McDonald et al., 2007), protocols are structured processes used to give equal time and weight to every voice and perspective in the group. Protocols provide an agreed-upon and trustworthy process for staying together at the table to surface sensitive issues, to examine teacher and student work samples, and to read and discuss a wide variety of texts, including video, audio recordings, performances, lectures, expert panels, and visual art.

Protocols often originate in or borrow heavily from now-familiar K–12 literacy strategies such as Think/Pair/Share or Save the Last Word for Me. Others have been created as needed to examine student and teacher work samples or to excavate and explore teacher dilemmas. Protocols are also developed in the field and refined by critical friendship practitioners. While all protocols strive to create conditions that value and make equitable access for all participants, several with an explicit equity orientation have been developed in recent years as an acknowledgment that cross-racial dialogue requires extra-careful attention to ways of listening and talking together.[4]

Our study group consistently identified the use of protocols with fidelity (e.g., sticking to the outlined procedures, careful selection of the right protocol for the situation, not veering off onto tangents or allowing one person to do all the talking, etc.) as essential to the group's ability to continue meeting voluntarily over a two-year period. The use of protocols distributes air time, maintains a sharp, productive focus, and purposely shares facilitation responsibilities evenly across the group, resulting in productive, reflective, and relevant engagements each time the group meets.

Sample Agenda

While each meeting of a critical friendship or intentional learning community will reflect the unique needs and ways of being of each group, there is a general pattern that has persisted in our own practice. In Table 1 we provide an archived agenda draft co-created for and with our study group for a meeting at a group member's house. Susan drafted the agenda and sent it out to the members for adjustment and feedback prior to the meeting. She also facilitated the opening of the meeting, known as *opening moves*, and helped the group monitor time. Jamie provided facilitative support for Cori, who presented a professional dilemma to the group. Other members (Careth, Jannine, and Michael) led other portions of the meeting. It is important to note that the names used here are the actual first names of our group members for two reasons:

1. They prefer that we use their first names and have explicitly provided permission for the use of their names in our publications (Adams & Buffington-Adams, 2016).

2. We are all really proud of the work we accomplished together, and naming our group members is one small way to honor them.

At the meeting, all members receive a printed version of the agenda, which

---

4   To view this list of emerging equity-oriented protocols, see School Reform Initiative (n.d.): http://www.schoolreforminitiative.org/protocols/?wpfb_cat=28#wpfb-cat-28

allows them to jot down personal notes and observations in the "So what?" and "Now what?" sections. Significant attention is paid to opening and closing the meeting purposefully with an eye toward the ongoing development of relationships within the group. This particular group negotiated a "soft start" time that allowed for chatting informally, getting a snack, and settling in, but a "hard stop" time at which they agreed to close the meeting so the members could head home on time.

The largest bloc of time scheduled for this meeting is dedicated to a professional dilemma presentation using a Consultancy protocol to structure the process, with approximately ten minutes reserved for debriefing the experience of the protocol and giving warm, positive, and cool, constructive feedback to the facilitator of the protocol. Keeping the focus of meetings on examining student and/or teacher work or professional dilemmas ensures that the group does not drift off into unstructured and unproductive chatter.

What	So What?	Now What?
Description/ What we are doing	Interpretation/ Meaning	Application/ Why it matters
Opening Moves, Susan facilitating Soft Opening 6:30–6:45 • Connections Hard Start 6:45, led by Jannine • Reflection Summary from Previous Meeting • Agenda Review • Agreements Review Prompt: What revisions to our agreements do we need to do our best work tonight?		
Cori's Dilemma using the Consultancy[5] protocol, Jamie facilitating the protocol Debrief of the process and facilitative feedback 7:00–8:00		

Reflection on Our Practice, Careth facilitating
Reflective Writing 8:00–8:20
5-minute Quick Writes and Round Robin Read-Alouds
around these questions:
   *Question 1: How do your will, skill, capacity, and
   knowledge qualify you to teach for equity?
   Question 2: Where do you find yourself right now
   in the struggle for equity in your school?*		

Closing Moves, Michael facilitating Scheduling Our Next Meeting 8:30 Reflective Close: *What do you need from this group? What does this group provide for you?*		

TABLE 1. Sample Meeting Agenda

---

5 To view the Consultancy protocol, visit School Reform Initiative (n.d.): http://www.schoolreforminitiative.org/?wpfb_dl=620

Group members regularly noted that the use of agendas and the focus on work or dilemmas meant the meetings were worth the investment of some personal time approximately once per month for two years.

Next, the group moves into a reflection activity designed to surface and share current thinking about each member's growing commitment to equity in education and to deepening each member's comfort with serving as an ad hoc equity leader in her/his school. This is not a free-form discussion space but is instead meant to provide time and safety for speaking and listening across racial difference.

Finally, rather than simply adjourning the meeting, a careful and deliberate plan for ending the meeting, known as *closing moves*, closes the loop by ensuring the meeting ends on time as promised. It also ensures that the next meeting date, time, and location are established before the meeting formally concludes. Individual written reflections are captured on carbon forms so that a copy can be shared with the meeting facilitator. Prior to the next meeting, the facilitator reviews the responses and prepares a summary for the group, indicating any adjustments in the agreements or the next agenda necessary in response to member feedback. For example, if a member indicates she would like more time for socializing or less time spent on quick writes, the group can decide how to address this request. This level of transparency and shared ownership is yet another important component of trust-building for the longevity of the group.

Study Group Findings

As we have written elsewhere (Adams, 2013; Adams & Buffington-Adams, 2016), when teachers are supported in creating and sustaining spaces dedicated to cross-racial dialogue, they in turn begin to structure their classrooms in ways that support students in building the same skills. And the skills students gain through such experiences are those they will need to navigate a diverse citizenship, engage in their own transformative learning, and work toward more equitable futures (Adams & Buffington-Adams, 2016).

As the group met consistently over two years, the members increasingly found the courage to share freely the inequitable practices they observed in their schools and articulate the impact of their own racial biases on Black and Brown students. They developed a shared discourse, using phrases like "going out onto a skinny branch" and about "getting real" with one another to signal moves into issues of potential discomfort. They bolstered, challenged, and cheered on one another, urging each other to interrupt and to eliminate discipline or teaching practices that disproportionately impact students of color. And while each person frequently felt isolated and alone in her or his school, they found great comfort in knowing that each of the others was "out there" working hard, too.

All members reported that while membership and participation in the group was sometimes exhausting and very challenging, they inevitably left our meetings feeling recharged, recommitted, and refocused on their shared commitments. Sadly, they also agreed that this was the first time any of them had been allowed to talk about race and schooling across racial differences in a professional setting. Careth, a Jamaican American member of the group, said it was the first time in more than 20 years of living in the United States that she felt a sense of belonging, and she compared it to being back home in Jamaica with her family.

The group identified a significant paradox they believed was present between them: "We are the same, but we are different." The members believed this tension created a productive yet palpable space in which to discuss race, similar to the conditions created by the learning environment paradox that Parker Palmer (2007) describes as being both "hospitable, yet charged." The presence of this paradox enabled them to delve deeply into complex and painful personal histories and bring that pain redemptively into the light of scrutiny. These are the very conditions educators need to learn to create in schools and classrooms if we hope to maintain and sustain productive and transformative conversations about race and schooling.

Implications

A primary implication of this work is a shift in how our society has come to view teachers—from a technician to an intellectual (Zeichner & Liston, 1996). It has been argued that the sit-and-get model of professional development is a symptom of the de-professionalization of the field and a distinct indicator that teachers are not perceived as intelligent individuals equipped with the knowledge and skills to identify and effectively address the barriers to learning in their classrooms and schools (Apple, 1986). Creating spaces for and maintaining cross-racial dialogue in the service of dismantling systemic racism, however, requires faith in teachers' abilities to grapple with difficult topics, pose critical questions, and take transformative action. In short, it means viewing teachers as capable, highly skilled public intellectuals who can be trusted with the care and preparation of future generations.

As part and parcel of trusting teachers to engage in critical, intellectual work, they must also have the freedom to form their own dialogic groups rather than being assigned to a particular body of individuals simply because they teach the same grade level or subject or have similar teaching schedules, as is often the PLC practice. Working with colleagues who are willing to hold confidences, to demonstrate respect and empathy, and who will keep the focus on improving professional practice are crucial elements in developing professional learning spaces in which teachers are safe to engage in risky, transformative learning. So, too, teachers must be respected as professionals who know what questions, dilemmas, or topics are most pertinent for them to address. They must be permitted to identify agendas that address their specific goals and professional needs without fear that choosing to delve into potentially controversial or contentious issues will result in evaluative consequences.

Just as teachers must be given the autonomy to decide with whom they can work and on what they want to focus, they must also be given the gift of time in which to do that work, since transformative learning requires significant time and rarely flourishes within strict schedule boundaries. Transformative adult learning thus requires not only regular, ample meeting time, but also requires long-term patience with the approach—something that certainly stands in contrast to the pressures to produce results quickly and efficiently.

Another significant implication of this work is its translation to the classroom setting. Once teachers have experienced participating in and contributing to supportive, cross-racial dialogic groups, they not only approach their classrooms with new perspectives, but with new practices and skill sets as well. In the case of our study group, every teacher applied the group processes and protocols to their own individual schools and classrooms (Adams, 2013). For example, what could be better in teaching students about democratic engagement than to teach them how to co-construct and implement classroom agreements? Two of the study group members did just that in a sixth-grade science classroom and in a ninth-grade reading classroom.

While co-constructed agendas are rarely seen in the realm of teacher professional development, they are even rarer in the K–12 classroom, where the expectation is that the teacher or administration determines the goals and pace of learning. Nonetheless, the use of shared agendas in the K–12 classroom adjusts classroom power dynamics in ways that provide space for student voice and agency, as well as creating opportunities for students to practice important life skills such as self-monitoring, setting goals, and compromising.

After experiencing how protocols structured the various ways in which one both attends to and responds to material, the teachers in our study group also began to implement specific protocols in their classrooms based on their immediate challenges or needs. Protocols obviously assist students in analyzing material—typically a stated content-area standard for most disciplines. Perhaps more importantly, however, protocols also support students in building the capacity to attend to learning for understanding rather than simply learning as preparation for responding, a skill that provides the foundation for students' eventual transformative learning and action as well. Whether using opening moves with students as a space in which they were welcome to share their burdens and celebrations, or teaching students to ask probing[6] questions as a means of stretching their classmates' thinking, our study group members leveraged protocols to hone students' abilities to engage one another critically and compassionately.

Conclusion

We are proponents of engaging teachers in deep intellectual work because we believe that transformative adult learning should be the point of professional development and is key to anti-racist work. Co-constructed agreements, shared agendas, and turn-taking protocols are effective in creating safe spaces in which educators can become vulnerable in order to tackle the ways in which systemic racism shapes each of our perspectives and practices. When teachers are given the space to build communities of trust wherein they can engage in critical questions as intellectuals and professionals, transformative learning is possible. When these shared experiences result in revised personal understandings and perspectives, teachers are better positioned to make similar learning conditions more accessible to students and to inspire them to ask critical questions about the world that they stand to inherit. These critical, potentially liberatory practices hold the promise of moving us forward in the work of dismantling the persistent, destructive, and systemic racism that continues to plague and shape our schools and societies.

---

6 To learn about probing questions, visit School Reform Initiative (n.d.): http://www.schoolreforminitiative.org/?wpfb_dl=340

Note:

The authors wish to extend deep respect, gratitude, and affection to our study group colleagues and friends: Jannine, Michael, Careth, and Cori. Thank you for allowing us to share your stories. Our professional and personal lives are richer for walking this journey together.

References

Adams, S.R. (2013). *The meaning of race-based professional development: A critical feminist ethnography.* Ph.D. dissertation, Indiana University. Retrieved from http://search.proquest.com/docview/1324465698?accountid=9807 (1324465698)

Adams, S.R., & Buffington-Adams, J. (2016). *Race and pedagogy: Creating collaborative spaces for teacher transformations.* Lanham, MD: Rowman & Littlefield.

Adams, S.R., & Peterson-Veatch, R. (2012). Critical friendship and sustainable change: Creating liminal spaces to experience discomfort together. In J. Faulkner (Ed.), *Disrupting pedagogies and teaching the knowledge society: Countering conservative norms with creative approaches* (pp. 32–45). Hershey, PA: IGI Global.

Apple, M. (1986). *Teachers and texts.* New York, NY: Routledge & Kegan Paul.

Dufour, R. (2004). What is a "professional learning community"? *Educational Leadership, 61*(8), 6–12.

Dufour, R. (2011, February). Work together: But only if you want to. *Phi Delta Kappan, 92*(5), 57–61.

Dufour, R., & Eaker, R. (1998). *Professional learning communities at work: Best practices for enhancing student achievement.* Alexandria, VA: Association for Supervision and Curriculum Development.

Kegan, R. (2000). What "form" transforms? A constructive-developmental approach to transformative learning. In Jack Mezirow and Associates (Ed.), *Learning as transformation: Critical perspectives on a theory in progress* (pp. 35–70). San Francisco, CA: Jossey-Bass.

Kegan, R., & Lahey, L.L. (2001, November). Immunity to change: How to overcome it and unlock the potential in yourself and your organization. *Harvard Business Review*, 85–92.

Lewin, K. (1948). *Resolving social conflicts: Selected papers on group dynamics* (Gertrude W. Lewin, ed.). New York, NY: Harper & Row.

McDonald, J., Mohr, N., Dichter, A., & McDonald, E.C. (2007). *The power of protocols: An educator's guide to better practice* (2nd ed.). New York, NY: Teachers College Press.

Mezirow, J. (1991). *Transformative dimensions of adult learning*. San Francisco, CA: Jossey-Bass.

Mezirow, J. (2000). Learning to think like an adult: Core concepts of transformation theory. In Jack Mezirow and Associates (Ed.), Learning as transformation: *Critical perspectives on a theory in progress* (pp. 3–34). San Francisco, CA: Jossey-Bass.

Palmer, P.J. (2007). *The courage to teach: Exploring the inner landscape of a teacher's life*. San Francisco, CA: Jossey-Bass.

School Reform Initiative. (n.d.). Retrieved from www.schoolreform initiative.org

Singleton, G., & Linton II, C. (2006). *Courageous conversations about race: A field guide for achieving equity in education*. Thousand Oaks, CA: Corwin Press.

Zeichner, K.M., & Liston, D.P. (1996). *Reflective teaching: An introduction*. Mahwah, NJ: Lawrence Erlbaum Associates.

CHAPTER EIGHT

CHANGING NARRATIVES:

Understanding the Struggle of Muslim Americans Today

WAFA MOHAMAD

EDUCATORS ENTER THEIR FIELDS for a variety of reasons, and I can assure you that the paycheck is not one of them. When you ask some educators, they may tell you they had an amazing teacher who made a difference in their lives. Others may tell you they saw something in the next generation of children that scared them, and they wanted to change it. If you were to ask me, I would say both.

I was in the seventh grade when I came across the teacher who changed my life. I was also in seventh grade when I noticed something changing within my own generation. I didn't like it. I didn't want it to continue. I wanted to do something about it. It was a Tuesday morning, to be exact, when I woke up with an odd feeling. I couldn't explain it, but I couldn't shake it off, either, so I jumped out of bed and walked around my house. My brother was not fast asleep in his room after a long night's work. My parents weren't in the kitchen eating breakfast like they always were. I immediately knew something wasn't quite right. I ran down to the family room in a panic. I asked why everyone was down there and not upstairs. Then I noticed that they were huddled around the television set, in a trance. They didn't turn to answer my question. I don't think they even heard me.

Like so many others on that day, the image I saw on that television would be ingrained in my brain forever. I saw the Twin Towers engulfed in smoke and flames. I asked my mom what happened, and I could see her lips moving, but I couldn't really hear what she was saying. I stared at the Twin Towers in disbelief. That day was Tuesday, September 11, 2001, and like so many others, this was the day that changed my life forever. But unlike so many others, this was day that I realized my multifaceted and forever-evolving identity would be put on trial forever.

An Identity Realized

I don't remember getting ready for school, going to school, or even getting back home that day. The only other memory I have of September 11, 2001, was my history class. My teacher sat in front of the classroom with her teacher's manual, just like she always did. We were getting ready to talk about the Civil War—I think. Before she could begin, a classmate asked a question. He or she asked what was happening in New York and why any-one would do that. As soon as I heard that question, I could feel a swarm of mixed emotions ranging from anxiety, to shame, to anger surround me and force me to slide into my seat slowly. I felt like everyone was staring at me through the backs of their heads.

Even though my family tried to keep to themselves as much as possible, all of my classmates had seen my mom. They knew she wore hijab. They knew we were Muslim. My history teacher, being the amazing teacher she was, did not ignore our questions. She welcomed them and created a sense of safety for my classmates and myself. She tried to foster an environment of inclusion and belonging, which played an essential part in forming my iden-tity at the time (La Barbera, 2015, p. 9). One student said something about how Muslims were at fault for this tragic event. The teacher made sure to remind him that not all Muslims were at fault, even if these men identified as Muslims. She connected it back to our studies about the Civil War and how not all White men wanted African Americans to be slaves.

I remember slowly sliding up in my chair, with a little bit of my pride gradually returning. The fear I felt, the embarrassment, the shame, and the confusion were slowly dissipating as I began to realize that she was right: this was not my fault. I do not believe the things those men believed. I was not them. I was me: Wafa Mohamad, a Muslim American born and raised in Chicago, Illinois. I realized I was a Muslim American who was a product of the Chicago Public School system *and* my Sunday school. I was a Muslim American who wanted to make this world a better place for everyone and wanted to live in the America that her parents had dreamed of: a land of diversity, freedom, opportunity, and possibility, a land where you can dream about the future with the freedom to let your mind wander as far as it possibly could.

Unwelcome Media Attention

As the years passed, I felt those dreams my parents had clung to slowly slipping away. I could see the country gradually changing. I felt as though every time I turned on the television, I was listening to another segment about terrorism on our own soil or abroad. If I wasn't listening to an hour-long story about possible Muslim terrorists, then I was listening to a 30-second segment on Muslim Americans being harassed or murdered on our own soil. I began to feel as though every time I heard the word "Muslim" on the news, it would either make me angry or make me cry. Either way, it was never good. Eventually, I realized the word "terrorism" was becoming synonymous with the word "Muslim."

Eighteen years after 9/11, I still fear that things are not getting any better. In fact, they are getting worse. Erin Kearns and fellow researchers (2017) looked at all the attacks listed in the Global Terrorism Database that occurred in the United States between 2011 and 2015. They found 89 attacks in their search, 12.4% of which were committed by Muslims. Then they examined U.S. media coverage for each attack. Of the 89 attacks, only 10 were committed by Muslims, 4 of whom were Muslim and foreign born. However, those four attackers received 32% of all media coverage. Kearns and colleagues determined that a Muslim perpetrator receives an average of 4½ times the coverage of a non-Muslim.

Eric Lichtblau (2016) confirmed my fears when he published an article stating that "hate crimes against Muslim Americans have soared to their highest levels since the aftermath of the Sept. 11, 2001 attacks." Vanita Gupta (2016), the head of the Civil Rights Division of the U.S. Justice Department, attested to this phenomenon:

We saw it after 9/11, and we continue to see an uptick in allegations of hate-related incidents today. We see criminal threats against mosques; harassment in schools; and reports of violence targeting Muslim Americans, Sikhs, people of Arab or South-Asian descent and people perceived to be members of these groups. (qtd. in Lichtblau, 2016)

The 260 hate crimes reported against Muslims nationwide in 2015 reflected an increase of 78% in such incidents. These hate crimes were usually targeted at people perceived to be Arabs and/or people who wore traditional Muslim clothing. That number reflected the largest increase in such crimes since a 2001 report of 481 incidents after the September 11 tragedy. However, because these numbers were compiled using official reports to the FBI, this same report indicates that even these numbers could reflect a drastic undercount.

Katayoun Kishi, a research associate focusing on global restrictions on religion at the Pew Research Center, reported that the FBI "collects hate crime data from about 15,000 law enforcement agencies that voluntarily participate, which means the annual statistics likely *undercount* the number of hate crimes in a given year" (Kishi, 2017). In order to balance this undercount, the Council on American-Islamic Relations (CAIR, 2018) recently released a quarterly report based on data compiled between April 1, 2018, and June 30, 2018. During this quarter, the Council received 1,006 reports of potential bias incidents and determined that 431 of these contained identifiable elements of anti-Muslim bias. The Bureau of Justice Statistics, using national telephone surveys, identified 293,790 general hate crimes, whereas the FBI reported only 6,573 that same year (Levin, 2016).

These underreported hate crimes, along with the increasing media attention that is used to portray Muslims as a "threat," is proving to be a double-edged sword for Muslim Americans around the nation. Brian Levin (2016), the director of the Center for the Study of Hate and Extremism at California State University in San Bernardino, believes that part of the blame for this increase in hate crimes may be attributable to our politicians.

Islamophobia in the Political Arena

Brian Levin (2016), looking specifically at hate crimes reported in the United States in 2014 and 2015, noted that there was a "moderate weekly rise in hate searches on Google like 'kill all Muslims' after Mr. Trump's proposed Muslim ban" (p. 26). Eric Lichtblau (2016) also observed that the frequency of these violent occurrences "increased immediately after [President Donald] Trump's most incendiary comments...In a few cases, people accused of hate crimes against Muslims and others have even cited Mr. Trump." He goes on to explain that the "political vitriol from candidates like Donald J. Trump, who has called for a ban on immigration by Muslims and a national registry of Muslims in the United States" is one reason for this profound distrust and the rise in hate crimes against Muslims. A number of experts in hate crimes—including James Nolan, a former FBI crime analyst who teaches at West Virginia University, and Mark Potok, a senior fellow at the Southern Poverty Law Center, which monitors extremism and hate groups—have also expressed this same concern.

On the other hand, in an email to Reuters, Kelly Love, a White House spokesperson, insisted that "President Trump has repeatedly condemned violence, racism, and hate groups" (Malone, 2018). However, the words of Donald Trump seem to tell a different story. Jenna Johnson and Abigail Hauslohner (2017) successfully debunked Love's sentiments when they reported an exchange Donald Trump had with an audience member at a Rochester, New Hampshire, post-rally debate. The exchange went as follows:

"We have a problem in this country, it's called Muslims," the man said. "We know our current president is one. You know, he's not even an American. Birth certificate, man."

"Right," Trump said, then adding with a shake of his head: "We need this question? This first question."

"But any way," the man said. "We have training camps... where they want to kill us."

"Uh huh," Trump said.

"That's my question: When can we get rid of them?" the man said.

Trump responded: "We're going to be looking at a lot of different things. You know, a lot of people are saying that, and a lot of people are saying that bad things are happening out there. We're going to look at that and plenty of other things."

This man begins by stating that there is a problem within our own country and that Muslims are the problem. He goes on to explain to President Trump that Muslims are trying to kill Americans and blatantly asks President Trump when "we" can get rid of "them." Nowhere in this conversation did President Trump condemn violence against Muslims. On the contrary, he tells this audience member that "we're going to be looking at that" (Johnson & Hauslohner, 2017). Instead of using this opportunity to build some bridges and foster an open dialogue, he uses it to establish his campaign on the basis of an anti-dialogue, as I like to call it. He does not foster conversations that can create peaceful dialogue and negotiations across the aisle, let alone across the street.

In March 2016, President Trump told CNN, "I think Islam hates us" (Johnson & Hauslohner, 2017). In June, he said, "There's no real assimilation by even second- and third- generation Muslim Americans". At a rally in Alabama on November 21, 2015, Trump insisted that when the World Trade Center came tumbling down, he "watched in Jersey City, N.J., where thousands and thousands of people were cheering as that building was coming down". The next day, he stated that this event was well covered and continued to insist this was true even after this comment was proven to be a lie. President Trump has even gone as far as quoting a discredited poll that found that "Muslims in the United States agreed that violence against Americans is justified as part of the global jihad". These are just a few of the 36 incidents of Trump's hateful rhetoric as recorded by the *Washington Post*. I can't help but wonder how many Islamophobic statements Trump has made that were not documented and how many of them have been burned into the hearts of the perpetrators involved in hate crimes against Muslim Americans.

Surrounded by all of this negative rhetoric and misinformation, I have found a new type of frustration taking over. I couldn't believe I had a president who had the audacity to say things such as "Islam hates us." I couldn't wrap my brain around the fact that someone in such a position could be so irresponsible with his words, knowing that millions around the world not only clung on to his words, but also looked to his office for hope and inspiration. Instead of using the power his office has given him to create a world of peaceful dialogue, he is promoting a "them-versus-us" mentality where Muslims are looked at as outsiders prone to violence, actively pursuing a vendetta against the world. I was tired of hearing all of this negativity attached to the phrases "Muslim" and "Muslim American."

A part of me hoped our media would hold him accountable for his blatant lies and exaggerations. I always looked to media outlets to help me stay up to date with the latest in politics and world news. Naturally, I hoped they would be the beacon for the American people as well, but the night they announced that Donald Trump would become the 45th President of the United States was the night I lost hope that our media would change this rhetoric. With a positive change in rhetoric coming from the media or leaders like President Trump clearly unlikely, I realized the Muslim American narrative needed to be changed by Muslim Americans. We couldn't wait around for someone else to do it. The only questions left to ask was: "Is it possible?" and "How long would this take?"

Changing the Narrative

Shirin Sinnar, a professor of law at Stanford University who studies the effect of counter-terror policies on minority and immigrant populations, believes the normalization of President Trumps' rhetoric is dangerous. She told *The Independent* that "the administration's anti-Muslim and anti-immigrant rhetoric and policies can fuel white supremacist violence directed at Muslims, immigrants, or people of colour by legitimising such hate" (Sampathkumar, 2017). Statistics have supported Sinnar's claims. The Council on Arab American Relations reported 300 U.S. hate crimes targeting Muslims in 2017 alone (Malone, 2018).

With hates crimes on the rise, I feared that taking hold of the Muslim American narrative to tell my story positively, and the stories of millions of Muslim Americans across the nation, was looking dismal. Then I saw a glimmer of hope in the most tragic way after the deaths of Deah, Yusor, and Razan in Chapel Hill, North Carolina. That particular incident was pivotal in changing my perspective on Muslim Americans and the impact our media was having on our lives.

Deah and Yusor were young newlyweds, and Razan was Yusor's sister. Razan was studying architecture at North Carolina State University. Deah was a dental student at the University of North Carolina. Yusor was contemplating a career in dentistry while attending North Carolina State College. They both volunteered for various dental clinics to help refugees, as well as working to feed the homeless and organizing health fairs. They enjoyed all-American sports, horror movies, and game nights with friends (Talbot, 2015).

Deah, Yusor, and Razan were all determined to make a positive impact on this world through their volunteer efforts. They were an integral part of their community—Muslim Americans in every sense of the word. On Tuesday, February 10, 2015, Deah, Yusor, and Razan's dreams were snatched away by the rifle fire of their neighbor, Craig Hicks. The moment the news of their deaths broke, people began "the work of assigning meaning" to their pointless deaths (Talbot, 2015). The Chapel Hill police released a statement saying that their investigation had led them to the conclusion that the killings had likely been motivated by an ongoing dispute over parking. While the media and local authorities tried to paint a picture of a pointless and tragic death over a parking dispute, Deah, Yusor, and Razan's families were not convinced. The facts of the case made their families skeptical:

1. Hicks had flashed his gun at the newlyweds when threatening them at their door.

2. Hicks presented himself as a "libertarian gun enthusiast" and an "anti-theist" who wanted "religion to go away," and the families found this rhetoric to be trivializing. (Talbot, 2015)

While the deaths of Deah, Yusor, and Razan were pointless, I do not believe they were meaningless. For the first time in my life, I was able to turn on the news and hear about the positive impact three Muslim Americans had had on the world. Media coverage surrounding their deaths was substantial, and this time it was not all negative. As news stations told the story of their lives as Muslim Americans and the positive impact they had made, the public was able to see an example of Muslim Americans, not just Muslims. America was mourning the death of one of their own.

Barakat's sister Suzanne became a familiar face after regularly speaking to news outlets, and she wasn't holding back. She addressed Margaret Talbot, a reporter for *The New Yorker*, during an informal interview and implored Talbot and her readers to "[start] talking about how real Islamophobia is—that it's not just a word tossed around for political purposes but that it has literally knocked on our doorstep and killed three of our

American children" (Talbot, 2015). The thought of someone knocking on someone's front door and ending their life was disturbing. The reality that a man fueled by hate could so easily wipe out half of a family was terrifying. While this was not the first time Muslim Americans were attacked, and though the perpetrator was not accused of a hate crime, this was the first time that the public was outraged by it. This was the first time I could remember the deaths of American Muslims on American soil resonating with so many people.

The resounding evidence of public outrage and mourning over the deaths of Deah, Yusor, and Razan was also manifested in the huge crowd that gathered on a football field for Yusor, Deah, and Razan's funeral. It was at this same funeral that Yusor's father, Mohammed, addressed a group of 5,000 broken-hearted Americans, saying:

> We have no doubt why they died. We are not seeking any revenge. Our children are much more valuable than any revenge. When we say that this was a hate crime, it's all about protecting all other children in the U.S.A.—it is about making this country that they loved, and where they lived and died, peaceful for everybody else. (Talbot, 2015)

Mohammed stressed that, while they believe this was a hate crime, they were simply seeking the protection of our American children. Mohammed's speech was significant because, while his children had strong ties to their grandparents' homeland, Mohammed did not use that to dissociate his children from their American identity. In fact, he embraced it, an act that allowed spectators like me to do so as well. Moreover, he did not focus on the fact that police continued to deny that this was a hate crime. Instead, he focused on the importance of labeling it a hate crime, because with that label comes the protection he believed his children needed but never received.

Anna Bigelow, a North Carolina State professor of Islamic Studies and published author, added to Mohammed's sentiments:

> Whether Hicks was motivated in a particular way might not be the issue. Just as maybe it's not the issue whether any of the cops in Ferguson or on Staten Island actually were personally motivated by

racial animus in the moment. African-Americans know that this is part of a bigger picture and a systemic feeling of insecurity vis à vis the cops. And Muslim Americans have that feeling vis à vis a certain sector of the society that is becoming more vocal and increasingly comfortable expressing not just its dislike for Islam but its profound distrust. (Bigelow; qtd. in Talbot, 2015)

Bigelow echoes Mohammed's need for protection and security, but she argues that the label itself is not the issue. The concern is with a feeling of security that is lacking for a huge portion of our society. However, I would argue that the label and the sense of security go hand in hand.

Two years after the Chapel Hill shootings, we witnessed the death of another innocent Muslim American, Nabra Hassane, a 17-year-old high school student who died from wounds she suffered after being beaten to death on the side of the road after leaving her mosque at the conclusion of nightly prayers. Again, the police investigation concluded that this was a senseless crime that was not religiously or racially motivated. It was at that time that Jonathan Blitzer chimed in on the importance of keeping Muslim Americans feeling safe. He says:

There's an important political element at issue, too: if law enforcement fails to call something a hate crime in the face of striking evidence, as many say was the case in Chapel Hill, a community can be left feeling unprotected. (Blitzer, 2017)

With Eraqi (2015a, p.93) estimating "that there are currently 1.7 to 3.6 million Arab-Americans and approximately 7 million Muslim-Americans living in the United States," that is a substantial part of the American population to leave unprotected.

It was after these incidents that I realized that this is exactly what Muslim Americans need. We need to have a more accurate, humanized understanding of a population that has been dehumanized for far too long. The only way to do so is to make sure that Americans are hearing more humanizing stories that showcase the positive impact that Muslim Americans have had on U.S. culture. These types of stories would help to protect every part of our society and restore a trust that has been destroyed in the wake of 9/11. It is time for the national rhetoric to change.

Institutional Changes

Columbia University Historian Edward Said has contended that this change in rhetoric is possible if we understand that the roots of such prejudice trace back to colonial times. Said argued that the portrayal of Arabs as the "other" is nothing new, and that discrimination against Arabs was the product of British colonization in the Middle East. In his book *Orientalism*, Said proposed that the Western study of the East was based on self-affirmation of European identity instead of an objective study (Said, 1978).

Given Said's work, Eraqi (2015a) argues that combatting such deeply rooted prejudices will be an uphill battle. However, Eraqi believes it is still possible. In order to eradicate a prejudice that has been embedded in our society for generations, an institutional change needs to occur and, according to Eraqi, the best place to begin is in our schools.

While the purpose of schools is still up for debate today, many agree that their main objective is to create responsible citizens who are involved in their communities and their government. Further, their involvement should focus on having a positive impact on society. In 1934 John Dewey wrote:

> the purpose of education has always been to everyone, in essence, the same—to give the young the things they need in order to develop in an orderly, sequential way into members of society...whether this education goes in a one-room school in the mountains of Tennessee or in the most advanced, progressive school in a radical community. (p. 97)

Although Dewey's idea is nearly a century old, it still rings true today. Ensuring that our students can be functional citizens in society and have a positive impact is essential. However, Dewey goes on to explain that if the goal of education is to adjust its curriculum according to society, then there arises a need to understand what that society is. What are its strengths and weaknesses, and what are the habits and beliefs of the society?

While it has become apparent that Muslim Americans are being harmed in myriad ways, Eraqi argues that the best way to create these institutional changes must begin with our schools. Through multicultural education and social justice education, we can begin to break the "others" narrative of which Said speaks. However, in a 2015 study of American textbooks, Eraqi (2015b) found that our schools are doing a great job of reinforcing the colonial image of Arabs that was spoken of by Said so many years ago.

Eraqi (2015b) analyzed the top five adopted U.S. social studies textbooks published by McDougal Littell, Teachers' Curriculum Institute (TCI), Glencoe McGraw-Hill, Pearson Prentice Hall, and McGraw-Hill. Eraqi found that the U.S. social studies curriculum was maintaining the social oppression of the Arab and Muslim American community. She determined that of the five textbooks she examined, there was only one that discussed Arab and Muslim contributions to the European exploration of the New World (p. 77). It was not until the textbooks reached the Post-World War II era that a chapter finally discussed Arabs again; this time it was in regard to conflicts within the Arab or Muslim World, and even then they emphasized stereotypes already being perpetuated by U.S. media. None of the textbooks specifically addressed Arab or Muslim American immigrants or citizens. Eraqi concludes her study by stating that:

> The analysis of the five textbooks demonstrates that publishers have included many ethnic groups, their cultural traditions, contributions and achievements; however, Arabs, Muslims, and Arab- and Muslim-Americans are still greatly ignored... Only one text specifically mentioned Arab-Americans, comparing Arab-American stereotyping and discrimination in the aftermath of 9/11, to anti-Japanese sentiments after the attacks on Pearl Harbor. (p. 77)

Other studies have shown similar results. In 2011, Saleem and Thomas examined how 12 social studies textbooks portrayed Arab culture and declared that publishers used propaganda to associate terrorism with Islam, consequently identifying Arabs, Muslims, and Islam as "other" (p. 30–31). In addition, Sewall (2008) found that many of the textbooks he examined contained errors involving the misrepresentation of Islamic figures, along with the general population of Muslims in the Middle East.

Eraqi went on to emphasize just how damaging these textbooks can be in framing students' consciousness toward Muslim culture. She argues:

"Historical events can be portrayed differently within each textbook. It also means that students will analyze texts to develop their own understanding of historical events and characters. It can also appeal to readers' emotions or influence their behavior" (2015b, p. 68). Therefore, Eraqi (2015a) urges teachers to "work together to prepare a generation of active citizens who better understand their diverse classmates, neighbors, and other citizens that they share this world with" (p. 98). While these changes cannot be enacted overnight, there is always something that administrators and teachers can do in the meantime.

In her text *Un-standardizing Curriculum*, Christine Sleeter (2017) discusses the importance of "transformative intellectual knowledge," arguing that it is essential to multicultural education because "most textbooks are examples of additive rather than transformed curriculum" (p. 81). Therefore, textbooks must be questioned critically and supplemented with different resources (p. 81). While it may be difficult for teachers to find supplemental resources, it is not impossible. Eraqi recently published an article entitled "Arab-American and Muslim American Contributions: Resources for Secondary Social Studies Teachers" (2015a) that reveals substantial contributions that Arab and Muslim Americans have made to the United States. In addition, she also suggests activities that teachers could conduct with students in the classroom using the information provided. Studies have also shown that making such changes to our curriculum can have a positive effect on the way students perceive Muslims (Klepper, 2014). Klepper states that "students generally showed more tolerance toward Muslims, and they developed a more nuanced view of the place of women in Islamic societies and of Islamic extremism" (p. 120).

Writing Our Own Narratives

While I believe that scholars such as Eraqi, Klepper, and Saleem and Thomas make a strong case for changing the content of textbooks, prominent historical figures such as Edward Said and Paulo Freire might have disagreed. In his book *Pedagogy of the Oppressed* (1970), Freire maintained that a structure must permit dialogue, and if it does not, then a change must be made. For far too long the need for this change has been ignored. It is time to bring this issue to the forefront of our conversations. Fortunately, the emergence of publications such as Said's *Islamophobia Studies Journal* at the University of California in Berkeley and organizations such as the Institute for

Social Policy and Understanding (ISPU), the Council on American-Islamic Relations (CAIR), the Arab American Anti-Discrimination Committee (Triple ADC), and the Islamic Society of North America (ISNA) allows for the beginning of structural changes in the United States. These organizations not only bring issues of Arab and Muslim discrimination in America to the forefront of the conversation; they also empower Muslim Americans like me to be their own advocates by telling their own stories.

Growing up, I was surrounded by Muslim American adults who decided to live in the shadows of American society as "others." They lived in fear of speaking out and showing the world that they, too, had a rightful place and a rightful voice. While I used to believe that this was rooted in the 9/11 tragedy and America's subsequent War on Terror, historians such as Edward Said have shown that this mentality was rooted in the very fabric of our society long before 2001. It was not until I began seeing the rise of organizations such as CAIR and Triple ADC that I realized that living in the shadows was not the only option. It was not until I saw Dalia Mogahed, the Director of Research at ISPU and previous advisor to President Barack Obama, deliver her TED Talk, "What It's Like to Be a Muslim in America" that I finally understood the power of our words, because the power of her words resonated with me for years. She inspired me to show the world that "Muslims, like all other Americans, aren't a tumor in the body of America, we're a vital organ" (Mogahed, 2016).

Conclusion

At this moment in history, it appears that American students and citizens will not become more tolerant toward Muslim and Arab Americans through their own volition. This is especially so if U.S. media, as well as school curricula, choose to focus on negative, often destructive, dehumanizing images of Arab and Muslim Americans. By disrupting the narrative and fostering a more socially just perspective, this historically dehumanized population can be seen as more than a threat to the very fabric of the United States. However, if the media, along with educators, fail to provide students with an accurate and humanized view of Muslim and Arab Americans, it is unlikely that the United States will remain a nation committed to the highest ideals of human equality and social progress. Educators must work with students to foster a disposition of tolerance and acceptance for Muslim and Arab Americans.

References

Blitzer, J. (2017, June 23). A Muslim community responds to a murder, hate crime or not. *The New Yorker*. Retrieved from https://www.newyorker.com/news/news-desk/a-muslim-community-responds-to-a-murder-hate-crime-or-not

Council on American-Islamic Relations. (2018). *Civil Rights Data Quarter Two update: Anti-Muslim bias incidents April–June 2018*. Washington, DC: CAIR.

Dewey, J. (1934). Individual psychology and education. *The Philosopher, 12*(1), 1–6.

Eraqi, M. (2015a). Arab-American and Muslim-American contributions: Resources for secondary social studies teachers. *Multiple Perspectives, 17*(2), 93–98.

Eraqi, M. (2015b). Inclusion of Arab-Americans and Muslim Americans within secondary U.S. history textbooks. *Journal of International Social Studies, 5*(1), 64–80.

Freire, P. (1970). *Pedagogy of the oppressed*. Boulder, CO: Continuum.

Johnson, J., & Hauslohner, A. (2017, May 20). "I think Islam hates us": A timeline of Trump's comments about Islam and Muslims. Retrieved from https://www.washingtonpost.com/news/post-politics/wp/2017/05/20/i-think-islam-hates-us-a-timeline-of-trumps-comments-about-islam-and-muslims/?noredirect=on&utm_term=.73d3097a15d3

Kearns, E., et al. (2017, March 5). Why do some terrorist attacks receive more media attention than others? *Justice Quarterly*. doi:10.1080/074188 25.2018.1524507

Kishi, K. (2017, November 15). *Assaults against Muslims in U.S. surpass 2001 level*. Retrieved from http://www.pewresearch.org/fact-tank/2017/11/15/assaults-against-muslims-in-u-s-surpass-2001-level/

Klepper, A. (2014). High school students' attitudes toward Islam and Muslims: Can a social studies course make a difference? *The Social Studies, 105*(3), 113–123.

La Barbera, M.C. (Ed.). (2015). Identity and migration: An introduction. In *Identity and migration in Europe: Multidisciplinary perspectives* (pp. 1–14). Switzerland: Springer International Publishing.

Levin, B. (2016). *Special status report: Hate crime in the United States.* San Bernardino, CA: Center for the Study of Hate & Extremism.

Lichtblau, E. (2016, September 17). Hate crimes against American Muslims most since post-9/11 era. *The New York Times.* Retrieved from https://www.nytimes.com/2016/09/18/us/politics/hate-crimes-american-muslims-rise.html

Malone, S. (2018, April 23). U.S. anti-Muslim hate crimes rose 15 percent in 2017: Advocacy group. *Reuters.* Retrieved from https://www.reuters.com/article/us-usa-islam-hatecrime/u-s-anti-muslim-hate-crimes-rose-15-percent-in-2017-advocacy-group-idUSKBN1HU240

Mogahed, D. (2016). *What it's like to be Muslim in American* [TED Talk Transcript]. Retrieved from https://www.ted.com/talks/dalia_mogahed_what_do_you_think_when_you_look_at_me

Said, E. (1978). *Orientalism.* New York, NY: Vintage Books, 1978.

Saleem, M.M., & Thomas, M.K. (2011). The reporting of the September 11th terrorist attacks in American social studies textbooks: A Muslim perspective. *High School Journal, 95*(1), 15–33.

Sampathkumar, M. (2017). Majority of terrorists who have attacked America are not Muslim, new study finds. *Independent.* Retrieved from http://www.independent.co.uk/news/world/americas/us-politics/terrorism-right-wing-america-muslims-islam-white-supremacists-study-a7805831.html

Sewall, G. T. (2009). Islam in the classroom: What the textbooks tell us. New York, NY: American Textbook Council.

Sleeter, C.E., & Carmona, J.F. (2017). *Un-standardizing curriculum: Multicultural teaching in the standards-based classroom.* New York, NY: Teachers College Press.

Talbot, M. (2015, June 22). The story of a hate crime: What led to the murder of three Muslim students in Chapel Hill? *The New Yorker.* Retrieved from https://www.newyorker.com/magazine/2015/06/22/the-story-of-a-hate-crime

CHAPTER NINE

RESTORATIVE JUSTICE:

The Alternative to Excessive Suspensions and Expulsions and the Zero-Tolerance Policy

KIMBERLY R. JAMES, RUNELL J. KING, AND JOVAN T. THOMAS

FOR MANY YEARS, SCHOOL disciplinary practices have raised concerns for African American students. Empirical evidence has been presented to support the notion of increased suspension and expulsion rates among African American students, which unequivocally contributes to an increase in students being funneled into the school-to-prison pipeline (Fenning & Rose, 2007; Morris & Perry, 2016). The school-to-prison pipeline is the result of several formal policies implemented through legislation, namely the abuse of zero-tolerance policies under the No Child Left Behind Act of 2002 (NCLB). Since the implementation of NCLB, zero-tolerance policies have been used to enforce out-of-school suspensions and expulsions for nonviolent offenses such as truancy and willful disobedience. As a result, students habitually suspended and expelled and are forced to enroll in alternative schools or remain absent from school for long periods of time, eventually causing them to drop out altogether. Out-of-school youth often commit crimes that move them into the juvenile justice system and, eventually, the criminal justice system. Minorities make up the primary population of individuals who fall victim to the school-to-prison pipeline, as a result of policies enforced under NCLB (Juvenile Law Center, 2011).

School Discipline Practices

Mainstream society and television are two of the outlets that, over the years, have played a part in what we conceptualize as appropriate school discipline. For many decades, schools have used various forms of discipline to regulate student behavior (detention, in-school suspension, out-of-school suspension, expulsion, etc.) both inside and outside of the classroom. Overall, the research suggests that, among racial or ethnic groups, Black students are disproportionally impacted by exclusionary discipline practices, thus linking poor behavior to low socio-economic status (SES). According to the American Psychological Association (APA), SES is defined as the combination of education, income, and occupation (American Psychological Association, 2014). Low SES affects society as a whole and is linked to higher levels of aggression, hostility, perceived threat, and perceived discrimination for youth. Consequently, Louisiana is ranked second-highest in the nation in terms of poverty level, with 21.1% of its population living below the poverty line (Adelson, 2012). Therefore, the state is well known for its poor ratings in education. The overrepresentation of ethnic minority students, particularly African American males, in the exclusionary discipline consequences of suspension and expulsion has been consistently documented during the past three decades (Fenning & Rose, 2007). Morris and Perry (2016) asserted that school discipline is a crucial but under-examined factor in achievement differences by race. High suspension and expulsion rates continue to increase across the nation, and the effects are becoming more evident in student achievement. Though large racial disparities in discipline exist, this pattern has never been examined empirically as an explanation of racial gaps in school performance. Further, Fenning and Rose (2007) examined the overrepresentation of African American students in exclusionary discipline. Despite high suspension and expulsion rates of African American students, research also supports the claim that other groups, such as children of poverty (Casella, 2003) and those with academic problems (Balfanz, Spirikakis, Neild, & Legters, 2003), are also likely to be pushed out of school through exclusionary discipline consequences.

In some states, school systems receive federal funding through grant projects to hire school resource officers or law enforcement officers. While the presence of these officers may serve to eliminate school violence, school administrators misuse their presence by referring students for minor infractions. For example, a federal civil rights lawsuit was filed against officials in Meridian, Mississippi, by the U.S. Department of Justice for systematically violating the due process rights of children (Equal Justice Initiative, 2012). Practices like this are not isolated to small cities like Meridian. These incidents occur in most minority communities across the country, all of them in an effort to divide the lines of societal existence to exclude and oppress. This further supports the concept that exclusionary discipline policies serve as a mechanism to imprison minority students, reinforce the school-to-prison pipeline, and add to the dilemma of mass incarceration. Further, the education system upholds policies that deliberately persecute minority students and enforce practices that render children incapable of learning in an environment that induces progressive growth and development. Consequently, the government has successfully used public policy to reinforce a racially cast social system whose primary goal is to enforce guidelines that strengthen the school-to-prison pipeline (Alexander, 2010). The public education system is void of any effort to employ a restorative justice system that eliminates exclusionary policies and racial disparities among minority students.

The Zero-Tolerance Policy

The exploitation of the zero-tolerance policy is parallel to the barriers imposed during the Civil Rights Movement to hinder integration in public schools. The existence of policies like NCLB, which are created for the sole purpose of separating one race from another, is evidence that racism is still dominant in America. Welch and Payne (2010) establish the racial threat imposed in school discipline. In a study that supports the previous assertions, sanctions imposed on Black students are more rigid and punitive than those imposed on White students. These practices are most prevalent in urban schools where rigorous security and surveillance are imposed to restrict and confine students in an environment that mirrors that of a prison (Welch & Payne, 2010). A trend is identified among students who are subject to such punitive discipline—90% are ethnic minority, poor, and most likely male. Michelle Alexander, author of *The New Jim Crow: Mass Incarceration in the Age of Colorblindness* (2010), provided a detailed narrative offering evidence regarding the current state of minorities in the criminal justice system. She described a troubling historical pattern in the criminal justice system of theory-associated laws created to limit the advancement and freedom (socially, economically, and politically) of people of color. The dialogue cites the deception of public policies—for example, the War on Drugs Act of 1986—that promote an institutionalized form of racism. These policies contributed to the current problem of mass incarceration and racial segregation through the disproportionate imprisonment of minorities for nonviolent crimes that require rehabilitation instead of the harsh, disparate sentences imposed. Likewise, zero-tolerance policies have been aligned with crime-related politics, where exclusionary discipline is considered a just consequence of misbehavior, even though these practices are considered ineffective as a corrective measure (Gonzalez, 2011). The result of exclusionary discipline policies is to place minority students in a vulnerable situation, subjected to traditions of racial disparity, neglect, and exploitation.

The Advancement Project (2005) confirms that zero-tolerance policies are a definite link in the school-to-prison pipeline. Research supports the theory that involving police in suspension and expulsion remedies for minor violations likely leads students to the juvenile justice system and eventually to the criminal justice system. The report maintains that the zero-tolerance policy is overused and abused by school administrators and indicates the lasting implications and harm it has on students. A student who commits a minor offense should not be grouped with students who commit more serious offenses. These measures likely place students at greater risk for entry into the criminal justice system by overexposure to police involvement and resulting desensitization. The study further provides evidence that Black students are more likely to be arrested than White students by at least 30%, lending legitimacy to discriminatory practices as designed by the zero-tolerance policy.

The school-to-prison pipeline is a phenomenon that mainly plagues the African American community (Terrell, 2016). Over the past two decades, school discipline has grown increasingly harsh and impersonal. Many schools and states are willing to exclude students—both temporarily and permanently—for almost any type of behavior (Black, 2016). The origin of the term "zero tolerance" dates back to the early 1980s, when state and federal efforts to combat drug abuse intensified (Tseng & Becker, 2016). According to Tseng and Becker, zero-tolerance policies (ZTPs) were implemented as a deterrent to serious crimes. Generally, zero-tolerance policies assign predetermined punishments and retroactively apply them to specific offenses without regard to the severity of the crimes.

School discipline is a necessary component of a functioning school environment. However, recent evidence suggests that current approaches to school discipline may have negative consequences for students and schools (Curran, 2016). One of the primary criticisms of zero-tolerance discipline is that such policies do not produce equitable outcomes for all students. Recent research has demonstrated significant gaps in disciplinary rates by race. The suspension rate for Black students (16%) is more than three times that for White students (5%) (U.S. Department of Education, Office for Civil Rights [OCR], 2014; Curran, 2016).

"Zero tolerance," as conceived, implies one-way communication or domination: one powerful group or alliance of dominant social and political actors sets the stage for "appropriate" ways of seeing, feeling, being, thinking, acting, and relating in public spaces—specifically, public schools (Robbins, 2005). Another issue arises when differing punishments are meted out to African Americans versus their Caucasian counterparts for the same infraction (Terrell, 2016). Furthermore, African American students are subjected to more office referrals and tougher punishments than Caucasian students for the same infractions (Milner, 2013).

The use of zero-tolerance policies as a form of school discipline and their racialized and gendered outcomes has been well documented (e.g., Crenshaw, Ocen, & Nanda, 2015; Raffaele Mendez & Knoff, 2003; Skiba & Rausch, 2006; Wallace, Goodkind, Wallace, & Bachman, 2008; Hines-Datiri & Andrews, 2017). In recent years, the criticism of zero-tolerance policies has expanded to include allegations that the policies are contributing to racial disparities in discipline. Nationally representative data demonstrates that Black students experience exclusionary discipline (suspensions and expulsions) at a significantly higher rate than their White peers (U.S. Department of Education, Office for Civil Rights, 2014; Curran, 2016). A report by the U.S. Department of Education, Office for Civil Rights (2014) indicated that Black boys have a higher incidence of suspensions (ranging from two to three), while Black girls have higher rates of punishment than female students across all racial and ethnic categories—rates that, in fact, exceed those of a majority of male students (Hines-Datiri & Andrews, 2017).

Zero tolerance is an education policy and practice that undermines the life chances of students, particularly African American students. The practice of zero tolerance and its consequences on students of color cannot be understood outside the criminal justice practice of zero tolerance, its consequences on African Americans and communities of color, and the dominating political climate that rationalizes social exclusion (Robbins, 2005, p. 1). Quintana and Mahgoub (2016) found that ethnic and racial disparities in education have been demonstrated across a wide range of academic and educational outcomes over a long period of time. Consequently, educational disparities are associated with limited access to educational and social capital resources and differential treatment of ethnic and racial minority students by educators.

Restorative Justice

In order to stabilize the imbalance of the suspension and expulsion rates of African American students in public schools and negate the zero-tolerance policy, restorative justice practices need implementation in the public school sector because they have proven to be a positive alternative to the utilization of the zero-tolerance policy (Song & Swearer, 2016; McCluskey et al., 2008a). The term restorative justice was introduced by Albert Eglash, an American psychologist who initiated a program that focused on human restoration between the offender and the victim (Andrioni, Popp, & Petrica, 2016; Eglash, 1957). Eglash (1957) examined three types of justice: retributive, distributive, and restorative. Retributive justice focused solely on the punishment of the offense, while distributive justice promoted clinical therapy and behavioral treatment for offenders (Fathurokhmandan & Fauzi, 2015). These types of justice, however, focused solely on the offender. Restorative justice, in contrast, concentrated on the effects of the crime on the victim.

Eglash (1957) considered restorative justice as an alternative to retributive justice (Braithwaite, 1996), and he created the restorative justice program based on the 12 steps of Alcoholics Anonymous and the group therapy sessions within those steps (Maruna, 2014). Eglash (1957) implemented his restorative justice program on delinquent youth and adults who were on probation and had narrative testimonials and group therapy support (Maruna, 2014; O'Reilly, 1997). In addition, Eglash (1957) added creative restitution from steps 8 and 9, where the offenders have to make amends to their victims, and Step 10, where they have to confess to the crime they committed and seek forgiveness from the people they harmed (Maruna, 2014).

Eglash (1957) believed that creative restitution was a "constructive contribution instead of painful or uncomfortable punishment, because the offender has to give more of himself or herself through the process" (p. 619). Moreover, as the offenders are providing their stories to others, their narratives would assist in curbing the negative behavior of others who are at risk of being in prison. Eglash stated that creative restitution is a "growth process for offenders, not a punishment given by a judge and imposed on an offender" (p. 621), and that process would stop any recurring behaviors that could result in the offender being returned to prison. The open discussion instilled in restorative justice or restitution "redefined past responsibility in terms of damage or harm done and redefined present responsibility in terms of our ability or capacity for constructive remedial action" (Eglash, 1977, p. 92). The process of restorative justice or creative restitution from Eglash's perspective is aimed at the rehabilitation of the offender, but John Braithwaite further advanced the practice to involve the victims and their families in the restorative justice process.

Braithwaite (1996) defined restorative practice as being victim-centered, where the victims are violated based on the criminal activity perpetrated on them, and those victims need mental and emotional rehabilitation after the offense. In addition, restorative practice would "restore any lost sense of empowerment as a result of crime" (p. 15). Restorative justice is recognized as deliberate justice because "it is about people deliberating over the consequences of crimes, and how to deal with them and prevent their recurrence" (p. 16) instead of allowing the traditional practice of involving lawyers in determining the consequences of the crime without consulting with the victim. When people are violated, they feel disrespected by their offender, and the disrespect they feel from the violation causes feelings of shame for them, creating "a shame-rage spiral wherein victims reciprocate indignity with indignity through vengeance or by their own criminal acts" (p. 16). Restorative justice reinstates balance between the victim and offender by answering questions about why the violation occurred and the thought process of the offender during the violation. Restorative justice restores harmony between the victim and the offender with a "remedy grounded in dialogue which takes account of underlying injustices" (p. 17), and it allows the dialogue between the victim and the offender to continue until the victim feels a sense of harmony and forgiveness toward the offender and the violation. Restorative justice offers restoration for the family and friends of the victims by allowing them to provide social support to the victims of the crimes.

Although Braithwaite concentrated on restorative justice being victim- centered, he stressed the importance of offenders and the community being rehabilitated in the process. Restorative justice rebuilds dignity within the offender as he or she identifies the actions taken in the course of the violation and "accepts responsibility for the bad consequences suffered by the victim and apologizing with sincerity" (p. 18). Further, offenders' self-esteem can be restored through restorative justice in regard to their future, such as employment, educational aspirations, and future success. Restorative justice involves the offender's family because it allows the family to "stand beside him [the offender] during justice rituals, sharing the shame for what has happened, which causes more shame to occur inside of the offender for shaming his or her parents" (p. 19). Because of the shame of letting his or her family down because of the crime, an act of forgiveness from those loved ones can rebuild the dignity of the offender.

Since restorative justice was implemented in the criminal justice system, there has been a benefit to offenders and victims alike upon completion of the process. Recidivism rates have been reduced drastically since the implementation of restorative justice (Johnson et al., 2015); likewise, victims who participated in the restorative justice process expressed great satisfaction with fairness and justice through this process than the traditional justice system process. Data showed that offenders were more satisfied with the restorative justice system than the traditional justice process, and more offenders completed the restorative justice program successfully than the requirements from the traditional justice process (Johnson et al., 2015; De Beus & Rodriguez, 2007; Sherman & Strang, 2007; Latimer, Dowden, & Muise, 2005).

As a result of the positive data generated by restorative justice practices in the criminal justice system, the process has been implemented in public school systems around the world. Restorative justice began in "Australia and New Zealand in the late 1980s and early 1990s, and it started in the United States in Minnesota and Pennsylvania in the 1990s" (McMorris et al., 2011, p. 5). The public schools that participated in restorative justice utilized the practice to minimize the number of suspensions and expulsions in the school and to stop the school-to-prison pipeline that the zero-tolerance policy had created. Furthermore, schools' administrations executed restorative justice as a "non-punitive disciplinary method that focused on restoring relationships, and all parties involved in the conflict were included in the restorative process" (Hurley, Guckenburg, Persson, Fronius, & Petrosino, 2015, p. 1), which involved the whole school and community in order to reshape the culture and climate of public schools and to provide positive strategies for handling student conflicts.

Restorative Justice Strategies
Restorative justice consisted of various practices and strategies, including mediation (Ahlin, Gibbs, Kavanaugh, & Lee, 2015; Zehr, 1995), family/ group counseling (Ahlin et al., 2015; Alder & Wundersitz, 1994), and group therapy circles (Ahlin et al., 2015; Jaccoud, 1998; Stuart, 1996). One restorative justice strategy used in the process is restorative conferences, which are "structured meetings between offenders, victims and both parties' family and friends, and they deal with the consequences of the crime or wrongdoing and decide how best to repair the harm" (Wachtel, 2013, p. 6). Likewise, it allows both the victim and the offender to solve their own problems with the support of family and friends. Restorative conferences provide the victims with the opportunity to confront their offender, express their feelings about the issue, and inquire as to the motivations behind the violation. In addition, this method gives the offender the opportunity to "apologize, make amends and agree to financial restitution or personal or community service work" (p. 6).

Within the restorative conference, the victim and the offender meet, along with the parents of those involved, and they openly discuss any issues they may have with one another and ways to resolve the problem without revisiting it. Next, a facilitator guides the conversation and may use leading questions in order to summarize the events related to the violation, the emotional effects the situation had on the victim, and options for resolving the animus between the victim and the offender (Lea, Bowlby, & Holt, 2015; McCluskey et al., 2008b). The restorative conference assigns accountability and responsibility to the ones involved instead of allowing them to accept the punishment followed under the zero-tolerance policy. Likewise, it assists with "rebuilding relationships damaged by crime and other conflicts and offers students a means to rebuild their dignity through mature reparation of harm" (Schiff, 2013, p. 7).

Another restorative strategy is "restorative circles," which involve a facilitator, author, receiver, and the community. The facilitator brings together everyone involved in the conflict, and the offender and the victim are labeled as author and receiver based on the "bidirectionality of conflict and the complexity of roles" (Ortega, Lyubansky, Nettles, & Espelage, 2016, p. 460). Before the restorative circle begins, the facilitator conducts a separate, pre-circle meeting with the author and the receiver. Next, the facilitator meets with the family and friends involved. The restorative circle then starts with the facilitator helping to instigate a dialogue between the author and the receiver so that they can "understand each other, take responsibility for their choices, and generate actions or agreements for moving forward" (p. 460). After the restorative circle ends, the author and the receiver reflect about what they have heard and understood in the course of the meeting, and a post-circle is done to "check in on the agreed actions and how things have been going since the circle" (p. 460).

The final restorative strategy used in restorative justice is family group conferencing or family group decision making, where the "extended family and friends of the family have an opportunity to take responsibility for their own loved ones" (Wachtel, 2013, p. 9). This strategy of allowing the extended family and friends to make decisions that may affect the family member's well-being displays familial and community support for the distressed family member. Further, this option creates "empowerment for the family to fix their own problems which facilitates healing" (p. 9). During the family group conferencing or family group decision making, the facilitator informs the family about the details of the case, the family and community members create a plan for the child, and professionals analyze the plan to ensure that it is within legal boundaries. After the plan is approved, professionals and family members "monitor the plan's progress, and often follow-up meetings are held" (p. 9).

Effects of Restorative Justice
The implementation of restorative justice in public schools has led to significant reductions in their suspension and expulsion rates, and it has created a positive school climate (Song & Swearer, 2016; High Hopes Campaign, 2012; Wong, Cheng, Ngan, & Ma, 2011; Sumner, Silverman, & Frampton, 2010; Lewis, 2009); in addition, the students who were involved in restorative justice showed improvement in their self-esteem and attitude. School attendance was affected by restorative justice—indeed, some schools that practice restorative justice reported a "50-percent reduction in absenteeism during the first year of implementation and a decrease in tardiness of about 64 percent" (Hurley et al., 2016, p. 22). Restorative justice affected the

school climate in that the schools using it reported that the social-emotional atmosphere of the school improved substantially (Hurley et al., 2016; Jain, Bassey, Brown, & Kalra, 2014). Schools that practiced restorative justice saw major increases in academic achievement and graduation rates; likewise, graduation rates rose significantly compared to the smaller change brought about under the traditional methods (Hurley et al., 2016; Jain et al., 2014).

The suspension and expulsion rate of African-American students in public schools is higher than for any other group of students and results in an increase in both academic failure and dropout rates among this group of students. The zero-tolerance policy provides only for suspensions and expulsions when school rules are broken, while failing to offer positive accountability and responsibility for students' actions. As a way to curb the high percentage of suspensions and expulsions of African American students resulting from this zero-tolerance policy, restorative justice offers a prime solution. It provides the victim, the offender, and the parents of the students the opportunity to work collaboratively to address the issue between the offender and the victim, the reasons why the issue arose in the first place, the feelings surrounding the problem, and effective strategies for rebuilding a positive relationship between the offender and the victim. Thanks to the process of restorative justice, the suspension and expulsion rates in public schools that practice this strategy have been significantly reduced, along with the improvement of school climate and rates of academic achievement.

References

Adelson, J. (2012, September 12). Louisiana ranks poorly on latest income, health insurance statistics. *The Times Picayune*. Retrieved from: http://www.nola.com/politics/index.ssf/2012/09/louisiana_ranks_poorly_on_late.html

The Advancement Project (2005). *Education on lockdown: The schoolhouse to jailhouse track*. Retrieved from https://b.3cdn.net/advancement/5351180e24cb166d02_mlbrqgxlh.pdf

Ahlin, E., Gibbs, J., Kavanaugh, P., & Lee, J. (2015). Support for restorative justice in a sample of U.S. university students. *International Journal of Offender Therapy and Comparative Criminology, 61*(2), 229–245.

Alder, C., & Wundersitz, J. (1994). New directions in juvenile justice reform in Australia. In C. Alder & J. Wundersitz (Eds.), *Family conferencing and juvenile justice: The way forward or misplaced optimism?* (pp. 15–44). Canberra: Australian Institute of Criminology.

Alexander, M. (2010). *The new Jim Crow: Mass incarceration in the age of colorblindness.* New York, NY: The New Press.

American Psychological Association. (2014). *Children, youth and families & socioeconomic status.* Retrieved from http://www.apa.org/pi/ses/resources/publications/factsheet-cyf.aspx

Andrioni, F., Popp, L.E., & Petrica, I. (2016). Juvenile delinquency in the Jiu Valley at the junction with the probation service and restorative justice. *The Fifth International Conference multidisciplinary perspectives in the quasi-coercive treatment of offenders.* Timisoara-Romania: Filodiritto Editore.

Balfanz, R., Spiridakis, K., Neild, R.C., & Legters, N. (2003). High-poverty secondary schools and the juvenile justice system: How neither helps the other and how that could change. *New Directions for Student Leadership, 2003*(99), 71–89.

Black, D.W. (2016). *Ending zero tolerance: The crisis of absolute school discipline.* New York, NY: New York University Press.

Braithwaite, J. (1996). Restorative justice and a better future. *The Dalhousie Review, 76*(1), 9–31.

Casella, R. (2003). Punishing dangerousness through preventive detention: Illustrating the institutional link between school and prison. *New Directions for Student Leadership, 2003*(99), 55–70.

Crenshaw K.W., Ocen, P., & Nanda, J. (2015). *Black girls matter: Pushed out, overpoliced, and underprotected.* New York, NY: African American Policy Forum, Center for Intersectionality and Social Policy Studies.

Curran, F.C. (2016). Estimating the effects of state zero tolerance laws on exclusionary discipline, racial discipline gaps, and student behavior. *Educational Evaluation and Policy Analysis, 38*(4), 647–668.

De Beus, K., & Rodriguez, N. (2007). Restorative justice practice: An examination of program completion and recidivism. *Journal of Criminal Justice,* *35,* 337–347.

Eglash, A. (1957). Creative restitution: A broader meaning for an old term. *Journal of Criminal Law, Criminology, and Police Science, 48,* 619–622.

Eglash, A. (1977). Beyond restitution: Creative restitution. In Hudson, J. & Galaway, B. (Eds.). *Restitution in criminal justice: A critical assessment of sanctions.* Lanham, MD: Lexington Books.

Equal Justice Initiative (2012). *Department of Justice sues Mississippi officials for operating school to prison pipeline.* Retrieved from http://www.eji. org/node/709

Fathurokhmandan, F., & Fauzi, A. (2015). Islamic criminal law as a bridge of contention between public and individual interest within restorative justice. *Journal Media Hukum, 22*(1), 36–56.

Fenning, P., & Rose, J. (2007). Overrepresentation of African American students in exclusionary discipline: The role of school policy. *Urban Education, 42*(6), 536–559.

Gonzalez, T. (2011). Restoring justice: Community organizing to transform school discipline policies. *Davis Journal of Juvenile Law & Policy, 15*(1), 1–36.

High Hopes Campaign. (2012). *Restorative justice in Chicago public schools.* Chicago, IL: Author.

Hines-Datiri, D., & Andrews, D.J. (2017). The effects of zero tolerance policies on Black girls: Using critical race feminism and figured worlds to examine school discipline. *Urban Education,* 1–20. Retrieved from https://doi. org/10.1177/0042085917690204

Hurley, N., Guckenburg, S., Persson, H., Fronius, T., & Petrosino, A. (2015). *What further research is needed on restorative justice in schools?* Retrieved from https://jprc.wested.org/wp-content/uploads/2015/07/Restorative_Justice_ Future_Research.pdf

Jaccoud, M. (1998). Restoring justice in native communities in Canada. In

L. Walgrave (Ed.), *Restorative justice for juveniles: Potentialities, risks, and problems* (pp. 285–299). Leuven, Belgium: Leuven University Press.

Jain, S., Bassey, H., Brown, M., & Kalra, P. (2014). *Restorative justice implementation and impacts in Oakland schools* (prepared for the Office of Civil Rights, U.S. Department of Education). Oakland, CA: Oakland Unified School District, Data in Action.

Johnson, T., Quintana, E., Kelly, D., Graves, C., Schub, O., Newman, P., & Casas, C. (2015). Restorative justice hubs concept paper. *Revisita de Mediacion, 8*(2), 1–11.

Juvenile Law Center (2011). *Federal policy, ESEA reauthorization and the school to prison pipeline.* Retrieved from: http://www.jlc.org/resourcespub licationsfederal-policy-esea-reauthorization-and-school-prison-pipeline

Latimer, J., Dowden, C., & Muise, D. (2005). The effectiveness of restorative justice practices: A meta-analysis. *Prison Journal, 85*(2), 127–144.

Lea, J., Bowlby, S., & Holt, L. (2015). Reconstituting social, emotional and mental health difficulties? The use of restorative approaches to justice in schools. In P. Kraftl (Ed.), *Children's emotions in policy and practice: Mapping and making spaces of childhood* (pp. 242–258). London: Palgrave Macmillan.

Lewis, S. (Ed.). (2009). *Improving school climate: Findings from schools implementing restorative practices.* Bethlehem, PA: International Institute for Restorative Practices.

Maruna, S. (2014). The role of wounded healing in restorative justice: An appreciation of Albert Eglash. *Restorative Justice, An International Journal, 2*(1), 9–23.

McCluskey, G., Lloyd, G., Kane, J., Stead, J., Riddell, S., & Weedon, E. (2008a). Can restorative practices in schools make a difference? *Educational Review, 60*(4), 405–417.

McCluskey, G., Lloyd, G., Kane, J., Stead, J., Riddell, S., & Weedon, E. (2008b). "I was dead restorative today": From restorative justice to restorative approaches in school. *Cambridge Journal of Education, 38*(2), 199–216.

McMorris, B., Eggert, R., Beckman, K., Gutierrez, S., Gaona, V., Abel, S., Friedman, M., Lenertz, J., Schwanke, C., & Burns, J. (2011). *A pilot program evaluation of the family and youth restorative conference program.* Retrieved from http://www.minneapolismn.gov

Milner, R. (2013). Why are students of color (still) being punished more severely and frequently than White students? *Urban Education, 48*(4), 483–489.

Morris, E.W., & Perry, B.L. (2016). The punishment gap: School suspension and racial disparities in achievement. *Social Problems, 63*(1), 68–86.

O'Reilly, E. (1997). *Sobering tales: Narratives of alcoholism and recovery.* Amherst, MA: University of Massachusetts Press.

Ortega, L., Lyubansky, M., Nettles, S., & Espelage, D. (2016). Outcomes of a restorative circles program in a high school setting. *Psychology of Violence, 6*(3), 459–468.

Quintana, S.M., Mahgoub, L. (2016). Ethnic and racial disparities in education: Psychology's role in understanding and reducing disparities. *Theory into Practice, 55*(2), 94–103.

Raffaele Mendez, L.M., & Knoff, H.M. (2003). Who gets suspended from school and why? A demographic analysis of schools and disciplinary infractions in a large school district. *Education & Treatment of Children, 26,* 30–51.

Robbins, C. (2005). Zero tolerance and the politics of racial injustice. *Journal of Negro Education, 74*(1), 2–17. Retrieved from http://www.jstor.org. libezp.lib.lsu.edu/stable/40027226

Schiff, M. (2013). Dignity, disparity and desistance: Effective restorative justice strategies to plug the "school-to-prison pipeline." In *Center for Civil Rights Remedies National Conference. Closing the school to research gap: Research to Remedies Conference,* (pp. 1–18). Washington, DC.

Sherman, L., & Strang, H. (2007). *Restorative justice: The evidence.* London, UK: Smith Institute. Retrieved from www.restorativejustice.org

Skiba R.J., & Rausch, M.K. (2006). Zero tolerance, suspension, and expulsion: Questions of equity and effectiveness. In C.M. Evertson & C.S. Weinstein (Eds.), *Handbook of classroom management: Research, practice, and contemporary issues* (pp. 1063–1089). New York, NY: Routledge.

Song, S., & Swearer, S. (2016). The cart before the horse: The challenge and promise of restorative justice consultation in schools. *Journal of Educational and Psychological Consultation, 26*(4), 313–324.

Stuart, B. (1996). *Building community justice partnerships: Community peacemaking circles.* Ontario, Canada: Aboriginal Justice Section, Department of Justice of Canada.

Sumner, M.D., Silverman, C.J., & Frampton, M.L. (2010). *School-based restorative justice as an alternative to zero-tolerance policies: Lessons from West Oakland.* Berkeley, CA: Thelton E. Henderson Center for Social Justice, University of California, Berkeley, School of Law.

Terrell, S.C. (2016). *Zero tolerance or zero efficiency? The detrimental effects of educational policies that adversely affect African American males.* Unpublished honors thesis, Texas State University, San Marcos, Texas.

Tseng M., & Becker, C.A. (2016). Impact of zero tolerance policies on American K–12 education and alternative school models. In G.A. Crews (Ed.), *Critical examinations of school violence and disturbance in K–12 education.* Hershey, PA: Information Science Reference.

U.S. Department of Education. Office for Civil Rights. (2014). *Civil rights data collection—Data snapshot: School discipline* (Issue Brief No. 1). Retrieved from http://ocrdata.ed.gov/Downloads/CRDC-School-Discipline-Snapshot.pdf

Wachtel, T. (2013). *Defining restorative.* Bethlehem, PA: International Institute for Restorative Practices. Retrieved from http://thaichristianfoundation.org

Wallace, Jr., J.M., Goodkind S., Wallace, C.M., & Bachman, J.G. (2008). Racial, ethnic, and gender differences in school discipline among U.S. high school students: 1991–2005. *Negro Educational Review, 59*(1–2), 47–62.

Welch, K. & Payne, A. (2010). Racial threat and punitive school discipline. *Social Problems, 57*(1), 25-48.

Wong, D.W., Cheng, C.K., Ngan, R.H., & Ma, S.K. (2011). Program effectiveness of a restorative whole-school approach for tackling school bullying in Hong Kong. *International Journal of Offender Therapy and Comparative Criminology, 55*(6), 846–862.

Zehr, H. (1995). Justice paradigm shift? Values and visions in the reform process. *Mediation Quarterly, 12*(3), 207–216.

J. Q. Adams is Emeritus Professor of Educational and Interdisciplinary Studies at Western Illinois University (WIU). He earned a B.Ph in 1975 from Grand Valley State University, a MA from Indiana University in 1977, and a Ph.D. in Educational Psychology from the University of Illinois in 1989. Adams is a five-time recipient of the WIU's "Faculty Excellence Award." In 2002 he received the Distinguished Alumni Award from the University of Illinois's College of Education. In 2005 he was selected as WIU's College of Education and Human Services "Teacher of the Year" and in 2008 he received Grand Valley State University College of Education's Alumni Leadership Award. In 2009 he was recognized as the G. Pritchy Smith's Multicultural Educator of the Year by the National Association for Multicultural Education, and in 2011 he was selected as WIU's Distinguished Faculty Lecturer. Dr. Adams' most recent publications/projects include the books *Multicultural Films: A Reference Guide, Dealing with Diversity: the Anthology* (2nd edition), and the videotape series *Effective Strategies for Learning and Teaching about Diversity in the U.S.A.* Adams' teleclass, "Dealing with Diversity" (3rd edition) has been taught in over 150 colleges and universities across the United States.

His experience and ongoing research have focused particularly on the effects of color hierarchy, race/ethnicity, and nationality in educational institutions, governmental agencies, and communities, as well as in business and industry. He is currently the founder and director of Academic Consulting for Excellence (www.aceconsultingmidwest.com).

Susan Adams is Associate Professor of Middle/Secondary Education at Butler University. A former high school ESL and Spanish teacher, Dr. Adams earned her Ph.D. in Literacy, Culture, and Language in Education from Indiana University. Her publications have appeared in *Theory into Practice, English Journal, SAGE Sociology of Education, Critical Literacy, The Brock Education Journal, Writing and Pedagogy,* and *The New Educator.* Her book *Race and Pedagogy: Creating Collaborative Spaces for Teacher*

Transformations (2016) was co-authored with Jamie Buffington-Adams. She is an intentional learning community national facilitator affiliated with School Reform Initiative and a Senior Student Garuda with Warriors for the Human Spirit.

Jamie Buffington-Adams is Associate Professor in the School of Education at Indiana University East, where she focuses on preparing future teachers to identify what they believe about teaching and learning and to work with students who struggle to find success in schools. A former jack-of-all-educational-trades, Dr. Buffington-Adams's broad experiences in special, remedial, and alternative education have developed into professional interests in emancipatory pedagogies for marginalized youth and curriculum theory. She currently serves on committees focused on ensuring the quality of academic offerings and addressing issues of diversity, equity, and student success across multiple aspects of campus life. She is a co-author of *Race and Pedagogy: Creating Collaborative Spaces for Teacher Transformations*. Her other publications are included in *SAGE Encyclopedia of Curriculum Studies, Review of Disability Studies: An International Journal, SAGE Encyclopedia of Deaf Studies*, and the forthcoming book *Radical Youth Pedagogy*.

Traci P. Baxley has worked in Pre-K–20 educational systems for over 25 years, earning a doctorate in Curriculum and Instruction with an area of specialization in literacy. Dr. Baxley's areas of scholarship include critical literacy, multicultural literature, and racial and identity development. Much of her scholarship and service is grounded in social justice education that addresses the opportunity gap and the academic and social successes of students of color and students in poverty.

Christina J. Cavallaro is a doctoral candidate in the Department of Curriculum, Culture, and Educational Inquiry. She attended the University of Florida, where she earned her bachelor's degree in elementary education and her master's degree in special education with a TESOL specialization. She uses culturally responsive and community-oriented approaches to examine the language of schooling as a means for providing access and educational opportunity to students within general education classrooms.

Sheron Fraser-Burgess is an Associate Professor of Social Foundations/ Multicultural Education at Ball State University and teaches courses in the undergraduate teacher licensure/professional education program and also philosophy and ethics courses in the master of arts and doctoral program in Educational Studies. As Provenzo (2012) states, in its attention to social justice, social and cultural foundations can make it possible for teacher candidates and practitioners to become responsible advocates for democratic education. Dr. Fraser-Burgess seeks to come alongside teacher candidates and practicing teachers in making the theory-to-practice connections that social justice in education requires, in addition to their acquisition of the knowledge, skills, and dispositions of their profession.

Michael Hernandez is a Denver native and a Denver Public Schools graduate who has been teaching Social Science at East High School since 1995, as well as a variety of courses that include Sociology, Social Problems, Contemporary Issues, Psychology, Civics, Economics, Honors Geography, Honors Ancient and Medieval History, and AP World History.

Maria Hernández Finch is an Associate Professor of Educational Psychology and currently directs the Master's and Educational Specialist programs in school psychology at Ball State University. Dr. Hernández Finch's primary research areas include the intersection of diversity, early learning, and assessment/identification, with a focus on equity and traditionally understudied and disenfranchised populations on both ends of the human exceptionality continuum. Current studies and grants focus on early gifted identification and twice exceptionality, investigating the developmental trajectories of individuals with Autism Spectrum Disorder, efficacious suicide prevention training, and culturally relevant and responsive intervention, consultation, research methods, and school support team collaboration.

Jessica A. Heybach is Associate Professor in the School of Education and Human Performance at Aurora University. Dr. Heybach is currently the department chair of Ed.D. Programs at AU, and teaches graduate courses in educational research, curriculum studies, and ethics and philosophy in education. Her scholarly interests include questions of justice and equity in education, how conceptions of teacher neutrality influence curriculum and instruction, and how visual culture informs human understandings of injustice. She has published in such journals as the *Education Policy Analysis Archives, Educational Studies, Education and Culture, Critical Questions in Education*, and *Philosophical Studies in Education*, and co-edited the book *Dystopia and Education: Insights into Theory, Praxis, and Policy* with Eric C. Sheffield.

Mary Beth Hines is an Associate Professor and Chair of the Department of Literacy, Culture, and Language Education at Indiana University, where she teaches undergraduate and graduate literacy courses. She has published a number of articles in *English Education, Teacher Development, The Curriculum Journal, English Teaching: Practice and Critique*, as well as a number of book chapters. Her work focuses on issues of social justice with linguistically and culturally diverse students in the English classroom.

Terry Husband is an Associate Professor of Early Childhood Literacy at Illinois State University in Normal, Illinois. He teaches undergraduate- and graduate-level courses related to literacy assessment, literacy instruction, and issues of diversity in K–12 contexts. Dr. Husband's research interests include issues of social justice in early childhood classrooms, literacy development in Black boys in P–5 classrooms, and multicultural children's literature. He spent 10 years as an urban early childhood educator prior to accepting his current position at Illinois State.

Kimberly R. James is a native of Jackson, Mississippi, who currently resides in Baton Rouge, Louisiana. In 2004, Dr. James earned her bachelor's degree in English at Tougaloo College in Jackson, Mississippi, and Masters of Education in Teaching Arts at Mississippi College in Clinton, Mississippi. In 2011, Dr. James entered the education field and began teaching in the Jackson Public School District. In 2014, she moved to Baton Rouge, Louisiana, and enrolled in Louisiana State University, where she began work on her Ph.D. in Educational Leadership and Research while teaching in the East Baton Rouge School Parish. Her 2016 dissertation focused on the experiences of African American single mothers while furthering their education. In 2017, Dr. James graduated with her Specialist Degree in Educational Leadership and Research from Louisiana State. She is currently the Academic

Dean of Instruction in the East Baton Rouge School Parish, where she provides instructional support to the teachers and administration. Dr. James is a member of Alpha Kappa Alpha Sorority, Inc., Gamma Omicron chapter.

Cole Kervin is a doctoral student in the Department of Curriculum, Culture, and Educational Inquiry at Florida Atlantic University. He earned his bachelor's degree in history education and Spanish from Illinois State University and his master's degree in curriculum and instruction from The University of Jamestown. His research interests involve using systemic functional linguistics and arts-based approaches with a focus on social justice.

Runell J. King is a native of White Castle, Louisiana, which is located about 20 miles outside of Baton Rouge, Louisiana. Dr. King began his tenure as one of the New Orleans schools' youngest Executive Leaders. He currently serves as the Executive Director of Data, Assessment, and School Accountability for the New Beginnings Schools Foundation Charter School Network. He is a 2013 graduate of Dillard University, where he earned his bachelor's degree in Sociology and Mathematics, and a graduate of Louisiana State University, where he earned master's degrees in Higher Education & Applied Statistics, and also a Ph.D. in Research Methods & Applied Statistics. Over the last three years, he has led New Orleans public schools toward a new era of academic achievement and boastful academic gains. For five years, Dr. King served in a variety of roles in Orleans Parish Schools, including Principal, Director of Academics, and Director of School Performance. He is a Fall 2011 initiate of the Beta Phi Chapter of Alpha Phi Alpha Fraternity Incorporated.

Paul Markson III has been teaching at East High School in Denver since 2005. He has taught Honors Geography, United States History, AVID courses, and Afro-American History (Honors/Regular). His constant interactions with his students leave him with a sense of hope and promise for the future.

Wafa Mohamad, a native of Chicago, is an elementary school teacher in the suburbs of that city. She is currently pursuing a doctorate in Leadership in

Curriculum and Instruction at Aurora University. Her research focuses on the experiences of Muslim American students and their subsequent participation in civil society. Her publications and presentations have specifically explored how media and curricula portray Muslims, as well as the subsequent effects of this portrayal on their identity formation.

Ritu Radhakrishnan is an Assistant Professor in the Department of Curriculum & Instruction and Chair of the School of Education Diversity Committee at the State University of New York in Oswego. Dr. Radhakrishnan is the coordinator of the Adolescence Social Studies Education Program and teaches courses in Childhood and Adolescence Social Studies Methods and Literacy Instruction and Assessment. In addition, she facilitates professional development at a K–8 and K-schools in central New York State. Her research focuses on examining forms of curriculum (hidden, explicit, and null) and incorporating critical pedagogy and aesthetics into the curriculum. Specifically, she is interested in how the application of critical pedagogy, through children's literature and aesthetics in the K–12 curriculum (and teacher education), can offer opportunities for social justice in education.

Maria B. Sciuchetti is an Assistant Professor of Special Education at Ball State University in Muncie, Indiana. She holds a PhD from the University of Texas in Special Education, Learning Disabilities and Behavior Disorder. In addition she also received master's degrees respectively from Rhode Island College in Special Education in Mild/Moderate Disabilities and in Elementary Education from Roger Williams University. Her primary research areas include academic and behavioral interventions for students from diverse backgrounds who exhibit challenging behaviors and preservice teacher preparation to meet the needs of this population. Her current projects explore the intersectionality of diversity, disability, and behavior and the implications these intersections have for school-based behavior policies and practices, as well as teacher preparation programs.

Sabrina F. Sembiante is an Assistant Professor of TESOL/Bilingual Education in the Curriculum, Culture, and Educational Inquiry Department at Florida Atlantic University. Dr. Sembiante holds a doctorate from the University of Miami in Language and Literacy Learning in Multilingual

Settings, with a focus on early childhood bilingualism. Her research centers on the instructional practices that support emergent to advanced bilingual students' developing bilingualism, biliteracy, and academic language development in school contexts. She frames her research from sociocultural and systemic functional linguistic perspectives.

Jovan T. Thomas is a native of Thibodaux, Louisiana, and holds a Bachelor of Science degree in Public Health from Dillard University in New Orleans. He attended Southern University in New Orleans, where he earned his master's degree in Social Work, and later transitioned to Higher Education, furthering his education by obtaining an Educational Specialist (Ed.S.) degree from Louisiana State University. Dr. Thomas recently earned his Doctor of Philosophy degree in Educational Leadership & Research with a Cognate in Higher Education Administration. His research is centered on the mentoring of young Black males, and the academic success of Black Male students who attend predominately White institutions.

Kiesha Warren-Gordon is an Associate Professor of Criminal Justice/Criminology at Ball State University. Her substantive areas include criminology, race, and ethnicity. Dr. Warren-Gordon's research explores the intersection of race and class in the miscarriage of justice, violence, and community engagement. Her teaching interests are victimology, multiculturalism, the death penalty, and criminal justice processes.

Kathryn Young is an Associate Professor in Secondary Education at Metropolitan State University of Denver and served as a Faculty Fellow with the Office of Institutional Diversity at the University for four years. Her research interests include Disability Studies in Education, Inclusive and Multicultural Education, and Microaggressions in Education and in the Workplace.